THE

CONJURE-MAN

DIES

A MYSTERY TALE OF DARK HARLEM

BY RUDOLPH FISHER

ANN ARBOR

THE UNIVERSITY OF MICHIGAN PRESS

First edition as an Ann Arbor Paperback 1992
All rights reserved
Published in the United States of America by
The University of Michigan Press
Originally published in New York in 1932
Manufactured in the United States of America

2005   10   9

Library of Congress Cataloging-in-Publication Data

Fisher, Rudolph, 1897–1934
    The conjure-man dies : a mystery tale of dark Harlem / Rudolph
Fisher. — 1st ed.
      p.   cm. — (Ann Arbor paperbacks)
    ISBN 0-472-09492-0 (clothbound : alk. paper). — ISBN
0-472-06492-4 (paperbound : alk. paper)
    ISBN-13 978-0-472-06492-2
    I. Title.
PS3511.17436C66 1992   91-44256
813′.52—dc20   CIP

THE
CONJURE-MAN
DIES

Ann Arbor Paperbacks

Waddell, *The Desert Fathers*
Erasmus, *The Praise of Folly*
Donne, *Devotions*
Malthus, *Population: The First Essay*
Berdyaev, *The Origin of Russian Communism*
Einhard, *The Life of Charlemagne*
Edwards, *The Nature of True Virtue*
Gilson, *Héloïse and Abélard*
Aristotle, *Metaphysics*
Kant, *Education*
Boulding, *The Image*
Duckett, *The Gateway to the Middle Ages*
(3 vols.): *Italy; France and Britain; Monasticism*
Bowditch and Ramsland, *Voices of the Industrial Revolution*
Luxemburg, *The Russian Revolution* and *Leninism or Marxism?*
Rexroth, *Poems from the Greek Anthology*
Zoshchenko, *Scenes from the Bathhouse*
Thrupp, *The Merchant Class of Medieval London*
Procopius, *Secret History*
Adcock, *Roman Political Ideas and Practice*
Swanson, *The Birth of the Gods*
Xenophon, *The March Up Country*
Buchanan and Tullock, *The Calculus of Consent*
Hobson, *Imperialism*
Kinietz, *The Indians of the Western Great Lakes, 1615–1760*
Lurie, *Mountain Wolf Woman, Sister of Crashing Thunder*
Leonard, *Baroque Times in Old Mexico*
Meier, *Negro Thought in America, 1880–1915*
Burke, *The Philosophy of Edmund Burke*
Michelet, *Joan of Arc*
Conze, *Buddhist Thought in India*
Arberry, *Aspects of Islamic Civilization*
Chesnutt, *The Wife of His Youth and Other Stories*
Zola, *The Masterpiece*
Chesnutt, *The Marrow of Tradition*
Aristophanes, *Four Comedies*
Aristophanes, *Three Comedies*
Chesnutt, *The Conjure Woman*
Duckett, *Carolingian Portraits*
Rapoport and Chammah, *Prisoner's Dilemma*
Aristotle, *Poetics*

Duckett, *Death and Life in the Tenth Century*
Langford, *Galileo, Science and the Church*
Milio, *9226 Kercheval*
Breton, *Manifestoes of Surrealism*
Scholz, *Carolingian Chronicles*
Wik, *Henry Ford and Grass-roots America*
Sahlins and Service, *Evolution and Culture*
Wickham, *Early Medieval Italy*
Waddell, *The Wandering Scholars*
Rosenberg, *Bolshevik Visions* (Part 1)
Mannoni, *Prospero and Caliban*
Shy, *A People Numerous and Armed*
Taylor, *Roman Voting Assemblies*
Hesiod, *The Works and Days; Theogony; The Shield of Herakles*
Raverat, *Period Piece*
Lamming, *In the Castle of My Skin*
Fisher, *The Conjure-Man Dies*
Strayer, *The Albigensian Crusades*
Lamming, *The Pleasures of Exile*
Lamming, *Natives of My Person*
Glaspell, *Lifted Masks and Other Works*
Grand, *The Heavenly Twins*
Allen, *Wolves of Minong*
Fisher, *The Walls of Jericho*
Lamming, *The Emigrants*
Kemble and Butler Leigh, *Principles and Privilege*
Thomas, *Out of Time*
Flanagan, *You Alone Are Dancing*
Kotre and Hall, *Seasons of Life*
Shen, *Almost a Revolution*
Meckel, *Save the Babies*
Laver and Schofield, *Multiparty Government*
Rutt, *The Bamboo Grove*
Endelman, *The Jews of Georgian England, 1714–1830*
Lamming, *Season of Adventure*
Radin, *Crashing Thunder*
Mirel, *The Rise and Fall of an Urban School System*
Brainard, *When the Rainbow Goddess Wept*
Brook, *Documents on the Rape of Nanking*
Mendel, *Vision and Violence*
Hymes, *Reinventing Anthropology*
Mulroy, *Early Greek Lyric Poetry*
Siegel, *The Rope of God*
Powelson, *The Moral Economy*
Buss, *La Partera*

THE
CONJURE-MAN
DIES

CHAPTER ONE

I

ENCOUNTERING the bright-lighted gaiety of Harlem's Seventh Avenue, the frigid midwinter night seemed to relent a little. She had given Battery Park a chill stare and she would undoubtedly freeze the Bronx. But here in this mid-realm of rhythm and laughter she seemed to grow warmer and friendlier, observing, perhaps, that those who dwelt here were mysteriously dark like herself.

Of this favor the Avenue promptly took advantage. Sidewalks barren throughout the cold white day now sprouted life like fields in spring. Along swung boys in camels' hair beside girls in bunny and muskrat; broad, flat heels clacked, high narrow ones clicked, reluctantly leaving the disgorging theaters or eagerly seeking the voracious dance halls. There was loud jest and louder laughter and the frequent uplifting of merry voices in the moment's most popular song:

> "I'll be glad when you're dead, you rascal you,
> I'll be glad when you're dead, you rascal you.
> What is it that you've got
> Makes my wife think you so hot?
> Oh you dog—I'll be glad when you're gone!"

An ironic song choice foreshadow

3

But all of black Harlem was not thus gay and bright. Any number of dark, chill, silent side streets declined the relenting night's favor. 130th Street, for example, east of Lenox Avenue, was at this moment cold, still, and narrowly forbidding; one glanced down this block and was glad one's destination lay elsewhere. Its concentrated gloom was only intensified by an occasional spangle of electric light, splashed ineffectually against the blackness, or by the unearthly pallor of the sky, into which a wall of dwellings rose to hide the moon.

Among the houses in this looming row, one reared a little taller and gaunter than its fellows, so that the others appeared to shrink from it and huddle together in the shadow on either side. The basement of this house was quite black; its first floor, high above the sidewalk and approached by a long graystone stoop, was only dimly lighted; its second floor was lighted more dimly still, while the third, which was the top, was vacantly dark again like the basement. About the place hovered an oppressive silence, as if those who entered here were warned beforehand not to speak above a whisper. There was, like a footnote, in one of the two first-floor windows to the left of the entrance a black-on-white sign reading:

"Samuel Crouch, Undertaker."

On the narrow panel to the right of the doorway the silver letters of another sign obscurely glittered on an onyx background:

"N. Frimbo, Psychist."

Between the two signs receded the high, narrow vestibule, terminating in a pair of tall glass-paneled doors.

Glass curtains, tightly stretched in vertical folds, dimmed the already too-subdued illumination beyond.

2

It was about an hour before midnight that one of the doors rattled and flew open, revealing the bareheaded, short, round figure of a young man who manifestly was profoundly agitated and in a great hurry. Without closing the door behind him, he rushed down the stairs, sped straight across the street, and in a moment was frantically pushing the bell of the dwelling directly opposite. A tall, slender, light-skinned man of obviously habitual composure answered the excited summons.

"Is—is you him?" stammered the agitated one, pointing to a shingle labeled "John Archer, M.D."

"Yes—I'm Dr. Archer."

"Well, arch on over here, will you, doc?" urged the caller. "Sump'm done happened to Frimbo."

"Frimbo? The fortune teller?"

"Step on it, will you, doc?"

Shortly, the physician, bag in hand, was hurrying up the graystone stoop behind his guide. They passed through the still open door into a hallway and mounted a flight of thickly carpeted stairs.

At the head of the staircase a tall, lank, angular figure awaited them. To this person the short, round, black, and by now quite breathless guide panted, "I got one, boy! This here's the doc from 'cross the street. Come on, doc. Right in here."

Dr. Archer, in passing, had an impression of a young

man as long and lean as himself, of a similarly light complexion except for a profusion of dark brown freckles, and of a curiously scowling countenance that glowered from either ill humor or apprehension. The doctor rounded the banister head and strode behind his pilot toward the front of the house along the upper hallway, midway of which, still following the excited short one, he turned and swung into a room that opened into the hall at that point. The tall fellow brought up the rear.

Within the room the physician stopped, looking about in surprise. The chamber was almost entirely in darkness. The walls appeared to be hung from ceiling to floor with black velvet drapes. Even the ceiling was covered, the heavy folds of cloth converging from the four corners to gather at a central point above, from which dropped a chain suspending the single strange source of light, a device which hung low over a chair behind a large desk-like table, yet left these things and indeed most of the room unlighted. This was because, instead of shedding its radiance downward and outward as would an ordinary shaded droplight, this mechanism focused a horizontal beam upon a second chair on the opposite side of the table. Clearly the person who used the chair beneath the odd spotlight could remain in relative darkness while the occupant of the other chair was brightly illuminated.

"There he is—jes' like Jinx found him."

And now in the dark chair beneath the odd lamp the doctor made out a huddled, shadowy form. Quickly he stepped forward.

"Is this the only light?"

"Only one I've seen."

Dr. Archer procured a flashlight from his bag and swept its faint beam over the walls and ceiling. Finding no sign of another lighting fixture, he directed the instrument in his hand toward the figure in the chair and saw a bare black head inclined limply sidewise, a flaccid countenance with open mouth and fixed eyes staring from under drooping lids.

"Can't do much in here. Anybody up front?"

"Yes, suh. Two ladies."

"Have to get him outside. Let's see. I know. Downstairs. Down in Crouch's. There's a sofa. You men take hold and get him down there. This way."

There was some hesitancy. "Mean us, doc?"

"Of course. Hurry. He doesn't look so hot now."

"I ain't none too warm, myself," murmured the short one. But he and his friend obeyed, carrying out their task with a dispatch born of distaste. Down the stairs they followed Dr. Archer, and into the undertaker's dimly lighted front room.

"Oh, Crouch!" called the doctor. "Mr. Crouch!"

"That 'mister' ought to get him."

But there was no answer. "Guess he's out. That's right—put him on the sofa. Push that other switch by the door. Good."

Dr. Archer inspected the supine figure as he reached into his bag. "Not so good," he commented. Beneath his black satin robe the patient wore ordinary clothing—trousers, vest, shirt, collar and tie. Deftly the physician bared the chest; with one hand he palpated the heart area while with the other he adjusted the ear-pieces of his stethoscope. He bent over, placed the bell of his instrument on the motionless dark chest, and listened a long time. He removed the instrument, disconnected first one, then the other, rubber tube at their junction with the bell, blew vigorously through them in turn, replaced them, and repeated the operation of listening. At last he stood erect.

"Not a twitch," he said.

"Long gone, huh?"

"Not so long. Still warm. But gone."

The short young man looked at his scowling freckled companion.

"What'd I tell you?" he whispered. "Was I right or wasn't I?"

The tall one did not answer but watched the doctor. The doctor put aside his stethoscope and inspected the patient's head more closely, the parted lips and half-open eyes. He extended a hand and with his extremely long fingers gently palpated the scalp. "Hello," he said. He turned the far side of the head toward him and looked first at that side, then at his fingers.

"Wh–what?"

"Blood in his hair," announced the physician. He procured a gauze dressing from his bag, wiped his moist fingers, thoroughly sponged and reinspected the wound. Abruptly he turned to the two men, whom until now he had treated quite impersonally. Still imperturbably, but incisively, in the manner of lancing an abscess, he asked, "Who are you two gentlemen?"

"Why—uh—this here's Jinx Jenkins, doc. He's my buddy, see? Him and me——"

"And you—if I don't presume?"

"Me? I'm Bubber Brown——"

"Well, how did this happen, Mr. Brown?"

" 'Deed I don' know, doc. What you mean—is somebody killed him?"

"You don't know?" Dr. Archer regarded the pair curiously a moment, then turned back to examine further. From an instrument case he took a probe and proceeded to explore the wound in the dead man's scalp. "Well—what do you know about it, then?" he asked, still probing. "Who found him?"

"Jinx," answered the one who called himself Bubber. "We jes' come here to get this Frimbo's advice 'bout a little business project we thought up. Jinx went in to see him. I waited in the waitin' room. Presently Jinx come bustin' out pop-eyed and beckoned to me. I went back with him—and there was Frimbo, jes' like you found him. We didn't even know he was over the river."

"Did he fall against anything and strike his head?"

"No, suh, doc." Jinx became articulate. "He didn't do nothin' the whole time I was in there. Nothin' but talk. He tol' me who I was and what I wanted befo' I could open my mouth. Well, I said that I knowed that much already and that I come to find out sump'm I didn't know. Then he went on talkin', tellin' me plenty. He knowed his stuff all right. But all of a sudden he stopped talkin' and mumbled sump'm 'bout not bein' able to see. Seem like he got scared, and he say, 'Frimbo, why don't you see?' Then he didn't say no more. He sound' so funny I got scared myself and jumped up and grabbed that light and turned it on him—and there he was."

"M-m."

Dr. Archer, pursuing his examination, now indulged in what appeared to be a characteristic habit: he began to talk as he worked, to talk rather absently and wordily on a matter which at first seemed inapropos.

"I," said he, "am an exceedingly curious fellow." Deftly, delicately, with half-closed eyes, he was manipulating his probe. "Questions are forever popping into my head. For example, which of you two gentlemen, if either, stands responsible for the expenses of medical attention in this unfortunate instance?"

"Mean who go'n' pay you?"

"That," smiled the doctor, "makes it rather a bald question."

Bubber grinned understandingly.

"Well here's one with hair on it, doc," he said. "Who got the medical attention?"

"M-m," murmured the doctor. "I was afraid of that. Not," he added, "that I am moved by mercenary motives. Oh, not at all. But if I am not to be paid in the usual way, in coin of the realm, then of course I must derive my compensation in some other form of satisfaction. Which, after all, is the end of all our getting and spending, is it not?"

"Oh, sho'," agreed Bubber.

"Now this case"—the doctor dropped the gauze dressing into his bag—"even robbed of its material promise, still bids well to feed my native curiosity—if not my cellular protoplasm. You follow me, of course?"

"With my tongue hangin' out," said Bubber.

But that part of his mind which was directing this discourse did not give rise to the puzzled expression on the physician's lean, light-skinned countenance as he absently moistened another dressing with alcohol, wiped off his fingers and his probe, and stood up again.

"We'd better notify the police," he said. "You men"—he looked at them again—"you men call up the precinct."

They promptly started for the door.

"No—you don't have to go out. The cops, you see"—he was almost confidential—"the cops will want to question all of us. Mr. Crouch has a phone back there. Use that."

They exchanged glances but obeyed.

"I'll be thinking over my findings."

Through the next room they scuffled and into the back of the long first-floor suite. There they abruptly came to a halt and again looked at each other, but now for an entirely different reason. Along one side of this room, hidden from view until their entrance, stretched a long narrow table draped with a white sheet that covered an unmistakably human form. There was not much light. The two young men stood quite still.

"Seem like it's—occupied," murmured Bubber.

"Another one," mumbled Jinx.

"Where's the phone?"

"Don't ask me. I got both eyes full."

"There 'tis—on that desk. Go on—use it."

"Use it yo' own black self," suggested Jinx. "I'm goin' back."

"No you ain't. Come on. We use it together."

"All right. But if that whosis says 'Howdy' tell it I said 'Goo'by.' "

"And where the hell you think I'll be if it says 'Howdy'?"

"What a place to have a telephone!"

"Step on it, slow motion."

"Hello!—Hello!" Bubber rattled the hook. "Hey operator! Operator!"

"My Gawd," said Jinx, "is the phone dead too?"

"Operator—gimme the station—quick. . . . Pennsylvania? No ma'am—New York—Harlem—listen, lady, not railroad. Police. *Please*, ma'am. . . . Hello—hey—send a flock o' cops around here—Frimbo's—the fortune teller's—yea—Thirteen West 130th—yea—somebody done put that thing on him! . . . Yea—O.K."

Hurriedly they returned to the front room where Dr. Archer was pacing back and forth, his hands thrust into his pockets, his brow pleated into troubled furrows.

"They say hold everything, doc. Be right over."

"Good." The doctor went on pacing.

Jinx and Bubber surveyed the recumbent form. Said Bubber, "If he could keep folks from dyin', how come he didn't keep hisself from it?"

"Reckon he didn't have time to put no spell on hisself," Jinx surmised.

"No," returned Bubber grimly. "But somebody else had time to put one on him. I knowed sump'm was comin'. I told you. First time I seen death on the moon since I been grown. And they's two mo' yet."

"How you reckon it happened?"

"You askin' me?" Bubber said. "You was closer to him than I was."

"It was plumb dark all around. Somebody could'a' snook up behind him and crowned him while he was talkin' to me. But I didn't hear a sound. Say—I better catch air. This thing's puttin' me on the well-known spot, ain't it?"

"All right, dumbo. Run away and prove you done it. Wouldn't that be a bright move?"

Dr. Archer said, "The wisest thing for you men to do is stay here and help solve this puzzle. You'd be called in anyway—you found the body, you see. Running away looks as if you were—well—running away."

"What'd I tell you?" said Bubber.

"All right," growled Jinx. "But I can't see how they could blame anybody for runnin' away from this place. Graveyard's a playground side o' this."

CHAPTER TWO

OF THE ten Negro members of Harlem's police force to be promoted from the rank of patrolman to that of detective, Perry Dart was one of the first. As if the city administration had wished to leave no doubt in the public mind as to its intention in the matter, they had chosen, in him, a man who could not have been under any circumstances mistaken for aught but a Negro; or perhaps, as Dart's intimates insisted, they had chosen him because his generously pigmented skin rendered him invisible in the dark, a conceivably great advantage to a detective who did most of his work at night. In any case, the somber hue of his integument in no wise reflected the complexion of his brain, which was bright, alert, and practical within such territory as it embraced. He was a Manhattanite by birth, had come up through the public schools, distinguished himself in athletics at the high school he attended, and, having himself grown up with the black colony, knew Harlem from lowest dive to loftiest temple. He was rather small of stature, with unusually thin, fine features, which falsely accentuated the slightness of his slender but wiry body.

It was Perry Dart's turn for a case when Bubber Brown's call came in to the station, and to it Dart, with four uniformed men, was assigned.

Five minutes later he was in the entrance of Thirteen

West 130th Street, greeting Dr. Archer, whom he knew. His men, one black, two brown, and one yellow, loomed in the hallway about him large and ominous, but there was no doubt as to who was in command.

"Hello, Dart," the physician responded to his greeting. "I'm glad you're on this one. It'll take a little active cerebration."

"Come on down, doc," the little detective grinned with a flash of white teeth. "You're talking to a cop now, not a college professor. What've you got?"

"A man that'll tell no tales." The physician motioned to the undertaker's front room. "He's in there."

Dart turned to his men. "Day, you cover the front of the place. Green, take the roof and cover the back yard. Johnson, search the house and get everybody you find into one room. Leave a light everywhere you go if possible—I'll want to check up. Brady, you stay with me." Then he turned back and followed the doctor into the undertaker's parlor. They stepped over to the sofa, which was in a shallow alcove formed by the front bay windows of the room.

"How'd he get it, doc?" he asked.

"To tell you the truth, I haven't the slightest idea."

"Somebody crowned him," Bubber helpfully volunteered.

"Has anybody ast you anything?" Jinx inquired gruffly.

Dart bent over the victim.

The physician said:

"There is a scalp wound all right. See it?"

"Yea—now that you mentioned it."

"But that didn't kill him."

"No? How do you know it didn't, doc?"

"That wound is too slight. It's not in a spot that would upset any vital center. And there isn't any fracture under it."

"Couldn't a man be killed by a blow on the head that didn't fracture his skull?"

"Well—yes. If it fell just so that its force was concentrated on certain parts of the brain. I've never heard of such a case, but it's conceivable. But this blow didn't land in the right place for that. A blow at this point would cause death only by producing intracranial hemorrhage——"

"Couldn't you manage to say it in English, doc?"

"Sure. He'd have to bleed inside his head."

"That's more like it."

"The resulting accumulation of blood would raise the intra—the pressure inside his head to such a point that vital centers would be paralyzed. The power would be shut down. His heart and lungs would quit cold. See? Just like turning off a light."

"O.K. if you say so. But how do you know he didn't bleed inside his head?"

"Well, there aren't but two things that would cause him to."

"I'm learning, doc. Go on."

"Brittle arteries with no give in them—no elasticity. If he had them, he wouldn't even have to be hit—just excitement might shoot up the blood pressure and pop an artery. See what I mean?"

"That's apoplexy, isn't it?"

"Right. And the other thing would be a blow heavy enough to fracture the skull and so rupture the blood vessels beneath. Now this man is about your age or mine—somewhere in his middle thirties. His arteries are soft—feel his wrists. For a blow to kill this man outright, it would have had to fracture his skull."

"Hot damn!" whispered Bubber admiringly. "Listen to the doc do his stuff!"

"And his skull isn't fractured?" said Dart.

"Not if probing means anything."

"Don't tell me you've X-rayed him too?" grinned the detective.

"Any fracture that would kill this man outright wouldn't have to be X-rayed."

"Then you're sure the blow didn't kill him?"

"Not by itself, it didn't."

"Do you mean that maybe he was killed first and hit afterwards?"

"Why would anybody do that?" Dr. Archer asked.

"To make it seem like violence when it was really something else."

"I see. But no. If this man had been dead when the blow was struck, he wouldn't have bled at all. Circulation would already have stopped."

"That's right."

"But of one thing I'm sure: that wound is evidence of too slight a blow to kill."

"Specially," interpolated Bubber, "a hard-headed cullud man——"

"There you go ag'in," growled his lanky companion.

"He's right," the doctor said. "It takes a pretty hefty

impact to bash in a skull. With a padded weapon," he
went on, "a fatal blow would have had to be crushing
to make even so slight a scalp wound as this. That's out.
And a hard, unpadded weapon that would break the
scalp just slightly like this, with only a little bleeding
and without even cracking the skull, could at most have
delivered only a stunning blow, not a fatal one. Do you
see what I mean?"

"Sure. You mean this man was just stunned by the
blow and actually died from something else."

"That's the way it looks to me."

"Well—anyhow he's dead and the circumstances
indicate at least a possibility of death by violence. That
justifies notifying us, all right. And it makes it a case
for the medical examiner. But we really don't know
that he's been killed, do we?"

"No. Not yet."

"All the more a case for the medical examiner, then.
Is there a phone here, doc? Good. Brady, go back there
and call the precinct. Tell 'em to get the medical examiner here double time and to send me four more men—
doesn't matter who. Now tell me, doc. What time did
this man go out of the picture?"

The physician smiled.

"Call Meridian 7–1212."

"O.K., doc. But approximately?"

"Well, he was certainly alive an hour ago. Perhaps
even half an hour ago. Hardly less."

"How long have you been here?"

"About fifteen minutes."

"Then he must have been killed—if he was killed—

say anywhere from five to thirty-five minutes before you got here?"

"Yes."

Bubber, the insuppressible, commented to Jinx, "Damn! That's trimming it down to a gnat's heel, ain't it?" But Jinx only responded, "Fool, will you hush?"

"Who discovered him—do you know?"

"These two men."

"Both of you?" Dart asked the pair.

"No, suh," Bubber answered. "Jinx here discovered the man. I discovered the doctor."

Dart started to question them further, but just then Johnson, the officer who had been directed to search the house, reappeared.

"Been all over," he reported. "Only two people in the place. Women—both scared green."

"All right," the detective said. "Take these two men up to the same room. I'll be up presently."

Officer Brady returned. "Medical examiner's comin' right up."

The detective said, "Was he on this sofa when you got here, doc?"

"No. He was upstairs in his—his consultation room, I guess you'd call it. Queer place. Dark as sin. Sitting slumped down in a chair. The light was impossible. You see, I thought I'd been called to a patient, not a corpse. So I had him brought where I knew I could examine him. Of course, if I had thought of murder——"

"Never mind. There's no law against your moving him or examining him, even if you had suspected murder—as long as you weren't trying to hide anything.

People think there's some such law, but there isn't."

"The medical examiner'll probably be sore, though."

"Let him. We've got more than the medical examiner to worry about."

"Yes. You've got a few questions to ask."

"And answer. How, when, where, why, and who? Oh, I'm great at questions. But the answers——"

"Well, we've the 'when' narrowed down to a half-hour period." Dr. Archer glanced at his watch. "That would be between ten-thirty and eleven. And 'where' shouldn't be hard to verify—right here in his own chair, if those two fellows are telling it straight. 'Why' and 'who'—those'll be your little red wagon. 'How' right now is mine. I can't imagine——"

Again he turned to the supine figure, staring. Suddenly his lean countenance grew blanker than usual. Still staring, he took the detective by the arm. "Dart," he said reflectively, "we smart people are often amazingly —dumb."

"You're telling me?"

"We waste precious moments in useless speculation. We indulge ourselves in the extravagance of reason when a frugal bit of observation would suffice."

"Does prescription liquor affect you like that, doc?"

"Look at that face."

"Well—if you insist——"

"Just the general appearance of that face—the eyes— the open mouth. What does it look like?"

"Looks like he's gasping for breath."

"Exactly. Dart, this man might—might, you understand—have been choked."

"Ch——"

"Stunned by a blow over the ear——"

"To prevent a struggle!"

"—and choked to death. As simple as that."

"Choked! But just how?"

Eagerly, Dr. Archer once more bent over the lifeless countenance. "There are two ways," he dissertated in his roundabout fashion, "of interrupting respiration." He was peering into the mouth. "What we shall call, for simplicity, the external and the internal. In this case the external would be rather indeterminate, since we could hardly make out the usual bluish discolorations on a neck of this complexion." He procured two tongue depressors and, one in each hand, examined as far back into the throat as he could. He stopped talking as some discovery further elevated his already high interest. He discarded one depressor, reached for his flashlight with the hand thus freed, and, still holding the first depressor in place, directed his light into the mouth as if he were examining tonsils. With a little grunt of discovery, he now discarded the flashlight also, took a pair of long steel thumb-forceps from a flap in the side of his bag, and inserted the instrument into the victim's mouth alongside the guiding tongue-depressor. Dart and the uniformed officer watched silently as the doctor apparently tried to remove something from the throat of the corpse. Once, twice, the prongs snapped together, and he withdrew the instrument empty. But the next time the forceps caught hold of the physician's discovery and drew it forth.

It was a large, blue-bordered, white handkerchief.

In which the mystery of
the handkerchief continues
and Frimbo's house goes
under investigation

CHAPTER THREE

I

"**D**OC," said Dart, "you don't mind hanging around with us a while?"

"Try and shake me loose," grinned Dr. Archer. "This promises to be worth seeing."

"If you'd said no," Dart grinned back, "I'd have held you anyhow as a suspect. I'm going to need some of your brains. I'm not one of these bright ones that can do all the answers in my head. I'm just a poor boy trying to make a living, and this kind of a riddle hasn't been popped often enough in my life to be easy yet. I've seen some funny ones, but this is funnier. One thing I can see—that this guy wasn't put out by any beginner."

"The man that did this," agreed the physician, "thought about it first. I've seen autopsies that could have missed that handkerchief. It was pushed back almost out of sight."

"That makes you a smart boy."

"I admit it. Wonder whose handkerchief?"

"Stick it in your bag and hang on to it. And let's get going."

"Whither?"

"To get acquainted with this layout first. Whoever's here will keep a while. The bird that pulled the job is probably in Egypt by now."

"That wouldn't be my guess."

"You think he'd hang around?"

"He wouldn't do the expected thing—not if he was bright enough to think up a gag like this."

"Gag is good. Let's start with the roof. Brady, you come with me and the doc—and be ready for surprises. Where's Day?"

The doctor closed and picked up his bag. They passed into the hallway. Officer Day was on guard in the front vestibule according to his orders.

"There are four more men and the medical examiner coming," the detective told him. "The four will be right over. Put one on the rear of the house and send the others upstairs. Come on, doc."

The three men ascended two flights of stairs to the top floor. The slim Dart led, the tall doctor followed, the stalwart Brady brought up the rear. Along the uppermost hallway they made their way to the front of the third story of the house, moving with purposeful resoluteness, yet with a sharp-eyed caution that anticipated almost any eventuality. The physician and the detective carried their flashlights, the policeman his revolver.

At the front end of the hallway they found a closed door. It was unlocked. Dart flung it open, to find the ceiling light on, probably left by Officer Johnson in obedience to instructions.

This room was a large bedchamber, reaching, except for the width of the hallway, across the breadth of the house. It was luxuriously appointed. The bed was a massive four-poster of mahogany, intricately carved and set off by a counterpane of gold satin. It occupied the mid-portion of a large black-and-yellow Chinese rug which covered almost the entire floor. Two upholstered chairs, done also in gold satin, flanked the bed, and a settee of similar design guarded its foot. An elaborate smoking stand sat beside the head of the bed. A mahogany chest and bureau, each as substantial as the four-poster, completed the furniture.

"No question as to whose room this is," said Dart.

"A man's," diagnosed Archer. "A man of means and definite ideas, good or bad—but definite. Too bare to be a woman's room—look—the walls are stark naked. There aren't any frills"—he sniffed—"and there isn't any perfume."

"I guess you've been in enough women's rooms to know."

"Men's too. But this is odd. Notice anything conspicuous by its absence?"

"I'll bite."

"Photographs of women."

The detective's eyes swept the room in verification. "Woman hater?"

"Maybe," said the doctor, "but——"

"Wait a minute," said the detective. There was a clothes closet to the left of the entrance. He turned, opened its door, and played his flashlight upon its contents. An array of masculine attire extended in orderly suspension—several suits of various patterns hanging from individual racks. On the back of the open door hung a suit of black pajamas. On the floor a half-dozen pairs of shoes were set in an orderly row. There was no suggestion of any feminine contact or influence; there was simply the atmosphere of an exceptionally well ordered, decided masculinity.

"What do you think?" asked Dr. Archer.

"Woman hater," repeated Dart conclusively.

"Or a Lothario of the deepest dye."

The detective looked at the doctor. "I get the deep dye—he was blacker'n me. But the Lothario——"

"Isn't it barely possible that this so very complete—er—repudiation of woman is too complete to be accidental? May it not be deliberate—a wary suppression of evidence—the recourse of a lover of great experience and wisdom, who lets not his right hand know whom his left embraceth?"

"Not good—just careful?"

"He couldn't be married—actively. His wife's influence would be—smelt. And if he isn't married, this over-absence of the feminine—well—it means something."

"I still think it could mean woman-hating. This other guess-work of yours sounds all bass-ackwards to me."

"Heaven forfend, good friend, that you should lose faith in my judgment. Woman-hater you call him and woman-hater he is. Carry on."

2

A narrow little room the width of the hallway occupied that extent of the front not taken up by the master bedroom. In this they found a single bed, a small table, and a chair, but nothing of apparent significance.

Frimbo
~~The~~ ~~apt~~ is clean and orderly
Very prepared... hiding something maybe?

26   THE CONJURE-MAN DIES

Along the hallway they now retraced their steps, trying each of three successive doors that led off from this passage. The first was an empty store-room, the second a white tiled bathroom, and the third a bare closet. These yielded no suggestion of the sort of character or circumstances with which they might be dealing. Nor did the smaller of the two rooms terminating the hallway at its back end, for this was merely a narrow kitchen, with a tiny range, a table, icebox, and cabinet. In these they found no inspiration.

But the larger of the two rear rooms was arresting enough. This was a study, fitted out in a fashion that would have warmed the heart and stirred the ambition of any student. There were two large brown-leather club chairs, each with its end table and reading lamp; a similarly upholstered divan in front of a fireplace that occupied the far wall, and over toward the windows at the rear, a flat-topped desk, upon which sat a bronze desk-lamp, and behind which sat a large swivel arm-chair. Those parts of the walls not taken up by the fireplace and windows were solid masses of books, being fitted from the floor to the level of a tall man's head with crowded shelves.

Dr. Archer was at once absorbed. "This man was no ordinary fakir," he observed. "Look." He pointed out several framed documents on the upper parts of the walls. "Here——" He approached the largest and peered long upon it. Dart came near, looked at it once, and grinned:

"Does it make sense, doc?"

"Bachelor's degree from Harvard. N'Gana Frimbo. N'Gana——"

"Not West Indian?"

"No. This sounds definitely African to me. Lots of them have that N'. The 'Frimbo' suggests it, too—mumbo—jumbo—sambo——"

"Limbo——"

"Wonder why he chose an American college? Most of the chiefs' sons'll go to Oxford or bust. I know—this fellow is probably from Liberia or thereabouts. American influence—see?"

"How'd he get into a racket like fortune telling?".

"Ask me another. Probably a better racket than medicine in this community. A really clever chap could do wonders."

The doctor was glancing along the rows of books. He noted such titles as Tankard's *Determinism and Fatalism, a Critical Contrast*, Bostwick's *The Concept of Inevitability*, Preem's *Cause and Effect*, Dessault's *The Science of History*, and Fairclough's *The Philosophical Basis of Destiny*. He took this last from its place, opened to a flyleaf, and read in script, "N'Gana Frimbo" and a date. Riffling the pages, he saw in the same script penciled marginal notes at frequent intervals. At the end of the chapter entitled "Unit Stimulus and Reaction," the penciled notation read: "Fairclough too has missed the great secret."

"This is queer."

"What?"

"A native African, a Harvard graduate, a student of

philosophy—and a sorcerer. There's something wrong with that picture."

"Does it throw any light on who killed him?"

"Anything that throws light on the man's character might help."

"Well, let's get going. I want to go through the rest of the house and get down to the real job. You worry about his character. I'll worry about the character of the suspects."

"Right-o. Your move, professor."

CHAPTER FOUR

MEANWHILE Jinx and Bubber, in Frimbo's waiting-room on the second floor, were indulging in one of their characteristic arguments. This one had started with Bubber's chivalrous endeavors to ease the disturbing situation for the two women, both of whom were bewildered and distraught and one of whom was young and pretty. Bubber had not only announced and described in detail just what he had seen, but, heedless of the fact that the younger woman had almost fainted, had proceeded to explain how he had known, long before it occurred, that he had been about to "see death." To dispel any remaining vestiges of tranquillity, he had added that the death of Frimbo was but one of three. Two more were at hand.

"Soon as Jinx here called me," he said, "I knowed somebody's time had come. I busted on in that room yonder with him—y'all seen me go—and sho' 'nough, there was the man, limp as a rag and stiff as a board. Y' see, the moon don't lie. 'Cose most signs ain't no 'count. As for me, you won't find nobody black as me that's less suprastitious."

"Jes' say we won't find nobody black as you and stop. That'll be the truth," growled Jinx.

"But a moonsign is different. Moonsign is the one sign you can take for sho'. Moonsign——"

"Moonshine is what you took for sho' tonight," Jinx said.

"Red moon mean bloodshed, new moon over your right shoulder mean good luck, new moon over your left shoulder mean bad luck, and so on. Well, they's one moonsign my grandmammy taught me befo' I was knee high and that's the worst sign of 'em all. And that's the sign I seen tonight. I was walkin' down the Avenue feelin' fine and breathin' the air——"

"What do you breathe when you don't feel so good?"

"——smokin' the gals over, watchin' the cars roll by—feelin' good, you know what I mean. And then all of a sudden I stopped. I store."

"You whiched?"

"Store. I stopped and I store."

"What language you talkin'?"

"I store at the sky. And as I stood there starin', sump'm didn't seem right. Then I seen what it was. Y' see, they was a full moon in the sky——"

"Funny place for a full moon, wasn't it?"

"——and as I store at it, they come up a cloud—wasn't but one cloud in the whole sky—and that cloud come up and crossed over the face o' the moon and blotted it out—jes' like that."

"You sho' 'twasn't yo' shadow?"

"Well there was the black cloud in front o' the moon and the white moonlight all around it and behind it. All of a sudden I seen what was wrong. That cloud had done took the shape of a human skull!"

"Sweet Jesus!" The older woman's whisper betokened the proper awe. She was an elongated, incredibly thin creature, ill-favored in countenance and apparel; her loose, limp, angular figure was grotesquely disposed over a stiff-backed arm-chair, and dark, nondescript clothing draped her too long limbs. Her squarish, fashionless hat was a little awry, her scrawny visage, already disquieted, was now inordinately startled, the eyes almost comically wide above the high cheek bones, the mouth closed tight over her teeth whose forward slant made the lips protrude as if they were puckering to whistle.

The younger woman, however, seemed not to hear. Those dark eyes surely could sparkle brightly, those small lips smile, that clear honey skin glow with animation; but just now the eyes stared unseeingly, the lips were a short, hard, straight line, the skin of her round pretty face almost colorless. She was obviously dazed by the suddenness of this unexpected tragedy. Unlike the other woman, however, she had not lost her poise, though it was costing her something to retain it. The trim, black, high-heeled shoes, the light sheer stockings, the black seal coat which fell open to reveal a white-bordered pimiento dress, even the small close-fitting black hat, all were quite as they should be. Only her isolating detachment betrayed the effect upon her of the presence of death and the law.

"A human skull!" repeated Bubber. "Yes, ma'am. Blottin' out the moon. You know what that is?"

"What?" said the older woman.

"That's death on the moon. It's a moonsign and it's never been known to fail."

"And it means death?"

"Worse 'n that, ma'am. It means three deaths. Whoever see death on the moon"—he paused, drew breath, and went on in an impressive lower tone—"gonna see death three times!"

"My soul and body!" said the lady.

But Jinx saw fit to summon logic. "Mean you go'n' see two more folks dead?"

"Gonna stare 'em in the face."

"Then somebody ought to poke yo' eyes out in self-defense."

Having with characteristic singleness of purpose discharged his duty as a gentleman and done all within his power to set the ladies' minds at rest, Bubber could now turn his attention to the due and proper quashing of his unappreciative commentator.

"Whyn't you try it?" he suggested.

"Try what?"

"Pokin' my eyes out."

"Huh. If I thought that was the onliest way to keep from dyin', you could get yo'self a tin cup and a cane tonight."

"Try it then."

" 'Tain't necessary. That moonshine you had'll take care o' everything. Jes' give it another hour to work and you'll be blind as a Baltimo' alley."

"Trouble with you," said Bubber, "is, you' ignorant. You' dumb. The inside o' yo' head is all black."

"Like the outside o' yourn."

"Is you by any chance alludin' to me?"

"I ain't alludin' to that policeman over yonder."

"Lucky for you he is over yonder, else you wouldn't be alludin' at all."

"Now you gettin' bad, ain't you? Jus' 'cause you know you got the advantage over me."

"What advantage?"

"How could I hit you when I can't even see you?"

"Well if I was ugly as you is, I wouldn't want nobody to see me."

"Don't worry, son. Nobody'll ever know how ugly you is. Yo' ugliness is shrouded in mystery."

"Well yo' dumbness ain't. It's right there for all the world to see. You ought to be back in Africa with the other dumb boogies."

"African boogies ain't dumb," explained Jinx. "They' jes' dark. You ain't been away from there long, is you?"

"My folks," returned Bubber crushingly, "left Africa ten generations ago."

"Yo' folks? Shuh. Ten generations ago, you-all wasn't folks. You-all hadn't qualified as apes."

Thus as always, their exchange of compliments flowed toward the level of family history, among other Harlemites a dangerous explosive which a single word might strike into instantaneous violence. It was only because the hostility of these two was actually an elaborate masquerade, whereunder they concealed the most genuine affection for each other, that they could come so close to blows that were never offered.

Yet to the observer this mock antagonism would have appeared alarmingly real. Bubber's squat figure sidled belligerently up to the long and lanky Jinx; solid as a fire-plug he stood, set to grapple; and he said with unusual distinctness:

"Yea? Well—yo' granddaddy was a hair on a baboon's tail. What does that make you?"

The policeman's grin of amusement faded. The older woman stifled a cry of apprehension.

The younger woman still sat motionless and staring, wholly unaware of what was going on.

CHAPTER FIVE

I

DETECTIVE DART, Dr. Archer, and Officer Brady made a rapid survey of the basement and cellar. The basement, a few feet below sidewalk level, proved to be one long, low-ceilinged room, fitted out, evidently by the undertaker, as a simple meeting-room for those clients who required the use of a chapel. There were many rows of folding wooden chairs facing a low platform at the far end of the room. In the middle of this platform rose a pulpit stand, and on one side against the wall stood a small reed organ. A heavy dark curtain across the rear of the platform separated it and the meeting-place from a brief unimproved space behind that led through a back door into the back yard. The basement hallway, in the same relative position as those above, ran alongside the meeting-room and ended in this little hinder space. In one corner of this, which must originally have been the kitchen, was the small door of a dumbwaiter shaft which led to the floor above. The shaft contained no sign of a dumbwaiter now, as Dart's flashlight disclosed: above were the dangling gears and broken ropes of a mechanism long since discarded, and below, an empty pit.

They discovered nearby the doorway to the cellar stairs, which proved to be the usual precipitate series

of narrow planks. In the cellar, which was poorly lighted
by a single central droplight, they found a large furnace,
a coal bin, and, up forward, a nondescript heap of
shadowy junk such as cellars everywhere seem to breed.

All this appeared for the time being unimportant,
and so they returned to the second floor, where the victim had originally been found. Dart had purposely left
this floor till the last. It was divided into three rooms,
front, middle and back, and these they methodically
visited in order.

They entered the front room, Frimbo's reception
room, just as Bubber sidled belligerently up to Jinx.
Apparently their entrance discouraged further hostili-
ties, for with one or two upward, sidelong glares from
Bubber, neutralized by an inarticulate growl or two
from Jinx, the imminent combat faded mysteriously
away and the atmosphere cleared.

But now the younger woman's eyes lifted to recognize
Dr. John Archer. She jumped up and went to him.

"Hello, Martha," he said.

"What does it mean, John?"

"Don't let it upset you. Looks like the conjure-man
had an enemy, that's all."

"It's true—he really is——?"

"I'm afraid so. This is Detective Dart. Mrs. Crouch,
Mr. Dart."

"Good-evening," Mrs. Crouch said mechanically and
turned back to her chair.

"Dart's a friend of mine, Martha," said the physician.
"He'll take my word for your innocence, never fear."

The older woman, refusing to be ignored, said impatiently, "How long you 'spect us to sit here? What we waitin' for? We didn' kill him."

"Of course not," Dart smiled. "But you may be able to help us find out who did. As soon as I've finished looking around I'll want to ask you a few questions. That's all."

"Well," she grumbled, "you don't have to stand a seven-foot cop over us to ask a few questions, do you?"

Ignoring this inquiry, the investigators continued with their observations. This was a spacious room whose soft light came altogether from three or four floor lamps; odd heavy silken shades bore curious designs in profile, and the effect of the obliquely downcast light was to reveal legs and bodies, while countenances above were bedimmed by comparative shadow. Beside the narrow hall door was a wide doorway hung with portières of black velvet, occupying most of that wall. The lateral walls, which seemed to withdraw into the surrounding dusk, were adorned with innumerable strange and awful shapes: gruesome black masks with hollow orbits, some smooth and bald, some horned and bearded; small misshapen statuettes of near-human creatures, resembling embryos dried and blackened in the sun, with closed bulbous eyes and great protruding lips; broad-bladed swords, slim arrows and jagged spear-heads of forbidding designs. On the farther of the lateral walls was a mantelpiece upon which lay additional African emblems. Dr. Archer pointed out a murderous-looking club, resting diagonally across one end of the mantel; it consisted of the lower half of a human femur, one extremity bulging into wicked-looking condyles, the other, where the original bone had been severed, covered with a silver knob representing a human skull.

"That would deliver a nasty crack."

"Wonder if it did?" said the detective.

2

They passed now through the velvet portières and a little isthmus-like antechamber into the middle room where the doctor had first seen the victim. Dr. Archer pointed out those peculiarities of this chamber which he had already noted: the odd droplight with its horizontally focused beam, which was the only means of illumination; the surrounding black velvet draping, its long folds extending vertically from the bottom of the walls to the top, then converging to the center of the ceiling above, giving the room somewhat the shape of an Arab tent; the one apparent opening in this drapery, at the side door leading to the hallway; the desk-like table in the middle of the room, the visitors' chair on one side of it, Frimbo's on the other, directly beneath the curious droplight.

"Let's examine the walls," said Dart. He and the doctor brought their flashlights into play. Like two offshoots of the parent beam, the smaller shafts of light traveled inquisitively over the long vertical folds of black velvet, which swayed this way and that as the two men pulled and palpated, seeking openings. The projected spots of illumination moved like two strange, twisting, luminous moths, constantly changing in size and shape, fluttering here and there from point to point, pausing, inquiring, abandoning. The detective and the physician began at the entrance from the reception room and circuited the black chamber in opposite directions. Presently they met at the far back wall, in whose midline the doctor located an opening. Pulling the hangings aside at this point, they discovered another door but found it locked.

"Leads into the back room, I guess. We'll get in from the hallway. What's this?"

"This" proved to be a switch-box on the wall beside the closed door. The physician read the lettering on its front. "Sixty amperes—two hundred and twenty volts. That's enough for an X-ray machine. What does he need special current for?"

"Search me. Come on. Brady, run downstairs and get that extension-light out of the back of my car. Then come back here and search the floor for whatever you can find. Specially around the table and chairs. We'll be right back."

3

They left the death chamber by its side door and approached the rearmost room from the hallway. Its hall door was unlocked, but blackness greeted them as they flung it open, a strangely sinister blackness in which eyes seemed to gleam. When they cast their flashlights into that blackness they saw whence the gleaming emanated, and Dart, stepping in, found a switch and produced a light.

"Damn!" said he as his eyes took in a wholly unexpected scene. Along the rear wall under the windows stretched a long flat chemical work-bench, topped with black slate. On its dull dark surface gleamed bright laboratory devices of glass or metal, flasks, beakers, retorts, graduates, pipettes, a copper water-bath, a shining instrument-sterilizer, and at one end, a gleaming black electric motor. The space beneath this bench was occupied by a long floor cabinet with a number of small oaken doors. On the wall at the nearer end was a glass-doored steel cabinet containing a few small surgical instruments, while the far wall, at the other end of the bench, supported a series of shelves, the lower ones bearing specimen-jars of various sizes, and the upper, bottles of different colors and shapes. Dart stooped and opened one of the cabinet doors and discovered more glassware, while Dr. Archer went over and investigated the shelves, removed one of the specimen-jars, and with a puzzled expression, peered at its contents, floating in some preserving fluid.

"What's that?" the detective asked, approaching.

"Can't be," muttered the physician.

"Can't be what?"

"What they look like."

"Namely?"

Ordinarily Dr. Archer would probably have indulged in a leisurely circumlocution and reached his decision by a flank attack. In the present instance he was too suddenly and wholly absorbed in what he saw to entertain even the slightest or most innocent pretense.

"Sex glands," he said.

"What?"

"Male sex glands, apparently."

"Are you serious?"

The physician inspected the rows of jars, none of which was labeled. There were other preserved biological specimens, but none of the same appearance as those in the jar which he still held in his hand.

"I'm serious enough," he said. "Does it stimulate your imagination?"

"Plenty," said Dart, his thin lips tightening. "Come on—let's ask some questions."

CHAPTER SIX

I

THEY returned to the middle chamber. Officer
Brady had plugged the extension into a hall socket
and twisted its cord about the chain which suspended
Frimbo's light. The strong white lamp's sharp radiance
did not dispel the far shadows, but at least it brightened
the room centrally.

Brady said, "There's three things I found—all on the
floor by the chair."

"This chair?" Dart indicated the one in which the
victim had been first seen by Dr. Archer.

"Yes."

The three objects were on the table, as dissimilar as
three objects could be.

"What do you think of this, doc?" Dart picked up
a small irregular shining metallic article and turned to
show it to the physician. But the physician was already
reaching for one of the other two discoveries.

"Hey—wait a minute!" protested the detective.
"That's big enough to have finger prints on it."

"My error. What's that you have?"

"Teeth. Somebody's removable bridge."

He handed over the small shining object. The physician examined it. "First and second left upper bicus-
pids," he announced.

"You don't say?" grinned Dart.

"What do you mean, somebody's?"

"Well, if you know whose just by looking at it, speak up. Don't hold out on me."

"Frimbo's."

"Or the guy's that put him out."

"Hm—no. My money says Frimbo's. These things slip on and off easily enough."

"I see what you mean. In manipulating that handkerchief the murderer dislodged this thing."

"Yes. Too bad. If it was the murderer's it might help identify him."

"Why? There must be plenty of folks with those same teeth missing."

"True. But this bridge wouldn't fit—really fit—anybody but the person it was made for. The models have to be cast in plaster. Not two in ten thousand would be identical in every respect. This thing's practically as individual as a finger print."

"Yea? Well, we may be able to use it anyhow. I'll hang on to it. But wait. You looked down Frimbo's throat. Didn't you notice his teeth?"

"Not especially. I didn't care anything about his teeth then. I was looking for the cause of death. But we can easily check this when the medical examiner comes."

"O.K. Now—what's this?" He picked up what seemed to be a wad of black silk ribbon.

"That was his head cloth, I suppose. Very impressive with that flowing robe and all."

"Who could see it in the dark?"

"Oh, he might have occasion to come out into the light sometime."

The detective's attention was already on the third object.

"Say——!"

"I'm way ahead of you."

"That's the mate to the club on the mantel in the front room!"

"Right. That's made from a left femur, this from a right."

"That must be what crowned him. Boy, if that's got finger prints on it——"

"Ought to have. Look—it's not fully bleached out like the specimens ordinarily sold to students. Notice the surface—greasy-looking. It would take an excellent print."

"Did you touch it, Brady?"

"I picked it up by the big end. I didn't touch the rest of it."

"Good. Have the other guys shown up yet? All right. Wrap it—here"—he took a newspaper from his pocket, surrounded the thigh bone with it, stepped to the door and summoned one of the officers who had arrived meanwhile. "Take this over to the precinct, tell Mac to get it examined for finger prints pronto—anybody he can get hold of—wait for the result and bring it back here —wet. And bring back a set—if Tynie's around, let him bring it. Double time—it's a rush order."

"What's the use?" smiled the doctor." You yourself said the offender's probably in Egypt by now."

"And you said different. Hey—look!"

He had been playing his flashlight over the carpet. Its rays passed obliquely under the table, revealing a grayish discoloration of the carpet. Closer inspection proved this to be due to a deposit of ash-colored powder. The doctor took a prescription blank and one of his professional cards and scraped up some of the powder onto the blank.

"Know what it is?" asked Dart.

"No."

"Save it. We'll have it examined."

"Meanwhile?"

"Meanwhile let's indulge in a few personalities. Let's see—I've got an idea."

"Shouldn't be at all surprised. What now?"

"This guy Frimbo was smart. He put his people in that spotlight and he stayed in the dark. All right— I'm going to do the same thing."

"You might win the same reward."

"I'll take precautions against that. Brady!"

Brady brought in the two officers who had not yet been assigned to a post. They were stationed now, one on either side of the black room toward its rear wall.

"Now," said Dart briskly. "Let's get started. Brady, call in that little short fat guy. You in the hall there— turn off this extension at that socket and be ready to turn it on again when I holler. I intend to sit pat as long as possible."

Thereupon he snapped off his flashlight and seated himself in Frimbo's chair behind the table, becoming now merely a deeper shadow in the surrounding dimness. The doctor put out his flashlight also and stood beside the chair. The bright shaft of light from the device overhead, directed away from them, shone full upon the back of the empty visitors' chair opposite, and on beyond toward the passageway traversed by those who entered from the reception room. They waited for Bubber Brown to come in.

2

Whatever he might have expected, Bubber Brown certainly was unprepared for this. With a hesitancy that was not in the least feigned, his figure came into view; first his extremely bowed legs, about which flapped the bottom of his imitation camels' hair overcoat, then the middle of his broad person, with his hat nervously fingered by both hands, then his chest and neck, jointly adorned by a bright green tie, and finally his round black face, blank as a door knob, loose-lipped, wide-eyed. Brady was prodding him from behind.

"Sit down, Mr. Brown," said a voice out of the dark.

The unaccustomed "Mr." did not dispel the unreality of the situation for Bubber, who had not been so addressed six times in his twenty-six years. Nor was he reassured to find that he could not make out the one who had spoken, so blinding was the beam of light in his eyes. What he did realize was that the voice issued from the place where he had a short while ago looked with a wild surmise upon a corpse. For a moment his eyes grew whiter; then, with decision, he spun about and started away from the sound of that voice.

He bumped full into Brady. "Sit down!" growled Brady.

Said Dart, "It's me, Brown—the detective. Take that chair and answer what I ask you."

"Yes, suh," said Bubber weakly, and turned back and slowly edged into the space between the table and the visitors' chair. Perspiration glistened on his too illuminated brow. By the least possible bending of his body he managed to achieve the mere rim of the seat, where, with both hands gripping the chair arms, he crouched as if poised on some gigantic spring which any sudden sound might release to send him soaring into the shadows above.

"Brady, you're in the light. Take notes. All right, Mr. Brown. What's your full name?"

"Bubber Brown," stuttered that young man uncomfortably.

"Address?"

"2100 Fifth Avenue."

"Age?"

"Twenty-six."

"Occupation?"

"Suh?"

"Occupation?"

"Oh. Detective."

"De—what!"

"Detective. Yes, suh."

"Let's see your shield."

"My which?"

"Your badge."

"Oh. Well—y'see I ain't the kind o' detective what has to have a badge. No, suh."

"What kind are you?"

"I'm a family detective."

Somewhat more composed by the questioning, Bubber quickly reached into his pocket and produced a business card. Dart took it and snapped his light on it, to read:

BUBBER BROWN, INC., *Detective*
(formerly with the City of
New York)
2100 Fifth Avenue
Evidence obtained in affairs of the
heart, etc. Special attention to cheaters and backbiters.

Dart considered this a moment, then said:

"How long have you been breaking the law like this?"

"Breaking the law? Who, me? What old law, mistuh?"

"What about this 'Incorporated'? You're not incorporated."

"Oh, that? Oh, that's 'ink'—that means black."

"Don't play dumb. You know what it means, you know that you're not incorporated, and you know that you've never been a detective with the City. Now what's the idea? Who are you?"

Bubber had, as a matter of fact, proffered the card thoughtlessly in the strain of his discomfiture. Now he chose, wisely, to throw himself on Dart's good graces.

"Well, y'see times is been awful hard, everybody knows that. And I did have a job with the City—I was in the Distinguished Service Company——"

"The what?"

"The D. S. C.—Department of Street Cleaning—but we never called it that, no, suh. Coupla weeks ago I lost that job and couldn't find me nothin' else. Then I said to myself, 'They's only one chance, boy—you got to use your head instead o' your hands.' Well, I figured out the situation like this: The only business what was flourishin' was monkey-business——"

"What are you talking about?"

"Monkey-business. Cheatin'—backbitin', and all like that. Don't matter how bad business gets, lovin' still goes on; and long as lovin' is goin' on, cheatin' is goin' on too. Now folks'll pay to catch cheaters when they won't pay for other things, see? So I figure I can hire myself out to catch cheaters as well as anybody—all I got to do is bust in on 'em and tell the judge what I see. See? So I had me them cards printed and I'm r'arin' to go. But I didn't know 'twas against the law sho' 'nough."

"Well it is and I may have to arrest you for it."

Bubber's dismay was great.

"Couldn't you jes'—jes' tear up the card and let it go at that?"

"What was your business here tonight?"

"Me and Jinx come together. We was figurin' on askin' the man's advice about this detective business."

"You and who?"

"Jinx Jenkins—you know—the long boy look like a giraffe you seen downstairs."

"What time did you get here?"

" 'Bout half-past ten I guess."

"How do you know it was half-past ten?"

"I didn't say I knowed it, mistuh. I said I guess. But I know it wasn't no later'n that."

"How do you know?"

Thereupon, Bubber told how he knew.

3

At eight o'clock sharp, as indicated by his new dollar watch, purchased as a necessary tool of his new profession, he had been walking up and down in front of the Lafayette Theatre, apparently idling away his time, but actually taking this opportunity to hand out his new business cards to numerous theater-goers. It was his first attempt to get a case and he was not surprised to find that it promptly bore fruit in that happy-go-lucky, care-free, irresponsible atmosphere. A woman to whom he had handed one of his announcements returned to him for further information.

"I should 'a' known better," he admitted, "than to bother with her, because she was bad luck jes' to look at. She was cross-eyed. But I figure a cross-eyed dollar'll buy as much as a straight-eyed one and she talked like she meant business. She told me if I would get some good first-class low-down on her big boy, I wouldn't have no trouble collectin' my ten dollars. I say 'O.K., sister. Show me two bucks in front and his Cleo from behind, and I'll track 'em down like a bloodhound.' She reached down in her stockin', I held out my hand and the deal was on. I took her name an' address an' she showed me the Cleo and left. That is, I thought she left.

"The Cleo was the gal in the ticket-box. Oh, mistuh, what a Sheba! Keepin' my eyes on her was the easiest work I ever did in my life. I asked the flunky out front what this honey's name was and he tole me Jessie James. That was all I wanted to know. When I looked at her I felt like givin' the cross-eyed woman back her two bucks.

"A little before ten o'clock Miss Jessie James turned the ticket-box over to the flunky and disappeared inside. It was too late for me to spend money to go in then, and knowin' I prob'ly couldn't follow her everywhere she was goin' anyhow, I figured I might as well wait for her outside one door as another. So I waited out front, and in three or four minutes out she come. I followed her up the Avenue a piece and round a corner to a private house on 134th Street. After she'd been in a couple o' minutes I rung the bell. A fat lady come to the door and I asked for Miss Jessie James.

" 'Oh,' she say. 'Is you the gentleman she was expectin'?' I say, 'Yes ma'am. I'm one of 'em. They's another one comin'.' She say, 'Come right in. You can go up—her room is the top floor back. She jes' got here herself.' Boy, what a break. I didn' know for a minute whether this was business or pleasure.

"When I got to the head o' the stairs I walked easy. I snook up to the front-room door and found it cracked open 'bout half an inch. Naturally I looked in—that was business. But, friend, what I saw was nobody's business. Miss Jessie wasn't gettin' ready for no ordinary caller. She look like she was gettin' ready to try on a bathin' suit and meant to have a perfect fit. Nearly had a fit myself tryin' to get my breath back. Then I had to grab a armful o' hall closet, 'cause she reached for a kimono and started for the door. She passed by and I see I've got another break. So I seized opportunity by the horns and slipped into her room. Over across one corner was——"

"Wait a minute," interrupted Dart. "I didn't ask for your life history. I only asked——"

"You ast how I knowed it wasn't after half-past ten o'clock."

"Exactly."

"I'm tellin' you, mistuh. Listen. Over across one corner was a trunk—a wardrobe trunk, standin' up on end and wide open. I got behind it and squatted down. I looked at my watch. It was ten minutes past ten. No sooner'n I got the trunk straight 'cross the corner again I heard her laughin' out in the hall and I heard a man laughin', too. I say to myself, 'here 'tis. The bathin'-suit salesman done arrived.'

"And from behind that trunk, y'see, I couldn't use nothin' but my ears—couldn't see a thing. That corner had me pretty crowded. Well, instead o' goin' on and talkin', they suddenly got very quiet, and natchelly I got very curious. It was my business to know what was goin' on.

"So instead o' scronchin' down behind the trunk like I'd been doin', I begun to inch up little at a time till I could see over the top. Lord—what did I do that for? Don' know jes' how it happened, but next thing

I do know is 'wham!'—the trunk had left me. There it was flat on the floor, face down, like a Hindu sayin' his prayers, and there was me in the corner, lookin' dumb and sayin' mine, with the biggest boogy in Harlem 'tween me and the door.

"Fact is, I forgot I was a detective. Only thing I wanted to detect was the quickest way out. Was that guy evil-lookin'? One thing saved me—the man didn't know whether to blame me or her. Before he could make up his mind, I shot out o' that corner past him like a cannon-ball. The gal yelled, 'Stop thief!' And the guy started after me. But, shuh!—he never had a chance —even in them runnin'-pants o' his. I flowed down the stairs and popped out the front door, and who was waitin' on the sidewalk but the cross-eyed lady. She'd done followed me same as I followed the Sheba. Musta hid when her man went by on the way in. But when he come by chasin' me on the way out, she jumped in between us and ast him where was his pants.

"Me, I didn't stop to hear the answer. I knew it. I made Lenox Avenue in nothin' and no fifths. That wasn't no more than quarter past ten. I slowed up and turned down Lenox Avenue. Hadn' gone a block before I met Jinx Jenkins. I told him 'bout it and ast him what he thought I better do next. Well, somebody'd jes' been tellin' him 'bout what a wonderful guy this Frimbo was for folks in need o' advice. We agreed to come see him and walked on round here. Now, I know it didn't take me no fifteen minutes to get from that gal's house here. So I must 'a' been here before half-past ten, y'see?"

4

Further questioning elicited that when Jinx and Bubber arrived they had made their way, none too eagerly, up the stairs in obedience to a sign in the lower hallway and had encountered no one until they reached the reception-room in front. Here there had been three men, waiting to see Frimbo. One, Bubber had recognized as Spider Webb, a number-runner who worked for Harlem's well-known policy-king, Si Brandon. Another, who had pestered Jinx with unwelcome conversation, was a notorious little drug-addict called Doty Hicks. The third was a genial stranger who had talked pleasantly to everybody, revealing himself to be one Easley Jones, a railroad man.

After a short wait, Frimbo's flunky appeared from the hallway and ushered the railroad man, who had been the first to arrive, out of the room through the wide velvet-curtained passage. While Jones was, presumably, with Frimbo, the two ladies had come in—the young one first. Then Doty Hicks had gone in to Frimbo, then Spider Webb, and finally Jinx. The usher had not himself gone through the wide doorway at any time—he had only bowed the visitors through, turned aside, and disappeared down the hallway.

"This usher—what was he like?"

"Tall, skinny, black, stoop-shouldered, and cock-eyed. Wore a long black silk robe like Frimbo's, but he had a bright yellow sash and a bright yellow thing on his head—you know—what d'y' call 'em? Look like bandages——"

"Turban?"

"That's it. Turban."

"Where is he now?"

"Don't ask me, mistuh. I ain't seen him since he showed Jinx in."

"Hm."

"Say!" Bubber had an idea.

"What?"

"I bet he done it!"

"Did what?"

"Scrambled the man's eggs!"

"You mean you think the assistant killed Frimbo?"

"Sho'!"

"How do you know Frimbo was killed?"

"Didn't—didn't you and the doc say he was when I was downstairs lookin' at you?"

"On the contrary, we said quite definitely that we didn't know that he was killed, and that even if he was, that blow didn't kill him."

"But—in the front room jes' now, didn't the doc tell that lady——"

"All the doctor said was that it looked like Frimbo had an enemy. Now you say Frimbo was killed and you accuse somebody of doing it."

"All I meant——"

"You were in this house when he died, weren't you? By your own time."

"I was here when the doc says he died, but——"

"Why would you accuse anybody of a crime if you didn't know that a crime had been committed?"

"Listen, mistuh, please. All I meant was, *if* the man

was killed, the flunky *might* 'a' done it and hauled hips. He could be in Egypt by now."

Dart's identical remark came back to him. He said less sharply:

"Yes. But on the other hand you might be calling attention to that fact to avert suspicion from yourself."

"Who—me?" Bubber's eyes went incredibly large. "Good Lord, man, I didn't leave that room yonder—that waitin'-room—till Jinx called me in to see the man—and he was dead then. 'Deed that's the truth—I come straight up the stairs with Jinx—we went straight in the front room—and I didn't come out till Jinx called me—ask the others—ask them two women."

"I will. But they can only testify for your presence in that room. Who says you came up the stairs and went straight into that room? How can you prove you did that? How do I know you didn't stop in here by way of that side hall-door there, and attack Frimbo as he sat here in this chair?"

The utter unexpectedness of his own incrimination, and the detective's startling insistence upon it, almost robbed Bubber of speech, a function which he rarely relinquished. For a moment he could only gape. But he managed to sputter: "Judas Priest, mistuh, can't you take a man's word for nothin'?"

"I certainly can't," said the detective.

"Well, then," said Bubber, inspired, "ask Jinx. He seen me. He come in with me."

"I see. You alibi him and he alibis you. Is that it?"

"Damn!" exploded Bubber. "You is the most suspicious man I ever met!"

"You're not exactly free of suspicion yourself," Dart returned dryly.

"Listen, mistuh. If you bumped a man off, would you run get a doctor and hang around to get pinched? Would you?"

"If I thought that would make me look innocent I might—yes."

"Then you're dumber'n I am. If I'd done it, I'd been long gone by now."

"Still," Dart said, "you have only the word of your friend Jinx to prove you went straight into the waiting-room. That's insufficient testimony. Got a handkerchief on you?"

"Sho'." Bubber reached into his breast pocket and produced a large and flagrant affair apparently designed for appearance rather than for service; a veritable flag, crossed in one direction by a bright orange band and in another, at right angles to the first, by a virulent green one. "My special kind," he said; "always buy these. Man has to have a little color in his clothes, y'see?"

"Yes, I see. Got any others?"

" 'Nother one like this—but it's dirty." He produced the mate, crumpled and matted, out of another pocket.

"O.K. Put 'em away. See anybody here tonight with a colored handkerchief of any kind?"

"No suh—not that I remember."

"All right. Now tell me this. Did you notice the

decorations on the walls in the front room when you first arrived?"

"Couldn't help noticin' them things—'nough to scare anybody dizzy."

"What did you see?"

"You mean them false-faces and knives and swords and things?"

"Yes. Did you notice anything in particular on the mantelpiece?"

"Yea. I went over and looked at it soon as I come in. What I remember most was a pair o' clubs. One was on one end o' the mantelpiece, and the other was on the other. Look like they was made out o' bones."

"You are sure there were two of them?"

"Sho' they was two. One on——"

"Did you touch them?"

"No *suh*—couldn't pay me to touch none o' them things—might 'a' been conjured."

"Did you see anyone touch them?"

"No, suh."

"You saw no one remove one of them?"

"No, suh."

"So far as you know they are still there?"

"Yes, suh."

"Who was in that room, besides yourself, when you first saw the two clubs?"

"Everybody. That was befo' the flunky'd come in to get the railroad man."

"I see. Now these two women—how soon after you got there did they come in?"

" 'Bout ten minutes or so."

"Did either of them leave the room while you were there?"

"No, suh."

"And the first man—Easley Jones, the railroad porter —he had come into this room before the women arrived?"

"Yes, suh. He was the first one here, I guess."

"After he went in to Frimbo, did he come back into the waiting-room?"

"No, suh. Reckon he left by this side door here into the hall."

"Did either of the other two return to the waiting-room?"

"No, suh. Guess they all left the same way. Only one that came back was Jinx, when he called me."

"And at that time, you and the women were the only people left in the waiting-room?"

"Yes, suh."

"Very good. Could you identify those three men?"

" 'Deed I could. I could even find 'em if you said so."

"Perhaps I will. For the present you go back to the front room. Don't try anything funny—the house is lousy with policemen."

"Lousy is right," muttered Bubber.

"What's that?"

"I ain't opened my mouth, mistuh. But listen, you don't think I done it sho' 'nough do you?"

"That will depend entirely on whether the women corroborate your statement."

"Well, whatever that is, I sho' hope they do it."

CHAPTER SEVEN

I

"**B**RADY, ask the lady who arrived first to come in," said Dart, adding in a low aside to the physician, "if her story checks with Brown's on the point of his staying in that room, I think I can use him for something. He couldn't have taken that club out without leaving the room."

"He tells a straight story," agreed Dr. Archer. "Too scared to lie. But isn't it too soon to let anybody out?"

"I don't mean to let him go. But I can send him with a couple o' cops to identify the other men who were here and bring them back, without being afraid he'll start anything."

"Why not go with him and question them where you find 'em?"

"It's easier to have 'em all in one place if possible—saves everybody's time. Can't always do it of course. Here comes the lady—your friend."

"Be nice to her—she's the real thing. I've known her for years."

"O. K."

Uncertainly, the young woman entered, the beam of light revealing clearly her unusually attractive appearance. With undisguised bewilderment on her pretty face, but with no sign of fear, she took the visitors' chair.

"Don't be afraid, Mrs. Crouch. I want you to answer, as accurately as you can, a few questions which may help determine who killed Frimbo."

"I'll be glad to," she said in a low, matter-of-fact tone.

"What time did you arrive here tonight?"

"Shortly after ten-thirty."

"You're sure of the time?"

"I was at the Lenox. The feature picture goes on for the last time at ten-thirty. I had seen it already, and when it came on again I left. It is no more than four or five minutes' walk from there here."

"Good. You came directly to Frimbo's waiting-room?"

"No. I stopped downstairs to see if my husband was there."

"Your husband? Oh—Mr. Crouch, the undertaker, is your husband?"

"Yes. But he was out."

"Does he usually go out and leave his place open?"

"Late in the evening, yes. Up until then there is a clerk. Afterwards if he is called out he just leaves a sign saying when he will return. He never," she smiled faintly, "has to fear robbers, you see."

"But might not calls come in while he is out?"

"Yes. But they are handled by a telephone exchange. If he doesn't answer, the exchange takes the call and gives it to him later."

"I see. How long did stopping downstairs delay you?"

"Only a minute. Then I came right up to the waiting-room."

"Who was there when you got there?"

"Four men."

"Did you know any of them?"

"No, but I'd know them if I saw them again."

"Describe them."

"Well there was a little thin nervous man who looked like he was sick—in fact he was sick, because when he got up to follow the assistant he had a dizzy spell and fell, and all the men jumped to him and had to help him up."

"He was the first to go in to Frimbo after you arrived?"

"Yes. Then there was a heavy-set, rather flashily-dressed man in gray. He went in next. And there were two others who seemed to be together—the two who were in there a few minutes ago when you and Dr. Archer came in."

"A tall fellow and a short one?"

"Yes."

"About those two—did either of them leave the room while you were there?"

"The tall one did, when his turn came to see Frimbo."

"And the short one?"

"Well—when the tall one had been out for about five or six minutes, he came back—through the same way that he had gone. It was rather startling because nobody else had come back at all except Frimbo's man, and he always appeared in the hall doorway, not the other, and always left by the hall doorway also. And, too, this tall fellow looked terribly excited. He beckoned to the short one and they went back together through the passage—into this room."

"That was the first and only time the short man left that room while you were there?"

"Yes."

"And you yourself did not leave the room meanwhile?"

"No. Not until now."

"Did anyone else come in?"

"The other woman, who is in there now."

"Very good. Now, pardon me if I seem personal, but it's my business not to mind my business—to meddle with other people's. You understand?"

"Perfectly. Don't apologize—just ask."

"Thank you. Did you know anything about this man Frimbo—his habits, friends, enemies?"

"No. He had many followers, I know, and a great reputation for being able to cast spells and that sort of thing. His only companion, so far as I know, was his servant. Otherwise he seemed to lead a very secluded life. I imagine he must have been pretty well off financially. He'd been here almost two years. He was always our best tenant."

"Tell me why you came to see Frimbo tonight, please."

"Certainly. Mr. Crouch owns this house, among others, and Frimbo is our tenant. My job is collecting rents, and tonight I came to collect Frimbo's."

"I see. But do you find it more convenient to see tenants at night?"

he
must
be
the
criminal!

⚹ "Not so much for me as for them. Most of them are working during the day. And Frimbo simply can't be seen in the daytime—he won't see anyone either professionally or on business until after dark. It's one of his peculiarities, I suppose."

"So that by coming during his office hours you are sure of finding him available?"

"Exactly."

"All right, Mrs. Crouch. That's all for the present. Will you return to the front room? I'd let you go at once, but you may be able to help me further if you will."

"I'll be glad to."

"Thank you. Brady, call in Bubber Brown and one of those extra men."

When Bubber reappeared, Dart said:

"You told me you could locate and identify the three men who preceded Jenkins?"

"Yes, suh. I sho' can."

"How?"

"Well, I been seein' that little Doty Hicks plenty. He hangs out 'round his brother's night club. 'Cose ev'ybody knows Spider Webb's a runner and I can find him from now till mornin' at Patmore's Pool Room. And that other one, the railroad man, he and I had quite a conversation before he come in to see Frimbo, and I found out where he rooms when he's in town. Jes' a half a block up the street here, in a private house."

"Good." The detective turned to the officer whom Brady had summoned:

"Hello, Hanks. Listen Hanks, you take Mr. Brown

there around by the precinct, pick up another man, and then go with Mr. Brown and bring the men he identifies here. There'll be three of 'em. Take my car and make it snappy."

Why is Jinx so cold and suspicious? who is he?

2

Jinx, behind a mask of scowling ill-humor, which was always his readiest defense under strain, sat now in the uncomfortably illuminated chair and growled his answers into the darkness whence issued Dart's voice. This apparently crusty attitude, which long use had made habitual, served only to antagonize his questioner, so that even the simplest of his answers were taken as unsatisfactory. Even in the perfectly routine but obviously important item of establishing his identity, he made a bad beginning.

he knows something about the murder

"Have you anything with you to prove your identity?"

"Nothin' but my tongue." *very snark*

"What do you mean?"

"I mean I say I'm who I is. Who'd know better?"

"No one, of course. But it's possible that you might say who you were not."

"Who I ain't? Sho' I can say who I ain't. I ain't Marcus Garvey, I ain't Al Capone, I ain't Cal Coolidge —I ain't nobody but me—Jinx Jenkins, myself."

"Very well, Mr. Jenkins. Where do you live? What sort of work do you do?"

"Any sort I can get. Ain't doin' nothin' right now."

"M-m. What time did you get here tonight?"

On this and other similar points, Jinx's answers, for all their gruffness, checked with those of Bubber and Martha Crouch. He had come with Bubber a little before ten-thirty. They had gone straight to the waiting-room and found three men. The women had come in later. Then the detective asked him to describe in detail what had transpired when he left the others and went in to see Frimbo. And though Jinx's vocabulary was wholly inadequate, so deeply had that period registered itself upon his mind that he omitted not a single essential item. His imperfections of speech became negligible and were quite ignored; indeed, the more tutored minds of his listeners filled in or substituted automatically, and both the detective and the physician, the latter perhaps more completely, were able to observe the reconstructed scene as if it were even now being played before their eyes.

3

The black servitor with the yellow headdress and the cast in one eye ushered Jinx to the broad black curtains, saying in a low voice as he bowed him through, "Please go in, sit down, say nothing till Frimbo speaks." Thereupon the curtains fell to behind him and he was in a small dark passage, whose purpose was obviously to separate the waiting-room from the mystic chamber beyond and thus prevent Frimbo's voice from reaching the circle of waiting callers. Jinx shuffled forward toward the single bright light that at once attracted and blinded. He sidled in between the chair and table and sat down facing the figure beneath the hanging light. He was unable, because of the blinding glare, to descry any characteristic feature of the man he had come to see; he could only make out a dark shadow with a head that seemed to be enormous, cocked somewhat sidewise as if in a steady contemplation of the visitor.

For a time the shadow made no sound or movement, and Jinx squirmed about impatiently in his seat, trying to obey directions and restrain the impulse to say something. At one moment the figure seemed to fade away altogether and blend with the enveloping blackness beyond. This was the very limit of Jinx's endurance—but at this moment Frimbo spoke.

"Please do not shield your eyes. I must study your face."

The voice changed the atmosphere from one of discomfiture to one of assurance. It was a deep, rich, calm voice, so matter of fact and real, even in that atmosphere, as to dispel doubt and inspire confidence.

"You see, I must analyze your mind by observing your countenance. Only thus can I learn how to help you."

Here was a man that knew something. Didn't talk like an African native certainly. Didn't talk like any black man Jinx had ever heard. Not a trace of Negro accent, not a suggestion of dialect. He spoke like a white-haired judge on the bench, easily, smoothly, quietly.

"There are those who claim the power to read men's lives in crystal spheres. That is utter nonsense. I claim the power to read men's lives in their faces. That is completely reasonable. Every experience, every thought, leaves its mark. Past and present are written there clearly. He who knows completely the past and the present can deduce the inevitable future, which past and present determine. My crystal sphere, therefore, is your face. By reading correctly what is there I know what is scheduled to follow, and so can predict and guard you against your future."

"Yes, suh," said Jinx.

"I notice that you are at present out of work. It is this you wish to consult me about."

Jinx's eyes dilated. "Yes, suh, that's right."

"You have been without a job several weeks."

"Month come Tuesday."

"Yes. And now you have reached the point where you must seek the financial aid of your friends. Being of a proud and independent nature, you find this difficult. Yet even the fee which you will pay for the advice I give you is borrowed money."

There was no tone of question, no implied request for confirmation. The words were a simple statement of fact, presented as a comprehensive résumé of a situation, expressed merely as a basis for more important deductions to follow.

"So far, you see, my friend, I have done nothing at all mysterious. All this is the process of reason, based on observation. And now, though you may think it a strange power, let me add that there is nothing mysterious either in my being able to tell you that your name is Jenkins, that your friends call you Jinx, that you are twenty-seven years old, and that you are unmarried. All these matters have passed through your mind as you sat there listening to me. This is merely an acuteness of mental receptivity which anyone can learn; it is usually called telepathy. At this point, Mr. Jenkins, others whom you might have consulted stop. But at this point—Frimbo begins."

There was a moment's silence. The voice resumed with added depth and solemnity:

"For, in addition to the things that can be learned by anyone, Frimbo inherits the bequest of a hundred centuries, handed from son to son through four hundred unbroken generations of Buwongo kings. It is a profound and dangerous secret, my friend, a secret my fathers knew when the kings of the Nile still thought human flesh a delicacy."

The voice sank to a lower pitch still, inescapably impressive.

"Frimbo can change the future." He paused, then continued, "In the midst of a world of determined, inevitable events, of results rigidly fashioned by the past, Frimbo alone is free. Frimbo not only sees. Frimbo and Frimbo alone can step in at will and change the course of a life. Listen!"

The voice now became intimate, confidential, shading off from low vibrant tones into softly sibilant whispers:

"Your immediate needs will be taken care of but you will not be content. It is a strange thing that I see. For though food and shelter in abundance are to be your lot sooner than you think, still you will be more unhappy than you are now; and you will rejoice only when this physical security has been withdrawn. You will be over-joyed to return to the uncertain fortunes over which you now despair. I do not see the circumstances, at the moment, that will bring on these situations, because they are outside the present content of your mind which I am contemplating. But these things even now impatiently await you—adequate physical necessaries, but great mental distress.

"Now then, when you have passed through that paradoxical period, what will you do? Let me see. It is but a short way—a few days ahead—but——" Into that until now completely self-assured tone crept a quality of puzzlement. It was so unexpected and incongruous a change that Jinx, up to this point completely fascinated, was startled like one rudely awakened from deep sleep. "It is very dark——" There was a long pause. The same voice resumed, "What is this, Frimbo?" Again a pause; then: "Strange how suddenly it grows dark. Frimbo ——" Bewilderment dilated into dismay. "Frimbo! Frimbo! *Why do you not see?*"

The voice of a man struck suddenly blind could not have been imbued with greater horror. So swift and definite was the transition that the alarmed Jinx could only grip the arms of his chair and stare hard. And despite the glaring beam, he saw a change in the figure beyond the table. That part of the shadow that had corresponded to the head seemed now to be but half its original size.

In a sudden frenzy of terror, Jinx jumped up and reached for the hanging light. Quickly he swung it around and tilted it so that the luminous shaft fell on the seated figure. What he saw was a bare black head, inclined limply sidewise, the mouth open, the eyes fixed, staring from under drooping lids.

He released the light, wheeled, and fled back to summon Bubber.

4

All this Jinx rehearsed in detail, making clear by implication or paraphrase those ideas whose original wording he was otherwise unable to describe or pronounce. The doctor emitted a low whistle of amazement; the detective, incredulous, said:

"Wait a minute. Let me get this straight. You mean to say that Frimbo actually talked to you, as you have related?"

" 'Deed he did."

"You're sure that it was Frimbo talking to you?"

"Jest as sure as I am that you're talkin' to me now. He was right where you is."

"And when he tried to prophesy what would happen to you a few days hence, he couldn't?"

"Look like sump'm come over him all of a sudden—claim he couldn't see. And when he seen he couldn't see, he got scared-like and hollered out jes' like I said: 'Frimbo—why don't you see?' "

"Then you say *you* tried to see *him*, and it looked as though his head had shrunken?"

"Yes, suh."

"Evidently his head-piece had fallen off."

"His which?"

Frimbo might have been murdered before anyone entered?

"Did you hear any sound just before this—like a blow?"

"Nope. Didn't hear nothin' but his voice. And it didn't stop like it would if he'd been hit. It jes' stopped like it would if he'd been tellin' 'bout sump'm he'd been lookin' at and then couldn't see no more. Only it scared him sump'm terrible not to be able to see it. Maybe he scared himself to death."

"Hm. Yea, maybe he even scared up that wound on his head."

"Well, maybe me and Bubber did that."

"How?"

"Carryin' him downstairs. We was in an awful hurry. His head might 'a' hit sump'm on the way down."

"But," said Dart, and Jinx couldn't know this was baiting, "if he was dead, that wound wouldn't have bled, even as little as it did."

"Maybe," Jinx insisted, "it stopped because he died jes' about that time—on the way down."

"You seem very anxious to account for his death, Jenkins."

"Humph," Jinx grunted. "You act kind o' anxious yourself, seems like to me."

"Yes. But there is this difference. By your own word, you were present and the only person present when Frimbo died. I was half a mile away."

"So what?"

"So that, while I'm as anxious as you are to account for this man's death, I am anxious for perhaps quite a different reason. For instance, I could not possibly be trying to prove my own innocence by insisting he died a natural death."

Jinx's memory was better than Bubber's.

"I ain't heard nobody say for sho' he was killed yet," said he.

"No? Well then, listen. We know that this man was murdered. We know that he was killed deliberately by somebody who meant to do a good job—and succeeded."

"And you reckon I done it?" There was no surprise in Jinx's voice, for he had long had the possibility in mind.

"I reckon nothing. I simply try to get the facts. When enough facts are gathered, they'll do all the reckoning necessary. One way of getting the facts is from the testimony of people who know the facts. The trouble with that is that anybody who knows the facts might have reasons for lying. I have to weed out the lies. I'm telling you this to show you that if you are innocent, you can best defend yourself by telling the truth, no matter how bad it looks."

"What you think I *been* doin'?"

"You've been telling a queer story, part of which we know to be absolutely impossible—unless——" The detective entertained a new consideration. "Listen. What time did you come into this room—as nearly as you can judge?"

"Musta been 'bout—'bout five minutes to eleven."

"How long did Frimbo talk to you?"

" 'Bout five or six minutes I guess."

"That would be eleven o'clock. Then you got Bubber. Dr. Archer, what time were you called?"

"Three minutes past eleven—according to the clock on my radio."

"Not a lot of time—three minutes—Bubber took three minutes to get you and get back. During those three minutes Jenkins was alone with the dead man."

"Not me," denied Jinx. "I was out there in the hall right at the head o' the stairs where the doc found me— wonderin' what the hell was keepin' 'em so long." This was so convincingly ingenuous that the physician agreed with a smile. "He was certainly there when I got here."

"During those few minutes, Jenkins, when you were here alone, did you see or hear anything peculiar?"

"No, 'ndeed. The silence liked to drown me."

"And when you came back in this room with the doctor, was everything just as you left it?"

"Far as I could see."

"M-m. Listen, doc. Did you leave the body at all from the time you first saw it until I got here?"

"No. Not even to phone the precinct—I had the two men do it."

"Funny," Dart muttered. "Damn funny." For a moment he meditated the irreconcilable points in Jinx's story—the immobility of Frimbo's figure, from which nevertheless the turban had fallen, the absence of any sound of an attack, yet a sudden change in Frimbo's speech and manner just before he was discovered dead; the remoteness of any opportunity—except for Jinx himself—to reach the prostrate victim, cram that hand-kerchief in place, and depart during the three minutes when Jinx claimed to be in the hall, without noticeably disturbing the body; and the utter impossibility of any man's talking, dead or alive, when his throat was plugged with that rag which the detective's own eyes had seen removed. Clearly Jenkins was either mistaken in some of the statements he made so positively or else he was lying. If he was lying he was doing so to protect himself, directly or indirectly. In other words, if he was lying, either he knew who committed the crime or he had committed it himself. Only further evidence could indicate the true and the false in this curious chronicle.

And so Dart said, rather casually, as if he were asking a favor, "Have you a handkerchief about you, Mr. Jenkins?"

" 'Tain't what you'd call strictly clean," Jinx obligingly reached into his right-hand coat pocket, "but——" He stopped. His left hand went into his left coat pocket. Both hands came out and delved into their respective trousers pockets. "Guess I must 'a' dropped it," he said. "I had one."

"You're sure you had one?"

"M'hm. Had it when I come here."

"When you came into this room?"

"No. When I first went in the front room. I was a little nervous-like. I wiped my face with it. I think I put it——"

"Is that the last time you recall having it—when you first went into the front room?"

"Uh–huh."

"Can you describe it?"

Perhaps this odd insistence on anything so unimportant as a handkerchief put Jinx on his guard. At any rate he dodged.

"What difference it make?"

"Can you describe it?"

"No."

"No? Why can't you?"

"Nothin' to describe. Jes' a plain big white handker-chief with a——" He stopped.

"With a what?"

"With a hem," said Jinx.

"Hm."

"Yea—hem."

"A white hem?"

"It wasn' no black one," said Jinx, in typical Har-lemese.

The detective fell silent a moment, then said:

"All right, Jenkins. That's all for the present. You go back to the front room."

Officer Brady escorted Jinx out, and returned.

"Brady, tell Green, who is up front, to take note of everything he overhears those people in there say. You come back here."

Obediently, Officer Brady turned away.

"Light!" called Dart, and the bluecoat in the hall pressed the switch that turned on the extension light.

In which the investigation continues
with interrogation of Mrs. Snead
and we are introduced to Mr. Crouch
the undertaker, who reveals the
existence of the arrogant butler

CHAPTER EIGHT

I

"**W**HAT do you think of Jenkins' story?" Dr. Archer asked.

"Well, even before he balked on the handkerchief," answered Dart, "I couldn't believe him. Then when he balked on describing the blue border, it messed up the whole thing."

"He certainly was convincing about that interview, though. He couldn't have just conjured up that story—it's too definite."

"Yes. But I'm giving him a little time to cool off. Maybe the details won't be so exact next time."

"As I figure it, he could be right—at least concerning the time the fatal attack occurred. It would be right at the end of the one-half hour period in which I first estimated death to have taken place. And in the state of mind he was in when Frimbo seemed to be performing miracles of clairvoyance, he might easily have failed to hear the attack. Certainly he could have failed to see it —he didn't see me standing here beside you."

"You're thinking of the crack on the head. You surely don't suppose Jenkins could have failed to see anyone trying to push that handkerchief in place?"

"No. But that could have been done in the minute

when he ran up front to get Bubber. It would have to be fast work, of course."

"Damn right it would. I really don't believe in considering the remote possibilities first. In this game you've got to be practical. Fit conclusions to the facts, not facts to conclusions. Personally I don't feel one way or the other about Jenkins—except that he is unnecessarily antagonistic. That won't help him at all. But I'm certainly satisfied, from testimony, that he is not the guilty party. His attitude, his impossible story, his balking on the blue-bordered handkerchief——"

"You think it's his handkerchief?"

"I think he could have described it—from the way he balked. If he could have described it, why didn't he? Because it belonged either to him or to somebody he wanted to cover."

"He was balking all right."

"Of course, that wouldn't make him guilty. But it wouldn't exactly clear him either."

"Not exactly. On the other hand, the Frimbo part of his story—what Frimbo said to him—is stuff that a man like Jenkins couldn't possibly have thought up. It was Frimbo talking—that I'm sure of."

"Through a neckful of cotton cloth?"

"No. When he was talking to Jenkins, his throat was unobstructed."

"Well—that means that, the way it looks now, there are two possibilities: somebody did it either when Jenkins went up front to get Bubber or when Bubber went to get you. Let's get the other woman in. All right,

Brady, bring in the other lady. Douse the glim, outside there."

Out went the extension light; the original bright horizontal shaft shot forth like an accusing finger pointing toward the front room, while the rest of the death chamber went black.

2

Awkwardly, not unlike an eccentric dancer, the tall thin woman took the spotlight, stood glaring a wide-eyed hostile moment, then disposed herself in a bristlingly erect attitude on the edge of the visitor's chair. Every angle of her meagre, poorly clad form, every feature of her bony countenance, exhibited resentment.

"What is your name, madam?"

"Who's that?" The voice was high, harsh, and querulous.

"Detective Dart. I'm sitting in a chair opposite you."

"Is you the one was in yonder a while ago?"

"Yes. Now——"

"What kind o' detective is you?"

"A police detective, madam, of the City of New York. And please let me ask the questions, while you confine yourself to the answers."

"Police detective? 'Tain't so. They don't have no black detectives."

"Your informant was either ignorant or color-blind, madam.—Now would you care to give your answers here or around at the police station?"

The woman fell silent. Accepting this as a change of heart, the detective repeated:

"What is your name?"

"Aramintha Snead."

"Mrs. or Miss?"

"Mrs." The tone indicated that a detective should be able to tell.

"Your address?"

"19 West 134th Street."

"You're an American, of course?"

"I is now. But I originally come from Savannah, Georgia."

"Occupation?"

"Occupation? You mean what kind o' work I do?"

"Yes, madam."

"I don't do no work at all—not for wages. I'm a church-worker though."

"A church-worker? You spend a good deal of time in church then?"

"Can't nobody spend too much time in church. Though I declare I been wonderin' lately if there ain't some things the devil can 'tend to better'n the Lord."

"What brought you here tonight?"

"My two feet."

Dart sighed patiently and pursued:

"How does it happen that a devoted church-worker like you, Mrs. Snead, comes to seek the advice of a man like Frimbo, a master of the powers of darkness? I should think you would have sought the help of your pastor instead."

"I did, but it never done no good. Every time I go to

the Rev'n the Rev'n say, 'Daughter take it to the Lord in prayer.' Well, I done like he said. I took it and took it. Tonight I got tired takin' it."

"Tonight? Why tonight?"

"Tonight was prayer-meetin' night. I ain' missed a prayer-meetin' in two years. And for two years, week after week—every night for that matter, but specially at Friday night prayer-meetin'—I been prayin' to the Lord to stop my husband from drinkin'. Not that I object to the drinkin' itself, y'understand. The Lord made water into wine. But when Jake come home night after night jes' drunk enough to take pleasure in beatin' the breath out o' me—that's another thing altogether."

"I quite agree with you," encouraged Dart.

In the contemplation of her troubles, Mrs. Snead relinquished some of her indignation, or, more exactly, transferred it from the present to the past.

"Well, lo and behold, tonight I ain't no sooner got through prayin' for him at the meetin' and took myself on home than he greets me at the door with a cuff side o' the head. Jes' by way of interduction, he say, so next time I'd be there when he come in. And why in who-who ain't his supper ready? So I jes' turn around and walk off. And I thought to myself as I walked, 'If one medicine don' help, maybe another will.' So I made up my mind. Everybody know 'bout this man Frimbo— say he can conjure on down. And I figger I been takin' it to the Lord in prayer long enough. Now I'm goin' take it to the devil."

"So you came here?"

"Yes."

"How did you happen to choose Frimbo out of all the conjure-men in Harlem?"

"He was the only one I knowed anything about."

"What did you know about him?"

"Knowed what he done for Sister Susan Gassoway's boy, Lem. She was tellin' me 'bout it jes' a couple o' weeks ago—two weeks ago tonight. We was at prayer-meetin'. Old man Hezekiah Mosby was prayin' and when he gets to prayin' they ain't no stoppin' him. So Sister Gassoway and me, we was talkin' and she told me what this man Frimbo'd done for her boy, Lem. Lem got in a little trouble—wild boy he is, anyhow—and put the blame on somebody else. This other boy swore he'd kill Lem, and Lem believed him. So he come to this Frimbo and Frimbo put a charm on him—told him he'd come through it all right. Well you 'member that case what was in the *Amsterdam News* 'bout a boy havin' a knife stuck clean through his head and broke off and the hole closed over and he thought he was jes' cut and didn't know the knife was in there?"

"Yes. Went to Harlem Hospital, was X-rayed, and had the knife removed."

"And lived! That was Lem Gassoway. Nothin' like it ever heard of before. Anybody else'd 'a' been killed on the spot. But not Lem. Lem was under Frimbo's spell. That's what saved him."

"And that's why you chose Frimbo?"

" 'Deed so. Wouldn't you?"

"No doubt. At just what time did you get here, Mrs. Snead?"

"Little after half-past ten."

"Did anyone let you in?"

"No. I did like the sign say—open and walk in."

"You came straight upstairs and into the waiting-room?"

"Yes."

"Did you see anybody?"

"Nobody but that other girl and them two fellers that was 'bout to fight jes' now and a couple o' other men in the room. Oh, yes—the—the butler or whatever he was. Evilest-lookin' somebody y'ever see—liked to scared me to death." ✳

"Did you notice anything of interest while you were waiting your turn?"

"Huh? Oh—yes. When one o' them other two men got up to go see the conjure-man, he couldn't hold his feet—must 'a' been drunker'n my Jake. 'Deed so, 'cause down he fell right in the middle o' the floor, and I guess he'd been there yet if them other men hadn't helped him up."

"Who helped him?"

"All of 'em."

"Did you notice the mantelpiece?"

"With all them conjures on it? I didn't miss."

"Did you see those two clubs with the silver tips?"

"Two? Uh–uh—I don't remember no two. I 'member one though. But I wasn't payin' much attention—might 'a' been a dozen of 'em for all I know. There was so many devilish-lookin' things 'round." ✳

"Did you see anyone with a blue-bordered white handkerchief—a man's handkerchief?"

"No, suh."

"You are sure you did not see any such handkerchief —in one of the men's pockets, perhaps?"

"What men is got in they pockets ain't none my business."

3

There were, at this point, sounds of a new arrival in the hall. The officer at the hall door was speaking to a man who had just appeared. This man was saying:

"My name is Crouch. Yes, I have the funeral parlor downstairs. I'd like to see the officer in charge."

"Ask Mr. Crouch in, Brady," called Dart. "Mrs. Snead, you may return to the front room, if you will."

"To the front room!" expostulated the woman. "How long do you expect me to stay in this place?"

"Not very long, I hope. Brady, take the young lady up front. Come right in, Mr. Crouch. Take that chair, will you please? I'm glad you came by."

"Whew! It's dark as midnight in here," said the newcomer, vainly trying to make out who was present. He went promptly, however, to the illuminated chair, and sat down. His manner was pleasantly bewildered, and it was clear that he was as anxious to learn what had occurred as were the police. He grasped at once the value of the lighting arrangement of which Dart had taken advantage and grinned. "Judas, what a bright light! Clever though. Can't see a thing. Who are you, if I may ask?"

Dart told him.

"Glad to know you—though so far you're just a voice.

Understand I've lost a tenant. Came back expecting to put the finishing touches on a little job down stairs, and found the place full of officers. Fellow in the door took my breath away—says Frimbo's been killed. How'd it happen?"

Dart's sharp black eyes were studying the undertaker closely. He observed a youngish man of medium build with skin the color of an English walnut, smooth, unblemished, and well cared for. The round face was clean shaven, the features blunt but not coarse, the eyes an indeterminate brown like most Negroes'. His hair was his most noteworthy possession, for it was as black and as straight as an Indian's and it shone with a bright gloss in the light that fell full upon it. His attire was quiet and his air was that of a matter-of-fact, yet genial business man on whom it would be difficult to play tricks. His manner, more than his inquiry, indicated that while there was no need of getting excited over something that couldn't be restored, still it was his right, as neighbor and landlord, to know just what had come about and how.

"Perhaps, Mr. Crouch," replied Dart, "you can answer your own question for us."

If the detective anticipated catching any twitch of feature that might have betrayed masquerading on the undertaker's part he was disappointed. Crouch's expression manifested only a curiosity which now became meditative.

"Well," he said reflectively, "let me see now. You know that he was killed, of course?"

"More than that. We know how he was killed. We

know when. We even have evidence of the assailant's identity."

"Assailant? Oh, he was assaulted then? One of his customers, probably. Why, say, if you know that much, you shouldn't have much trouble. It would be narrowed down to whoever was here at the time who wanted to kill him. But that's just your difficulty. Who'd want to kill him?"

"Exactly. That's where you may be able to help us. You knew Frimbo, of course?"

"Only as a landlord knows a tenant." Crouch smiled. "Even that isn't quite true," he amended. "Landlords and tenants are usually enemies. Frimbo, on the contrary, was the best tenant I've ever had. Paid a good rent, always paid it on time, and never asked for a thing. A rare bird in that respect. I'll hardly get another one like him."

"How long was he your tenant here?"

"Nearly two years now. Built himself up quite a following here in Harlem—at least he always had plenty of people in here at night."

"You've had your place of business here how long?"

"Five years this winter."

"And in spite of the fact that you and he have been neighbors for two years, you knew nothing about him personally?"

"Well," again Crouch smiled, "we weren't exactly what you'd call associated. The proximity was purely— geographical, would you call it? You know, of course, that this isn't my residence."

"Yes."

"To be frank, Frimbo always seemed—and I don't mean this geographically—a little above me. Pretty distant, unapproachable sort of chap. Part of his professional pose, I guess. Solemn as an undertaker—I honestly envied him his manner. Could have used it myself. Occasionally we'd meet and pass the time of day. But otherwise I never knew he was here."

"Your relations were purely of a business nature, then?"

"Quite."

"In that case you really had to see him only once a month—to collect his rent."

"At first, yes. But during the last few months I didn't even have to do that. My wife collects all the rents now."

"Isn't that rather a dangerous occupation for a woman? Carrying money about?"

"I suppose so. We hadn't thought about that angle of it. You know how women are—if they haven't anything much to do they get restless and dissatisfied. We haven't any kids and she has a girl to do the housework. When she asked me to let her collect the rents it struck me as quite sensible—something to occupy her time and give me a little more freedom. I'm on call at all hours, you see, so I appreciated a little relief."

"I see. That is probably why she was here tonight."

"Was she? That's good."

"Good? Why?"

"Why—I guess it sounds a little hard—but—of course I'm sorry for Frimbo and all—but death is such a common experience to me that I suppose I take it as a matter of course. What I meant was that at least he didn't die in our debt."

So bald a statement rendered even the illusionless Dart silent a moment, while Dr. Archer audibly gasped. Then the detective said:

"Well—evidently you didn't know Frimbo as well as I had hoped. You knew no one who would want him out of the way?"

"No. And whoever it was certainly didn't do me any favor."

"You were here earlier this evening, weren't you, Mr. Crouch?"

"Yes. I left about nine o'clock. From then until a few minutes ago I was at the Forty Club around the corner playing cards." He smiled. "You can easily verify that by one of the attendants—or by my friend, Si Brandon, whom I plucked quite clean."

"Tell me—could any one get into this room and out without being seen by people in the hall or in the waiting-room?"

"Indeed I don't know. This is the first time since Frimbo came that I've been in here."

"Is that so?"

"Yes."

"Even when you collected rents yourself, you never had to come in here?"

"No. I used to wait in the hall there. Frimbo's man would tell him I was here for the rent and he would send it out. I'd hand the receipt over to the man and that was all."

"I see."

"And there are no concealed passages in this house by which some one could get about undetected?"

"Not unless Frimbo put 'em in himself. I never bothered him or nosed around to see what he was up to. His lease required him to leave things at the end as he found them at the beginning and I let it go at that. But in a room like this I should think a lot of undetected movement would be easy for anyone who put his mind to it. The darkness and those wall drapes and all——"

"Of course. How long did the lease still have to run?"

"Three more years—and at a rate considerably higher than I'll be able to get from anyone now in this depression."

"Was there anything peculiar about your lease agreement—special features and such?"

"No. Nothing. Except perhaps the agreement about heating. I paid for the coal and he paid for the labor. That is, he had his man keep the fires. There's only one boiler, of course."

"His man would have to pass through your part of the house quite often then to tend the fire, put out ashes, and so on?"

"Yes—he did."

"Well, Mr. Crouch, I suppose that's all then for the present. Except that an apology is due you for making use of your parlor downstairs without permission. Dr. Archer here moved the victim down there to examine him better—before he knew he was dead."

"Oh, is that you there, doc? Look like anybody else in the dark, don't you? Don't mention it—glad to have been able to help out. Perhaps if you'd tell me the cir-

cumstances, officer, I might run across something of
value. Unless, of course, you have reasons for not dis-
closing what is known so far."

"Don't mind telling you at all," decided Dart. "The
victim was stunned by a blow with a hard object—a
sort of club—then stifled by a handkerchief pushed
down his throat."

"Judas Priest!"

"We have the handkerchief. The club is being examined for finger prints. It was last seen—prior to
Frimbo's death I mean—shortly after ten-thirty, resting
in its apparently usual place on the mantelpiece in the
front room. No one admits seeing it after that time
until we found it here on the floor beside this chair, in
which Frimbo's body was discovered. Testimony indicates that Frimbo was alive and talking as late as five
minutes to eleven. The club was removed therefore by
someone who was in the front room after ten-thirty and
used by someone who was out of the front room by
five minutes to eleven. Presumably the person who removed it was the person who used it. This person, of
course, could have hidden until five minutes to eleven in
the darkness or behind the drapes of the walls. But
certainly he was one of the people who passed from that
room into this room during that twenty-five-minute
period."

"Say—that's a swell method. Beats a maxim silencer,
doesn't it?"

"Well—I don't know. Leaves more evidence, apparently."

"Yes, but the more the evidence the more the possibility of confusion."

"True. But if the two clues we are studying—the ownership of the handkerchief and the identification of the finger prints—coincide, somebody'll be due for a toasting. On a specially designed toaster."

"I don't think you'll find any finger prints on your club though."

"Why not?"

"I'll bet the chap handled the club with the handkerchief."

"Hm—that's a good suggestion. But we'll have to wait for the results of the examination of the club to check that."

"Well," Crouch rose, "if I can think of anything or find anything that might help, I'll be glad to do so. I'm easy to get hold of if you need me again."

"Thank you, Mr. Crouch. I won't detain you." Dart called to the bluecoat at the hall door: "Pass Mr. Crouch out. Or did you say you had something to do downstairs, Mr. Crouch?"

"Well, I did, but it can wait till morning. I might be in your way now—searching around and all. Tomorrow'll be time enough—last few touches you know. Easier to handle a dead face than a live one—I've found that out."

"Interesting," commented Dart. "I never thought of an undertaker as a beautician."

"You'd be surprised. We can make the dark ones bright and the bright ones lighter—that seems to be the ambition in this community. We can fatten thin ones and reduce fat ones. I venture to say that, by the simplest imaginable changes, I could make Doc Archer there quite unrecognizable."

"The need," murmured the doctor, "may be present, but I trust the occasion does not soon arise."

"Well, good luck, officer. Good-night, doc. See you again sometime when things are brighter."

"Good-night."

"Good-night, Crouch."

4

"Why," asked Dr. Archer, "didn't you let him know his wife was still here?"

"She was here when the thing happened. I may need her. If I'd told him she was still here he'd have wanted to see her and she'd have wanted to leave with him."

"You could keep him too, then."

"Had no reason to keep him. His story checked perfectly with his wife's in spite of my efforts to trick him. And I can easily check his previous whereabouts, just as he said—he wouldn't have been so definite about 'em if they couldn't have been verified."

"He could pay liars."

"But he actually wasn't here. Brown, Jenkins, Mrs. Snead, or his wife—surely one of them would have mentioned him."

"That's so."

"And Frimbo was a goose that laid golden eggs for him."

"If it was anybody else besides Martha, I might be suspicious of——"

"Of what?"

"What she might have laid for Frimbo."

"Doctor—spare my blushes!" Then seriously, "But you're sure that she's an irreproachable character. And I'm just as sure Frimbo was not interested in women. That all argues against any outraged husband theory. There's absolutely no basis for it and even if there was, there's nothing that could possibly incriminate Crouch."

"You're right. But don't forget to check up." The doctor fell to ruminating in his wordy and roundabout way. "And keep your pupils dilated for more evidence. I have an impression—just an impression—that bright plumage oft adorns a bird of prey. Curious fellow, Crouch. Bright exterior, genial, cheerful even, despite his doleful occupation; but underneath, hard as a pawn-broker, with an extraordinarily keen awareness of his own possessions. Imagine a man congratulating himself on acquiring an extra month's rent before his tenant came to grief."

"Well, I don't know. Suppose a patient of yours died during an operation for which you had already col-lected the fee. Would you give back the fee—or would you be glad you had got it first?"

"I would desire with all my heart," murmured the doctor, "to reimburse the bereaved relatives. But since that would resemble an admission that my operation was at fault and would hence endanger my professional reputation, no course would remain except to rush speedily to the bank and deposit the amount to my credit."

"Self-preservation," grinned Dart. "Well, we can't blame Crouch for the same thing. He spoke bluntly, but maybe the man's just honest."

"Maybe everybody is," said Dr. Archer with a sigh.

CHAPTER NINE

I

MEANWHILE Bubber Brown, riding beside
Officer Hanks in Detective Dart's touring car
was evincing a decided appreciation of his new importance. Over his countenance spread a broad grin of satisfaction, and as the machine swung up the Avenue, he
reared back in his seat and surveyed his less favored fellow men with a superior air. The car swung into 135th
Street, pulled up at the curb in front of the station-
house, and acquired presently a new passenger in the
person of an enormous black giant named Small, who
managed to crowd himself into the tonneau. As it drew
away, Bubber could contain himself no longer.

"Hot damn!" he exclaimed. "In power at last!" As
the little five-passenger car started off again— "Y'all
s'posed to follow my directions now, ain't you?"

"Yep," said Hanks. "Where to now?"

"Henry Patmore's Pool Room—Fifth Avenue and
131st Street. And do me jes' one kind favor, will you
Mr. Hanks?"

"What?"

"See that red traffic light yonder?"

"Yep."

"Run on past it, will you please?"

Shortly they reached their objective, got out, and,

with Bubber expansively leading the way, entered Patmore's well-known meeting-place.

Patmore's boasted two separate entrances, one leading into the poolroom proper, the other into the barroom by its side. These two long, low rooms communicated within by means of a wide doorway in the middle of the intervening wall, and also by means of a small back gaming-room into which one might pass from either the speakeasy or the billiard parlor. It was into the poolroom that Bubber led the way. He and his uniformed escort paused just within the entrance to survey the scene. Two long rows of green-topped tables extended the length of the bare wooden floor. Players in shirt sleeves moved about, hats on the backs of their heads, cigarettes drooping from their lips; leaned far over the felt to make impossible shots, whooped at their successes, cursed their failures, thrust cue-points aloft to mark off scores, or thumped cue-butts upon the floor to signal an attendant.

One of these gentlemen, seeing the entrance of Bubber's familiar rotund figure flanked by two officers of the law, called sympathetically:

"Tough titty, short-order. What they got you for this time?"

"They ain't got me," responded Mr. Brown glowing with his new importance. "I got them. And you get fly, I'll get you, too. Now what you think o' that?"

"I think you jes' a pop-eyed liar," said the other, dismissing the matter to sight on a new shot.

Bubber asked the manager, standing nearby, "Say, boy, you seen Spider Webb?"

The one addressed looked at him and looked at the policemen. Then he inquired blandly, "Who'n hell is Spider Webb?"

"Damn!" Bubber murmured, pushing back his hat and scratching his head. "You boogies sho' get dumb in the presence of the law. Listen, this ain' nothin' on him —jes' want to get some dope from him, that's all. Y'see, I'm doin' a little detective work now"—he produced one of the cards he had shown Detective Perry Dart— "and I want Spider's slant on a little case."

"So I *got* to know him?" bridled the other.

"You did know him."

"Well, I done forgot him, then."

"Thanks, liar."

"You welcome—stool."

Ordinarily Bubber would have resented the epithet, which was much worse than the one he himself had used; but he was now in such lofty spirits that the opinion of a mere poolroom manager could not touch him.

"You all wait here," he suggested to the officers. "The Spider might try a fast one if he feels guilty."

But before this expedition had started, Hanks had caught a sign from Detective Dart that Mr. Bubber Brown must be brought back as well as those whom Mr. Brown identified; and so now Hanks offered an amendment:

"We'll leave Small at the door," he said, "and I'll come along with you."

So it was agreed, and Bubber with Hanks at his heels made his way to the back room of the establishment. As they approached it, Bubber saw the door open and Spider

Webb start out. Looking up, Webb recognized Bubber at a distance, stopped, noted the policeman, stepped back and quickly shut the door. Bubber reached the door and flung it open a few seconds later, but his rapid survey revealed a total and astonishing absence of Spider Webb.

"Where'd that boogy go?" inquired Bubber blankly.

"Who?" said the house-man, sitting on a stool at the mid-point of one side of the table, running the game.

"Spider Webb."

The house-man looked about. "Any o' you all seen Spider Webb?" he asked the surrounding atmosphere. The players were so intent on the game that they did not even seem to hear. Upon receiving no response, the house-man appeared to dismiss the matter and also became absorbed again in the fall of cards. Bubber and his policeman were decidedly outside the world of their consideration.

But the newly appointed champion of the law now caught sight of the door at the other end of the room leading into the bar which paralleled the poolroom. With more speed than consideration for those he swept past, he bustled along to the far end of the chamber, opened that door and burst forth into the long narrow barroom. Hanks was but a moment behind him, for Hanks was as concerned with keeping close to Bubber as Bubber was with overtaking Webb. The barroom, however, was as innocent of Spider Webb as had been the blackjack chamber, and Bubber was still expressing his bewilderment in a vigorous scratching of the back of his head when the gentleman pursued appeared. He came through the wide doorway by which the barroom communicated directly with the poolroom. He came, in other words, out of the poolroom. The mystery of how he managed to appear from a place where he certainly had not been—for had not Bubber and Hanks just traversed the poolroom?—was submerged in the more important fact that he was proceeding now very rapidly toward the street door.

"Spider! Hey, Spider!" called Bubber.

Mr. Webb halted and turned in apparent surprise. Bubber and the policeman overtook him.

"What's on your mind?" inquired the Spider quite calmly and casually, quite, indeed, as though he had not been in any hurry whatever and had no other interest in the world than the answer to his question.

"How did you get in yonder?" Bubber wanted to know.

"How," inquired Webb, "did you and your boy friend get in here?"

Bubber abandoned the lesser mystery to pursue his interest in the original one. "Listen. Somebody put that thing on Frimbo tonight. We all got to get together over there and find out who done it. Everybody what was there."

"Put what thing on him?"

"Cut him loose, man. Put him on the well-known spot."

"Frimbo——"

"Hisself."

"Killed him?"

"If you want to put it that way."

"Good-night!" Spider Webb's astonishment yielded to a sense of his own implication. "So what?" he inquired rather harshly.

"So you, bein' among those present, you got to return to the scene of the tragedy. That's all."

"Yea? And who knew I was on the scene of the tragedy?"

"Everybody knew it."

"Reckon the police knew it, huh? All they had to do was walk in, and they knew I'd been there, huh? The peculiar perfume I use or somethin'?" There was somber menace in Spider's tone.

"Well," admitted Bubber, "you know I been doin' a little private detective work o' my own, see? So I'm helpin' the police out on this case. Naturally, knowin' you was there, I knew you'd want to give all the information you could, see? Anything else would look like runnin' away, y'understand?"

"I see. You're the one I got to thank for this little consideration."

"I'm givin' you a chance to protect yo'self," said Bubber.

"Thanks," Webb responded darkly. "I'll do the same by you sometime. Be watchin' out for it."

"Let's go," suggested Officer Hanks.

They went into the poolroom and with Small, returned to the car at the curb.

2

"Know how to drive?" Hanks asked Bubber.

"Who me? Sho'. I can drive anything but a bargain."

"Take the wheel—and plenty o' time."

Bubber obeyed. Shortly the expedition arrived at its next port of call, the Hip-Toe Club on Lenox Avenue. Leaving Small and the ominously silent Spider Webb in the car, Officer Hanks and Bubber left to seek Doty Hicks.

"How you know he's here?" Hanks said.

"His brother runs the place. Spats Oliver, they call him. Real name's Oliver Hicks. Everybody knows him, and everybody knows Doty. Doty's been up for dope-peddlin' coupla times—finally the dope got him—now it's all he can do to get enough for himself. This is his hang-out."

"It would be," observed Hanks. They had passed under a dingy canopy and into a narrow entrance, had negotiated a precipitate and angular staircase, and so with windings and twistings had descended eventually into a reclaimed cellar. The ceiling was oppressively low, the walls splotched with black silhouetted grotesqueries, and the atmosphere thick with smoke. Two rows of little round white-topped tables hugged the two lateral walls, leaving between them a long narrow strip of bare wooden floor for dancing or entertainment. This strip terminated at a low platform at the far end of the room, whereon were mounted a pianist, a drummer, a banjo-player and a trumpeter, all properly equipped with their respective instruments and at the moment all performing their respective rites without restraint.

In the narrow strip of interspace, a tall brown girl was doing a song and dance to the absorbed delight of the patrons seated nearest her. Her flame chiffon dress, normally long and flowing, had been caught up bit by bit in her palms, which rested nonchalantly on her hips, until now it was not so much a dress as a sash, gathered about her waist. The long shapely smooth brown limbs below were bare from trim slippers to sash, and only a bit of silken underthing stood between her modesty and surrounding admiration.

With extraordinary ease and grace, this young lady was proving beyond question the error of reserving legs for mere locomotion, and no one who believed that the chief function of the hips was to support the torso could long have maintained so ridiculous a notion against the argument of her eloquent gestures.

Bubber caught sight of this vision and halted in his tracks. His abetting of justice, his stern immediate duty as a deputy of the law, faded.

"Boy!" he said softly. "What a pair of eyes!"

Sang the girl, with an irrelevance which no one seemed to mind:

> *I'll be standin' on the corner high*
> *When they drag your body by—*
> *I'll be glad when you're dead, you rascal you.*

"Where," said the unimpressionable Hanks, "is this bozo named Doty Hicks?"

"If he ain't here," returned Bubber, still captivated by the vision, "we'll jes' have to sit down and wait for him."

"I'll stand here. You look."

"I'm lookin'."

"For Hicks, if it ain't askin' too much."

Reluctantly obedient, Bubber moved slowly along the aisle, scanning the patrons at this table and that, acutely aware that his march was bringing him momentarily nearer the dancing girl. No one had he yet seen who faintly resembled Doty Hicks. The girl's number ended just as Bubber was on the point of passing her. As she terminated her dance with a flourish, she swung merrily about and chucked the newcomer under his plump chin.

"You're short and broad, but sweet, oh Gawd!"

Bubber, who was as much a child of the city as she, was by no means embarrassed. He grinned, did a little buck and wing step of his own, ended with a slap of his foot, and responded:

"You're long and tall and you've got it all!"

"O.K., big boy," laughed the girl and would have turned away, but he stopped her. Offering her one of his detective-cards, he said:

"Sis, if you ever need a friend, look me up."

She took the card, glanced at it, laughed again.

"Here on business, mister?"

"Business, no lie," he said ruefully. "Seen my friend Doty Hicks?"

"Oh—that kind o' business. Well who's that over in the corner by the orchestra?"

He looked, and there indeed was Doty Hicks, a little

wizened black fellow, bent despondently over the table at which he sat alone, his elbows resting on the white porcelain surface, which he contemplated in deep meditation, his chin in his hands.

"Thanks, sister. I'll do better when I can see more of you. Right now at present, duty calls." And lamenting the hardships of working for law and order, Bubber approached the disconsolate figure at the corner table.

Remembering how he had been received by Spider Webb, Bubber approached the present responsibility differently:

"Hello, Doty," he said pleasantly and familiarly.

Doty Hicks looked up, the protrusiveness of his eyes accentuated by the thinness of his face. He stared somewhat like a man coming out of anesthesia.

"Don't know you," he said in a voice that was tremulous but none the less positive. And he resumed his contemplation of the table top.

"Sure you know me. You and me was at Frimbo's tonight—remember?"

"Couldn't see Frimbo," said Doty. "Too dark." Whether he referred to the darkness of Frimbo's room or of Frimbo's complexion was not clear. Bubber went on:

"Frimbo's got somethin' for you."

"Yea—talk. Thass all. Lot o' talk."

"He ain't expected to live—and he wants to see you befo' he dies."

For a moment the little man made no sound, his great round eyes staring blankly at Bubber Brown. Then, in a hoarse, unsteady whisper he repeated:

"Ain't expected to live?"

"Not long." Bubber was pursuing the vague notion that by hiding the actuality of the death he would achieve easier coöperation and less enmity. "It took him sort o' sudden."

"Mean—mean Frimbo's dyin'?"

"Don't mean maybe."

Doty Hicks, unsteadily, jerkily, more like a mechanism than like a man, got to his feet, pushed back his chair, stood teetering a dizzy moment, then rubbed the back of his hand across his nose, shook his head, became steadier, and fixed Bubber with an unwavering stare, a look in which there was a hint of triumph and more than a hint of madness.

"It worked!" he said softly. "It worked!" A grin, vacant, distant, unpleasant to see, came over his wasted features. "It worked! What you know 'bout that?" said he.

Bubber did not care for this at all. "I don't know nothin' 'bout it, but if you comin', come on, let's go."

"If I'm comin'? You couldn't keep me 'way. Where is he?"

Bubber had to hold him by the arm on the way out, partly to support him, partly to restrain the trembling eagerness with which he sought to reach Frimbo ere the latter should die.

3

"Where," inquired Bubber of Officer Hanks as they wedged the diminutive Doty Hicks into the already well-occupied rear seat and resumed their journey, "are we go'n' put Brother Easley Jones—if any?"

"We'll have to drop these men off and come back for him."

"Won't need no car for him—told me he lived right there in the same block, a few houses from Frimbo."

"You know everybody, don't you?"

"Well, I recognized these two in the waitin'-room there tonight. Anybody that travels the sidewalks o' Harlem much as I do knows them by sight anyhow. This Easley Jones I struck up a conversation with on purpose. He was a jolly sort of a feller, easy to talk to, y' see, and when I found out he was a railroad man, I knew right off I might have a customer. Railroad men is the most back-bitten bozos in the world. They what you might call legitimate prey. That's, of co'se, if they married. Y' see, they come by it natural—they so crooked themselves. Any guy what lays over forty-eight hours one time in New York, where his wife is, and forty-eight hours another in Chicago, where she ain't, is gonna curve around a little in Chicago jes' to keep in practice for New York. Y' see what I mean?"

"Is that what this Easley Jones was doin'?"

"He didn't say. But he give me the number o' the house he rooms at in New York—his wife is in Chicago —and asked me to drop in and advise him some time."

"Some time'll be tonight."

"Right."

The two material witnesses were escorted back to Frimbo's and were left on the way upstairs in Officer

Small's care. Hanks and Bubber walked the short distance back along the block to the address Easley Jones had given. Bubber mounted the stoop and rang the bell of a dwelling much like that in which the African mystic had lived and died.

After a moment the dark hall lighted up, the door opened, and a large, yellow woman wearing horn-rimmed spectacles gazed inquisitively upon them.

"Mr. Jones in?" asked Bubber.

"Mr. who?"

"Mr. Jones. Mr. Easley Jones."

The lady glanced at the uniformed officer and said resolutely, "Don' nobody stay here by that name. You-all must have the wrong address." *why is everyone so afraid?*

"We don't want to arrest him, lady. We want him to help us find somebody, that's all. He's a friend o' mine —else how'd I know he lived here?"

The woman considered this. "What'd you say his name was?"

"Jones. Easley Jones. Light brown-skin feller with freckles all over his face and kinks all over his head. He's a railroad man—runs from here to Chicago—him and me used to work together. Yes ma'am. Sho' did."

The horn-rimmed lenses were like the windows of a fortress. "Sorry—y'all done made a mistake somewhere. No sech person lives in this house. Know a Sam Jones," she added helpfully, "that lives in Jamaica, Long Island. He's a butler—don' run on no road, but he commutes to New York mos' ev'y night."

"Too bad, lady, but we can't take no substitutes. If it ain't genuwine Easley, we can't use it. Thanks jes' the same. But if you do run across a Easley Jones, tell him Frimbo wants to see him again tonight—right away— please."

"Hmph!" responded the gracious lady and shut the door abruptly.

"That's funny, ain't it?" reflected Bubber as the two turned back toward the house of tragedy.

"It's all funny to me," confessed Officer Hanks. "It's all jes' a mess, what I mean. Everybody I've seen acts guilty."

"You ain't been lookin' at me, is you, brother?"

"You? You're mighty anxious to put it on somebody else—I see that."

Bubber sighed at the hopelessness of ever weaning a cop from indiscriminate suspicion.

CHAPTER TEN

I

THE officer who had taken the club to be examined for finger prints returned and reported that the examination was under way, that photographic reproductions would be sent over as soon as they were ready, and that a finger-print man would come with them to take additional data, make comparisons, and establish or eliminate such possible identities as Detective Dart might be seeking.

This officer was returned to his post as Doty Hicks and Spider Webb were ushered up the stairs by the gigantic Officer Small. Sensing their arrival, Dart had the extension light again turned off.

"If those are the men we're waiting for send them up front."

Accordingly, Small came in alone to report. "We got two of 'em. Little dopey guy and Spider Webb, the number-runner."

"Where are the others—Brown and Jones?"

"Brown's gone with Hanks to get Jones—right down the street here."

"Good. You wait outside, Small. Brady, bring Hicks —the little one—in first."

Doty Hicks, though of none too steady a gait, was by no means reluctant to come in. With his protruding eyes popping and mouth half open, he entered the shaft of light and stood peering into the well-nigh impenetrable blackness that obscured the seated detective and the doctor standing beside him.

Dart waited. After a long moment of fruitless staring, Doty Hicks whispered, "Is you dead yet?"

"No," said the detective softly.

"But you dyin', ain't you?" The little fellow was trembling. "They tol' me you was dyin'."

Dart followed the obvious lead, though he could only guess its origin.

"So you tried to kill me?"

A puzzled look came over Doty Hick's thin black face.

"You don't sound right. Yo' voice don't sound——"

"Sit down," said Dart.

Still bewildered, Hicks mechanically obeyed.

"Why did you try to kill me?"

Hicks stared dumbly, groping for something. Suddenly his features changed to an aspect of unwilling comprehension, then of furious disappointment. He leaned forward in his chair, catching hold of the edge of the table. "You ain't him!" he cried. "You ain't him! You tryin' to fool me! Where's he at—I got to see him die. I got to——"

"Why?"

"Else it ain't no use—I got to see him! Where's he at?"

"Take it easy, Hicks. Maybe we'll let you see him. But you'll have to tell us all about it. Now, what's the idea?"

A plaintive almost sobbing tone came into Doty's high, quavering voice.

"Who is you, mister? What you want to fool me for?"

"I don't want to fool you, Hicks. I want to help you. You can tell me all about it—you can trust me. Tell me the whole thing, and if it's straight, I'll let you see Frimbo."

"Lemme see him first, will you, mistuh? He may die before I get to him."

"If he isn't dead yet he won't die till you get to him. You'll have to tell your story first, so you better tell it quickly. Why did you come here tonight at ten-thirty? Why did you try to kill Frimbo, and why must you see him before he dies?"

Doty sank back in his chair. "All right," he said, dully. Then, quickened by the realization of the urgency, he leaned forward again. "All right—I'll tell you, I'll tell you. Listen." He paused.

"I'm listening."

Drawing a deep breath, Doty Hicks proceeded:

"Frimbo's a conjure-man. You know that."

"Yes."

"I come here tonight because Frimbo was killin' my brother." He hesitated. "Killin' my brother," he repeated. Then, "You know my brother—everybody knows my brother—Spats Oliver Hicks—runs the Hip-Toe Club on Lenox Avenue. Good guy, my brother. Always looked out for me. Even when I went dopey and got down and out like I is now, he never turned me down. Always looked out for me. Good guy. If it'd been

me Frimbo was killin', 'twouldn' matter. I'm jes' a dope
—nobody'd miss me. But he was killin' my brother, see?
Y'see, Frimbo's a conjure-man. He can put spells on
folks. One kind o' spell to keep 'em from dyin' like
that boy what got the knife stuck in his head. Another
kind to set 'em to dyin'—like he was doin' my brother.
Slow dyin'—misery all in through here, coughin' spells,
night sweats, chills and fever, and wastin' away. That's
what he was doin' to Spats."

"But why?" Dart couldn't help asking.

" 'Count o' my brother's wife. He's doin' it 'count o'
my brother's wife. Spats married a show-gal, see? And
hadn't been married a month befo' she met up with
some guy with more sugar. So she quit my brother for
the sugar-papa, see? And natchelly, bein' a regular man
and not no good-for-nothin' dope like me, my brother
went after her, see? He grabbed this sugar-daddy and
pulled him inside out, like a glove. And one day he met
the gal and asked her to come back and she called him
somethin' and he smacked her cross-eyed. Well, 'cose,
that give her a fever, and she come straight here to
Frimbo. She could get plenty o' what it took from the
new daddy, and she brought it with her. Frimbo told
her what to do. She made believe she was goin' back to
live with my brother, and he like a fool took her in.
She stayed jes' long enough to do what Frimbo'd told
her to do, whatever it was. Day she left, my brother had
a fit—jes' like a cat in a alley—a fit. And ever since,
he's been goin' from bad to worse. Doctor don' help,
nothin' don' help. Y'see, it's Frimbo's spell."

"And that's why you tried to kill him?"

"Yea—that's why."

"How did you go about it?"

Doty Hicks looked around him into the enshrouding darkness. He shook his head. "Can't tell you that. Can't tell nobody how—that'd break the spell. All I can tell you is that they's only one way to kill a conjure-man—you got to out-conjure him. You got to put a back-conjure on him, and it's got to be stronger 'n the one he put on the other feller. 'Cose you can't do it alone. Got to have help."

"Help? What kind of help?"

"Somebody has to help you."

"Who helped you with this?"

"Can't tell you that neither—that'd break the spell. Can I see him now?"

"Why do you have to see him before he dies?"

"That's part of it. I have to see him and tell him how come he's dyin', else it don't do no good. But if I see him and tell him how come he's dyin', then, soon as he die, my brother gets well. See? Jes' like that—gets well soon as Frimbo die."

"Did you pay the person to help you?"

"Pay him? Sho'—had to pay him."

"And do you realize that you are making a confession of deliberate murder—for which you may be sentenced to die?"

"Hmph! What I care 'bout that? I been tired livin' a long time, mistuh. But you couldn't prove nothin' on me. I did a stretch once and I know. You got to have evidence. I got it fixed so they ain't no evidence—not against me."

"Against somebody else, maybe?" Doty Hicks did not answer.

"Frimbo was a pretty wise bird. He must have known you wanted to conjure him—the way he could read people's minds. What did he say when you came in?"

"Didn't say nothin' for a while. I asked him to lay off my brother—begged him, if he had to conjure somebody, to conjure me—but he jes' set there in the dark like he was thinkin' it over, and then he begins talkin'. Say: 'So you want to die in place of your brother? It is impossible. Your brother is incurably ill.' Then he kep' quiet a minute and he say, 'You have been misinformed, my friend. You are under the impression that I have put an evil spell upon your brother. That is superstitious nonsense. I am no caster of spells. I am a psychist—a kind of psychologist. I have done nothing to your brother. He simply has pulmonary tuberculosis—in the third stage. He had had it for at least three months when your sister-in-law came to me for advice. I could not possibly be responsible for that, since until then I did not know of his existence.' 'Course I didn' believe that, 'cause my brother hadn' been sick a day till after his wife came here, so I kep' on askin' him to take off the spell, so he finally says that everything'll be all right in a few days and don' worry. Well, I figure he's jes' gettin' rid o' me, and I gets up like I'm on my way out and come through that side door there, but 'stead o' goin' on downstairs, I slips back in again and—and——"

"Put your counter-spell on him?"

"I ain' sayin'," said Doty Hicks, "I'm jes' tellin' you

enough so I can see him. I ain' sayin' enough to break the spell."

"And you refuse to say who helped you?"

"Not till I see Frimbo die; then I'll tell maybe. 'Twon' make no difference, then—the spell'll be broke. Now lemme see him, like you said."

"There's no hurry. You can wait up front a few minutes."

"You said if I tol' you——" Doty Hicks was changing from abjection and pleading to suspicion and anger. "What you want to say so for if you wasn't go'n'——"

"I said you must tell your story first. You've only told part of it. I also said that if Frimbo wasn't dead when you came in, he wouldn't be when you finished. That was true. He was already dead when you came in."

The face of the tremulous little man in the illumined chair was ordinarily ugly in a pitiful, dissolute, and rather harmless way. But as the meaning of Dart's statement now slowly sank into his consciousness that usual ugliness became an exceptionally evil and murderous ugliness. Doty Hicks leaned forward still further where he sat, his white eyes more protruding than ever, his breath coming in sharp gasps. And suddenly, as if a high tension current shot through him, he lurched to his feet and lunged forward toward Dart's voice.

"Gimme sump'm!" he screamed, his hands groping the table top in the dark. "Gimme sump'm in my hand! I'll bust yo' head open—you cheat! I'll——"

By that time Brady had him.

"Take him up front," instructed Detective Dart. "Have somebody keep a special eye on him. He's worth holding on to."

Struggling, cursing, and sobbing, Doty Hicks was dragged from the room.

2

"He wanted something with which to 'bust your head open,' " reflected Dr. Archer.

"So I noticed," said Detective Dart.

"Frimbo's head was—ever so slightly—'busted' open."

"Yes."

"Memory-suggestion?"

"Or coincidence? Anybody in a rage might want to get his hands on a weapon."

"With which to 'bust open' an offending cranium. No doubt. Rather over-effective way to 'put a spell' on a fellow though."

"Exactly. Wouldn't have to put a spell on him if you were going to brain him with a club."

"No. Yet—if you weren't going to brain him—if you just wanted him to keep still while the spell was being put on——"

"Yes—but a handkerchief is a pretty substantial thing, also, to use as a spell. And it wasn't put on. It was put in."

"In other words, whoever helped Doty Hicks, wasn't taking any chances."

"Something like that."

"Turn on the light a minute. I want to look at that—spell."

Dart gave the order. The extension lamp went on, throwing its sharp radiance into the darkness and giving an unnatural effect which disclosed well enough the men, the two chairs, the table, the black-hung walls, but somehow did not in any way relieve the oppressive somberness of the place—a light that cut through the shadow without actually dispelling it.

The physician stooped and, using his forceps, took the blue-bordered handkerchief out of his bag. He dropped it on the table, and with the instrument poked it about till it lay flat.

"What sort of a person," he meditated in a low tone, "would even think of using a device like that?"

Someone who shares as much medical / education experience as Frimbo

3

Whatever Dart might have answered was cut off by the unceremonious and rather breathless entrance of Bubber Brown. Hanks, like a faithful guardian, was at his heels.

"We got two of 'em—see 'em?" Bubber breathed. "Doty Hicks was no trouble—too anxious to get here. But that Spider Webb—we had to chase that nigger all over Pat's."

"Yes, thanks. But where's Easley Jones?"

"We went to where he said he lived, couple o' doors up the street. But the landlady claim she didn' know him. I think she got leery when she saw my boy's brass buttons here and jes' shut up on general principles. But we left word for him to come by."

"That's not so good. Guess we'll have to put out feelers for him."

"How come 'tain' so good?"

"Nobody's anxious to get mixed up in a murder case."

"How he know it's a murder case?" Bubber said, using the same logic Dart had used on him earlier. "All I said was Frimbo wanted to see him right away. If he don't know it's a murder case, he'll figure Frimbo's got some more advice for him or sump'm and come a-runnin'. If he do know it's a murder case, he's long gone anyhow, so leavin' the message can't do no more harm than's done already."

Dart looked at Bubber with new interest.

"That's good reasoning—as far as it goes," he remarked. "But the woman—the landlady—may have been telling the truth. Maybe Easley Jones doesn't live there."

"Well then," Bubber concluded promptly, "if he lied 'bout his address in the first place, he was up to sump'm crooked all along. He didn't *have* to invite me to come advise him 'bout his trouble, jes' 'cause he saw my card. I can see why his landlady would lie—to protect him— but there wasn't no reason for him to lie to me."

"Then what is your opinion, Brown?"

"My 'pinion's like this: I believe he gimme the right address. She'll tell him—if he's still there to tell. If he had anything to do with this he'll stay 'way. If he didn't have nothin' to do with it, and don't know it's happened, curiosity to see what else Frimbo wants will bring him back."

"In other words, if Easley Jones does come back, he isn't the man we're after. Is that it?"

"Yes, suh. That's it. And if he don't come back, whether it's 'cause he lied 'bout the address or 'cause he got the message and is scared to come—y'all better find him. He knows sump'm. Any man that runs away, well, all I say is, is been up to sump'm."

"The attendant seems to have run away," Dart reminded him.

"It's between the two of 'em then—less'n they show up."

"What about Doty Hicks? He's confessed."

"No!"

"Sure—while you were out."

"He did? Well, I don't pay that no mind. That nigger's crazy. Smokes too many reefers."

"There may be a good deal in what you say, Brown. Anyhow, thanks for your help. Just go up front and keep your eyes and ears open, will you?"

"Sho' will," Bubber promised, proud of his commendation. But as he was on the point of turning away, his eye fell on the table where the blue-bordered handkerchief lay.

"Jinx been in here, ain't he?" said he.

"Jenkins? Yes, why?"

"I see he left his handkerchief. Want me to give it to him?"

Dart and the physician exchanged glances.

"Is that his?" the detective asked, feigning mild surprise.

"Sho' 'tis. I was kiddin' him 'bout it tonight. Great big old ugly boogy like Jinx havin' a handkerchief with a baby blue border on it. Can y' imagine? A baby blue border!"

"But," Dart said softly, "I asked you before if you'd seen anybody here with a colored handkerchief, and you said no."

"Yea—but I thought you meant really colored—like mine. That's white, all 'cep'n' the hem. And anyhow, when you ast me if I'd seen any o' these people here with a colored handkerchief, I wasn't thinkin' 'bout Jinx. He ain't people. He never even crossed my mind. I was thinkin' 'bout them three men."

"Brady, ask Jenkins to come in again."

When Jinx returned, the unsuspecting Bubber, whose importance had by now grown large in his own eyes, did not wait for Dart to act. He picked up the handkerchief and thrust it toward Jinx saying:

"Here, boy, take your belongin's with you—don't leave 'em layin' 'round all over the place. You ain't home."

The tall, freckled, scowling Jinx was caught off guard. He looked doubtfully from the handkerchief to Bubber and from Bubber to the detective.

The detective was smiling quite guilelessly at him. "Take it if it's yours, Jenkins. We found it." Not even in his tone was there the slightest implication of any earlier mention of a handkerchief.

"Ole baby blue," mocked Bubber. "Take it boy, take it. You know it's yours—though it's no wonder you 'shamed to own it. Baby blue!"

But the redoubtable Jinx had by now grown normally wary.

" 'Tain' none o' mine," he growled. "Never seen it before. This here's the boy that goes in for colors."

"Well," grinned Bubber, unaware that he was driving nails in his friend's coffin, "it may not be yours, but you sho' was wipin' yo' face with it when you come in here tonight."

Dart was still smiling. "Never mind," he, remarked casually, "if it isn't Jenkins' he doesn't have to take it. That's all for the present. Just step up front again, will you please?"

A moment later, the doctor was saying, "Looks bad for Jenkins. If he'd accepted it right off, it would've been better for him."

"Right."

"But refusing to acknowledge it when it's now so clearly his—that's like being caught with the goods and saying 'I didn't take it.' "

"Jenkins is lying to cover up. That's a cinch."

"He may, of course—in ignorance—be just denying everything on general principles, without knowing specifically why himself."

"Yea," said Dart ironically. "He may. Brady, did you get that last down exactly?"

"Sho' did," said Brady.

"It wouldn't take much more," mused Dart, "to justify arresting our lanky friend, Jenkins."

"He hasn't admitted ownership of it."

"No. But knowing it's his, we can probably—er—persuade him to admit it, if necessary."

"But you've already got to hold that Hicks—on his own confession."

"His confession—if that's what it was—mentioned a sort of accomplice, as I remember it."

"So it did," reflected Dr. Archer.

"Jenkins might be that accomplice."

"Well—there's one strong argument against that."

"Name it."

"Jenkins' character. He just isn't the coöperating kind."

Detective Dart grinned.

"Doc, did you ever hear," he said, "of the so-called filthy lucre?"

Dr. Archer's serious face relaxed a little.

"I even saw some once," he murmured reminiscently.

CHAPTER ELEVEN

I

FROM the hall came the sound of an unsubdued and frankly astonished masculine voice, high-pitched in tone, firm, smooth in timbre, decidedly southern in accent, exclaiming:

"Great day in the mornin'! What all you polices doin' in this place? Policeman outside d' front door, policeman in d' hall, policeman on d' stairs, and hyer's another one. 'Deed I mus' be in d' wrong house! Is this Frimbo the conjure-man's house, or is it the jail?"

"Who you want to see?"

"There 'tis again. Policeman downstairs tole me come up hyer. Now you ask me same thing he did. Frimbo jes' sent for me, and I come to find out what he want."

"Wait a minute."

The officer thus addressed came in to Dart.

"Let him in," Dart said. But the order was unnecessary for the newcomer was already in.

Code switching

"Bless mah soul!" he ejaculated. "I never see so many polices in all my life. Look like a lost parade." He came up to the physician and the detective. "Which a one o' y'all is Mr. Frimbo?" he inquired. "When I was hyer befo' it was so dark I couldn' see, though 'cose I heard every word what was said. Fact, if one o' y'all is him,

123

jes' speak and I'll know it. Never fergit that voice as long as I got holes in my ears."

"You're Easley Jones?"

"At yo' service, brother."

"Mr. Frimbo is gone, Jones. Gone on a long journey."

"Is that a fact? Well, I'm a travelin' man myself. I run on the road—y' know—New York to Chicago. But say—how could he send me word to come back here if he's done gone away?"

"You received the message?"

"Sho' I did. Ha! That landlady o' mine's all right. Y' know, she figured I been up to sump'm, so she made out like she didn' know me when that cop come by jes' now. But I knowed I ain' done nothin' wrong, and I figured best thing to do was breeze on back and see what's up. Where's he gone, mistuh?"

"Frimbo's dead. He was killed while you were here tonight."

For the first time, the appearance of Easley Jones became definite, as if this statement had suddenly turned a floodlight full upon him. He was of medium height, dressed in dark clothing, and he carried a soft gray felt hat in his hand. The hat dropped to the floor, the man stood motionless, his brown eyes went widely incredulous and his light brown face, which was spattered with black freckles, grew pale so that the freckles stood out even blacker still. Loose-mouthed, he gazed upon the detective a long moment. Then he drew a deep breath, slowly bent his kinky head and recovered his hat, stood erect again, and sighed:

"Well I be dog-goned!"

"I'm a police officer. It was I who sent for you, not Frimbo. It speaks in your favor that you have come. If you will be kind enough to sit down there in that chair, I'd like to ask you a few questions."

"Ask *me* questions? 'Deed, brother, I don' know what good askin' me anythin's go'n' do you. Look like to me I ought to be askin' you the questions. How long he been daid?"

"Sit down, please."

There was no evading the quiet voice, the steadfast bright black eyes of the little detective. Easley Jones sat down. At a word from Dart, the extension light went out. Thereupon, Easley Jones promptly got up. He made no effort to conceal the fact that the absence of surrounding illumination rendered the situation decidedly uncomfortable for him.

"Why—this is jes' like it was befo'—befo'. Listen, brother, if you 'specks to get a straight tale out o' me, you better gimme plenty o' light. Dark as 'tis in hyer now, I can't make out what I'm sayin'."

"Nothing's going to hurt you. Just sit down and answer truthfully what I ask you."

"Aw right, mistuh. But tellin' a man somebody been killed, and then turnin' out all the lights and talkin' right from wha' he was—dat ain't no way to get the truth. I ain' 'sponsible for nothin' I say, I tell you that much, now. And jes' lemme hear one funny little noise and you'll find yo'self starin' at a empty chair."

"You won't get far, my friend."

"Who? I tol' you I was a travelin' man. If anything funny happen, I'm go'n' prove it."

"You run on the railroad?"

"Yas, suh. Dat is, I rides on it."

"Company?"

"Never has no company. No suh. Always go alone."

"What railroad company?"

"Oh. Pullman—natchelly."

"Porter, of course?"

"Now what else do the Pullman Company put nig-
gers on trains for?"

"How long've you been with them?"

"Ten years and five months yestiddy. Yestiddy was
the first o' February, wasn't it?"

"What run?"

"You mean now?"

"Yes."

"New York to Chicago over the Central."

"Twentieth Century?"

"Yas indeed—bes' train in the East."

"What's its schedule?"

"Two forty-five out o' New York, nine forty-five
nex' morning in Chicago."

"Same hours on the return trip?"

"Yas, suh. 'Cep'n' week-ends. I lay over Saturday
night and all day Sunday—one week in Chicago, nex'
week in New York. Tonight's my Saturday in New
York, y'see?"

"That's how you happened to choose tonight to see
Frimbo?"

"Uh-huh. Yea."

"What time did you get here tonight?"

"Ten-twenty on the minute."

"How can you say that so positively?"

"Well, I tole you I'm a railroad man. I does ev'ything by the clock. When I arrive someplace I jes' natchelly look at my watch—fo'ce o' habit, y'see."

"You went straight into the waiting-room?"

"Yea—they was a flunky standin' in the hall; he showed me in."

"Describe him."

"Tall, black, and cock-eyed."

"Which eye had the cast in it?"

"Right eye—no—lemme see—left—tell you the truth I don' know. I never could tell, when it come to folks like that, which eye is lookin' at me and which ain't. But it was one of 'em—I knows that."

"Who was present when you arrived?"

"Nobody. I was first."

"What did you do?"

"I sat down and waited. Nothin' else for me to, was they?"

"What happened?"

"Nothin'. Too much nothin'. I sat there waitin' a while, 'bout eight or ten minutes I guess, and then a little feller come in that looked—well, he looked kind o' dopey to me. Nex', right behind him, come a sporty lookin' gent in gray—kind o' heavy-set he was, and tight-lookin', like he don' want no foolishness. Then two other men come in together, a long thin one and a short thick one. We all set around a minute or so, and then this short one begin to walk around and look at them decorations and charms in yonder, and the tall one with him. He started talkin' to the tall one 'bout them little freakish-lookin' figures on the wall, and them knives and spears. He say, 'Boy, you know what them is?' His boy say, 'No, what?' He say, 'Them's the folks this Frimbo's done chopped loose, and these implements hyer is what he chopped 'em loose with.' So the other say, 'What of it?' And the little one say, 'Know how come he kilt 'em?' 'No,' the long boy says. So the little one say, ' 'Cause they was so ugly. That make it look bad for you, son.' Long boy say, 'Why?' Shorty say, ' 'Cause they was all better lookin' than you is!' I figgered he might know sump'm 'bout them things sho' 'nough, so I went over where he was and struck up a conversation with him. Turned out he was a sort o' home detective, and I figgered he might be of some use to me, so I invited him to come by and see me some time when I was in town. Said he would. Say—I guess that's how y'all knowed where to find me at, huh? He must 'a' tol' you."

"What particular decorations or charms did you and he discuss?"

"None of 'em. Started—but right off he handed me his card and we got to talkin' 'bout other matters and fust thing I know, there was the flunky ready to show me in to Frimbo. So I went back to my chair, picked up my hat, and follered the flunky. Thought I might see this li'l detective ag'in, but 'stead o' goin' out the way I come in, Frimbo tole me to go out by this side hall-door hyer."

"Did you see two clubs on opposite ends of the mantelpiece?"

"Clubs? Uh-uh. Not far as I 'member now. Them funny-faces and things on the wall—I 'member them. Wait a minute—you mean two bones?"

"Yes."

"B'lieve I did. One 'cross one end of the mantelpiece, and one 'cross the other. Yea—sho' I did."

"What did you wish to see Frimbo about, Mr. Jones?"

"Now right there, brother, is where you gettin' personal. But I reckon I kin tell you—though I don' want to see it in no papers."

"There are no reporters here."

"Well, then, y'see it's like this. I got a wife in Chicago. I figger she gets kind o' lonesome seein' me only every other week-end—that is, for any length o' time. Three four hours in the middle o' the day is jes' enough to say howdy and goo'by. So with all them evenin's full o' nothin' 'special to do, I got kind o' worried—y' understand? And one o' the New York boys on the train was tellin' me this Frimbo could tell the low-down on doings like that, so I figgered I'd come up and see him. So up I come."

"Did he give you the information you were looking for?"

" 'Deed he did, brother. He set my mind at rest."

"Just what was said when you came in to see him?"

"Well, I say I was hyer to ask 'bout my wife—was she true *to* me or f'ru *with* me. But he didn' say nothin' till he got good and ready, and then he didn' say much. Tole me I didn' have nothin' to worry 'bout—that he seen I had murder in my heart for somebody, but there wasn' no other mule in my stall sho' 'nough and to go on forgit it. 'Course them wasn' his 'zack words, but dass what he meant. So I went on——'cep'n' as I was 'bout to go down the stairs, the flunky 'peared in the hall there and collected my two bucks. Then I lef'."

Detective Dart turned his flashlight on the table where the blue-bordered handkerchief still lay.

"Ever see that before?"

The railroad porter leaned forward to inspect the object. "Seen one jes' like it," he admitted.

"When and where?"

"Tonight. In the front room yonder. That tall feller was wipin' his face with it when he fust come in. Couldn't miss it. 'Cose I can't say it's the self-same one——"

"That's all for the present, Jones. Thank you. Wait up front a few minutes, please."

"Yas, *suh*. And if they's anything I kin do, jes' lemme know. Who you reckon done it, chief?"

"When do you count up your tips, Jones?"

"Suh?"

"In the middle of the trip—or at the end?"

"Oh." Jones grinned widely, his round freckled face brightening. "I see what you mean. Yas, suh. I count 'em after the train's pulled in."

"Right. This train isn't in yet. But we know where it's headed and we know who's on board."

"O.K., brother engineer. But bring her in on time, please suh. I got me a little serious wringin' and twistin' to do later on tonight."

2

"I'm getting interested in the servant with the evil eye," murmured Dr. Archer. "Terribly careless of him to disappear like this."

"We'll find him, if it boils down that far."

"Are you by any manner of chance beginning to draw conclusions?"

"Not by chance, no. Getting tired?"

"The neurons of my pallium are confused but extraordinarily active. The soles of my feet, however, being, so to speak, at the other extreme as to both structure and function——"

"Brady, bring in Spider Webb and bring along a chair for Dr. Archer."

"Thoughtful of you," said Dr. Archer.

"Excuse me, doc. I forgot you were standing all this time."

"I only remember it in the intervals myself. And this is possibly the last. However, better tardy than when parallel lines meet—what's this?"

"Wait a minute, Brady. Lights, Joe," the detective called. "Who's there now? Oh, hello there, Tynes. This is our local finger-print hound, doc. What'd you find, Tynie?"

"They had some trouble," the Spaniard-like newcomer in civilian dress said, "gettin' a man up from downtown, and long as I was hangin' around——"

"Glad you were. Maybe we'll make a killing for our own office. Be nice to carry this through by ourselves. So what've you got?"

"I've got one isolated print. Smudgy, but definite. Didn't even have to bring it out—just photographed it like it was."

He reached into a small black Boston bag he was carrying. "Got the other stuff here, too." He brought forth a flat rectangular slab with a smooth metal surface a foot long and three inches wide, and placed it on the table, then a small roller with a handle, which he laid beside the slab. Next he withdrew a bundle wrapped in a silk cloth and handed it to Dart. "There's your bone or club or whatever it is. Next time wrap it in something soft like a silk handkerchief."

"Had a handkerchief all right," Dart said, "but it wasn't silk."

"Anything beats a newspaper—damn near scratched the thing useless."

"Don't hold us up for an argument, Tynie. Bring on your print."

"Well, there's probably lots of old finger marks on that bone—it's gooey as hell. But this one is new. It's a little spread, but there'd be no mistaking it."

He withdrew now a metal cigarette-case. "Best thing in the world to carry a moist print in—see?" He opened it, revealing, beneath either transverse guard, a single photograph of a thumb print. "The slight bulge accommodates the curl of the wet paper and the guards hold it in place without touching anything but the edges."

"Smart boy," said Dart.

"Smarter than that," said the physician, "if you can read those smudges."

"Now listen, young expert," said Dart, "hold that here a minute. After I see this next bird, I want you to print everybody here and see if you find a print identical with that one. If you do, there's a few free nights in jail for somebody."

"O.K., Perry."

"I hope so anyway—it'll save sending out an alarm for the tall dark gentleman with the cock-eye."

"External strabismus is the term," said the doctor gravely.

"The hell it is," said Dart. "Douse that light. All right Brady, let's have the Spider."

CHAPTER TWELVE

SPIDER WEBB, an alert mouse-faced gentleman, perhaps thirty-five years old, was of dusky yellow complexion, rather sharp yet negroid features, and self-assured bearing. He was decidedly annoyed at the circumstances which had thus involved him, and his deep-set green-gray eyes glowed with a malicious impatience as he sat facing the well-nigh invisible detective.

His curt answers to Dart's incisive questioning revealed nothing to contradict the essential points already established. But the eliciting of his reasons for coming tonight to see Frimbo opened an entirely new realm of possibility.

At first he surlily refused to discuss the interview between himself and the African. It had been strictly personal he said.

"No more personal," the detective suggested, "than being held for murder on suspicion, was it?"

Spider was silent.

"Or being arrested for number-running? You know we can get you there on several counts, don't you?"

"Can't help that. Whatever you know, you also know I can't talk. That's suicide."

"So's silence. Telling the truth, Spider, will get you out of this—if you're not guilty—out of this and several other counts I could hold you on. You've enjoyed a lot of freedom, but this is a matter of life and death. A man has been killed. You're suspected. You can't keep quiet but so long. You know that?"

Webb said nothing.

"Now if it really was a personal matter you came here on tonight, telling me about it won't affect your—er—professional standing. If it wasn't, it had something to do with your number game. I know about that already—you won't be telling me anything new. The only thing talking now will do is clear you if you're innocent. Silence is equal to a confession."

Spider's receding chin quivered a bit; he started to speak, but didn't.

"You can get plenty, you know, for withholding evidence, too."

"I'd rather go to jail," Spider growled, "than take lead."

"Oh. So you're afraid of getting shot? Then you do know something. You'd better spill it, Spider, now that you've gone that far. Who sent you here to get Frimbo?"

A little of Webb's assurance dropped away.

"Nobody. On the level. Nobody."

"The man behind you is Brandon. Did he send you?"

"I said nobody."

"Let's see now. Brandon has only one real competitor as a policy-king here in Harlem. That's Spencer. Spider, your silence means one of two things. Either Brandon or Spencer had it in for Frimbo. If it was Spencer, you won't talk because you did it. If it was Brandon, you're afraid to squeal because he might find out."

In the bright illumination of the horizontal beam of

light, Spider's face twitched and changed just enough to convince Dart that he was on the right track. He took a long chance:

"Spencer has been hit hard several times in the past month, hasn't he?"

"How—how'd you know?" came from the startled Spider.

"We watch such things, Spider. It helps us solve lots of crimes. Your chief, Brandon, however, has shown no signs of loss. He's going strong."

Again Spider Webb's expression betrayed a touch for the detective.

"Of course, if you let me do all the talking, Spider, I won't be able to give you any of the credit. I'll have to put you in jail just the same—on all the outstanding counts. Understand, the only reason you're not in jail now is that you might be of value in just such a case as this."

Uneasily, Spider stirred in his chair.

"You tried to escape coming here tonight, too, didn't you, Spider? In Pat's—when you saw a policeman with a man you had seen here earlier tonight. You tried to duck. I guess you're our man all right. Brady, put the bracelets on——"

"Wait a minute," said Spider. "Is this going to be on the level—no leaks?"

"Give you my word. Wait, Brady. Go ahead, Spider."

"O. K."

"Good. You're only protecting yourself," said Dart.

"This Frimbo was a smart guy—much too smart," Spider Webb began.

"Yes?"

"Yea. He had a system of playing the game that couldn't lose. I don't know how he did it—whether he worked out somethin' mathematical or was just a good guesser or what. But he could hit regular once a week without fail. And he played ten dollars a day, and I collected it."

"Go on."

"When he hit the third week in succession, the boss set up a howl. You know the percentage—six hundred to one. Hit for a dollar, you get six hundred minus the ten percent that goes to the runner. Hit for ten bucks, you're due six thousand minus the six hundred—five thousand four hundred dollars. Well, even a big banker like Brandon can't stand that—he only collects four grand a week."

"Only," murmured Dart.

"And when it happened the third week, it looked bad for me—I was gettin' six hundred out of each time this guy hit. I been with Brandon a long time, but he began to look at me awful doubtful. But he paid off—he always does—that's why he's successful at it. Also he told me, no more bets from this Frimbo. But then he begun to figure, and what he figured was this—that maybe he could use some o' this Frimbo's smartness for himself. Smart guy, Brandon. Here's what he did.

"First he accused me of playin' crooked. Runners try that once in a while, y' know. We have a list o' names on a slip, with the number and amount of money being played by each person beside the name. Well, the slips are s'posed to be turned in at nine forty-five every

A.M., but it takes some time to get 'em in. Ten o'clock, the clearing-house number on which the winner is based is announced downtown. There's ways of holdin' the slip just a few seconds after ten, having a buddy telephone the winning number up, say, to the house next door, or downstairs someplace, where another buddy signals what it is by tapping on the wall or a radiator or something. Then the runner adds the winning number to his list beside a fake name, collects the money later, and splits with his buddies. Brandon, of course, knows all them tricks, and accused me of 'em. I showed him I wasn't dumb enough to try it three weeks in succession. So he had to admit this Frimbo must be just smart.

"So he figured he could trust me and he told me what to do. I was to keep on takin' Frimbo's ten bucks a day, and the numbers he played. Brandon had some of his boys play the same numbers with Spencer—but for twenty bucks. Result—when the numbers hit, Brandon lost six grand to Frimbo and won twelve from Spencer. The rest of his income stood like it was before. Spencer couldn't stand more than two or three twelve-grand hits—he'd have to quit. That would clear the field for Brandon. Then he could just stop taking Frimbo's bets and be sitting pretty."

"So what?" inquired Detective Dart.

"So that's why I was here tonight, that's all. To get Frimbo's number."

"Did he give you the number?"

"Sure he did—right from where you're sitting now."

"And the ten bucks?"

"Nope. He never handles money himself. The flunky

collects all the people's fees as they go out of that door there. So I always got the ten bucks from the flunky. He'd either be waiting there or he'd come out in a moment."

"Come out? Out of where?"

"Out of the back room there."

"The back room? Oh. Could Spencer have learned of this and put Frimbo out of the way?"

"If he was smart enough. He'd be bound to get suspicious, no matter how Brandon played his twenty—it wouldn't look right. And he'd investigate. He'd check the bets each night before, find twenty bucks of the same number, and trace those players. But he'd have to pay 'em, once he'd taken the money. And he couldn't tell who not to take beforehand, either, because they could change their names, or if he did find a leak and got the lowdown, there'd be only one way out for him. He'd have to paralyze Frimbo or be ruined himself. Pure self-defense."

Perry Dart sat silent a moment, then said, "You know, doc, there's one thing that keeps worrying me. All these people agree up to now that Frimbo talked to them—talked to them personally about personal matters. How could a murdered man conduct an intelligent conversation *after* his death? That's why I haven't taken Jenkins already. The victim couldn't have been sitting here dead in the chair all the time, talking—through a stuffed neck."

"True," said the physician, "but the visitors preceding Jenkins might have found the man dead just as Jenkins did and slipped out without saying anything, to avoid incriminating themselves. Or the assistant might have been doing the talking through some trick or device, without knowing his master was dead. Everyone agrees the servant didn't come in here. So don't bank on the end of the conversation as the moment of death. Death could have occurred a half an hour or more earlier, without changing the testimony at all."

Another silence, then Dart said:

"Put on that light."

As the sharp radiance cut the shadow, Spider Webb exclaimed:

"Judas Priest! If I'd known you had all them listeners——"

"Don't worry—we'll see it doesn't cost you anything. Brady, bring everybody in here. All ready, Tynie?"

"All ready, Perry," said Tynes.

In which the Doctor.
finds a mysterious a dark Film on
the arm chair; The finger prints
found on the club are discarded to
be Jinx's who is held under
arrest for the
murder of Frimbo

CHAPTER THIRTEEN

I

IN THE crystalline underlighting from the glaring
extension, a thin brightness through which shot the
horizontal beam from Frimbo's curious illumination, a
semicircle of people stood facing the table. Behind it
now stood the detective and the physician. The latter
was busy with his handkerchief, wiping from his fingers
a dark film which had stuck to them while he had been
sitting in the chair which Brady had brought. It was
a small, erect wooden chair with short arms on one of
which he had rested a hand during Spider Webb's testimony. At the moment he paid the stuff no further
attention, considering it merely a sort of furniture
polish which had been too heavily applied, and had
become gummy on standing.

The detective was addressing the people facing him.
"I'm going to ask the coöperation of all of you folks.
Before doing so, I want you to know just what I have
in view." He paused a moment, considered, decided.
"Among the facts brought out by what we have found
and by your testimony are these: Frimbo, a man of
close habits and no definitely known special friends or
enemies, was killed here in this chair tonight between
ten-thirty and eleven o'clock. He was stunned by a
blow, presumably from this club, and then choked to

141

death by this handkerchief, which was removed from his throat in my presence by Dr. Archer."

He paused again to observe the effect of this announcement. Outstanding were two reactions, quite opposite: Mrs. Crouch's horrified expression, and Bubber Brown's astonished comment:

"Doggone! They's some excuse for chokin' on a fishbone—but a handkerchief!"

"There are several possible motives that have come to light. But before following these motives any further, we must establish or complete such evidence as we already have in hand. We have reliable testimony on the ownership of this handkerchief. We must now determine who handled this club. You all know the meaning of finger prints. On this club, we have found a fresh print which will have to be compared with certain of your finger prints. But first I want to give you a chance now to admit having hold of this weapon tonight—if you did. Is anyone here ready to admit that he—even accidentally—touched this club tonight?"

Everyone looked at everyone else. No one spoke but the irrepressible Bubber. "Not tonight," murmured he, "nor las' night, either."

"Very well, then. I shall have to ask you all to submit to what you may consider an indignity, but it's quite necessary. And any who objects will have to be arrested on suspicion and for withholding of evidence, and will then have to submit anyhow. You will please come forward to this table in turn, one by one, beginning with Mrs. Crouch on that end, and allow Officer Tynes to take your prints. These prints will not be held as police records unless you are arrested in connection with this case."

"Wait a minute." It was Dr. Archer who spoke. "Better take mine first, hadn't you? I'm a suspect, too."

Dart agreed. "Right you are, doc. Go ahead."

Tynes had prepared his flat slab meanwhile by touching to it a dab of thick special ink from a flexible tube, then rolling this to a thin smooth even film which covered the rectangular surface. Dr. Archer submitted his hand. Tynes grasped the physician's right thumb, laid its outer edge upon the inky surface, rolled it skillfully over with a light even pressure till its inner edge rested as had its outer, lifted it, and repeated the maneuver within a labeled space on a prepared paper blank. The result was a perfectly rolled thumb print.

"I'm pretty sure it's a thumb on the club," Tynes said, "but I'll take the others, too, for safety."

"By all means," said the tall physician gravely. And in a few minutes Tynes had filled all ten of the spaces on the blank. Then he produced a small bottle of gasoline and a bit of cheese cloth. "That'll take it off," he said. He looked at the prints. "Your left thumb's blurred. Must have been dirty."

"Yes. It was, now that you mention it. Gummy furniture polish or something on the arm of that chair I was sitting in."

"Never mind, it'll do. Next."

"Mrs. Crouch—if you don't mind," said Dart.

Martha Crouch stepped forward without hesitation. The others followed in turn. The dexterous Tynes required only a minute for each person: Mrs. Snead, highly disgruntled, but silent save for an occasional disgusted grunt, Spider Webb, sullen, Easley Jones, grinning, Doty Hicks, trembling, and Jinx Jenkins scowling. Bubber's turn came last. Jinx's paper with his name across the head lay in plain view among those scattered out to dry on the table. Bubber cocked his head sidewise and peered at it as he submitted his digits to Tynes.

"Listen, brother—ain't you made a mistake?" he asked.

"How?" said Tynes, working on.

"Honest now, them ain't Jinx's *finger* prints, is they?"

"Sure, they are."

"Go on, man. You done took the boy's foot prints. Ain' no fingers made look like that."

"They're his, though."

"Tell me, mistuh, does apes have finger prints?"

"I suppose so."

"Well, listen. When you get time, see if them there don't belong to a gorilla or sump'm. I've had my doubts about Jinx Jenkins for quite a long time."

2

Tynes gathered the papers indiscriminately, so that they were not in any known order, faced them up in a neat pile, and procured a large hand-glass from his bag. He was the center of attention—even the officers in the corners of the room drew unconsciously a bit nearer. The doctor insisted on his sitting in one of the two chairs, he and the detective both being now on their feet. Tynes complied, sitting at the end of the table toward the hall with his back to the door. The physician stood so that he could direct his flashlight from the side upon the objects of Tynes' observations.

The latter now removed from the cigarette case one of the two photographs of the print which he had found on the club. This he kept in his left hand, the hand-glass in his right, and holding the original so that it was beside each labeled space in turn, methodically began to compare under the glass, the freshly made prints with the photograph.

Intently, silently, almost breathlessly, the onlookers stood watching the bent shoulders, the sleek black head, the expressionless tan face of Tynes. The whole room seemed to shift a little each time he passed from one comparison to the next, to hang suspended a moment, then shift with him again. So complete was the silence that the sound of a fire-siren on the Avenue a quarter-mile away came clearly into the room, and so absorbed was everyone in this important procedure that occasional odd sounds below were completely ignored.

It appeared that Tynes was making two separate piles, one of which, presumably, contained cases dismissed as out of the question, the other of which contained cases to be further studied and narrowed down. The long moments hung unrelaxed; the observers stared with the same fascinated expectancy that might have characterized their watching of a burning fuse, whose spark too slowly, too surely, approached some fatal explosive.

Yet Tynes' work was proceeding very rapidly, facilitated by the fortunate accident that the original print belonged to one of the simpler categories. In an apparent eternity which was actually but a few minutes, he had reduced the final number to two papers. One of these he laid decisively aside after a short reinspection. The other he examined at one point long and carefully. He nodded his head affirmatively once or twice, drew a deep breath, put down his hand-glass, and straightened up. He handed the paper to Detective Perry Dart, standing behind the table.

"This is it, Perry. Right thumb. Exactly like the photograph."

Dart took the paper, held it up, looked at it, lowered it again. His bright black eyes swept the waiting circle, halted.

"Jenkins," he said quietly, "you're under arrest."

CHAPTER FOURTEEN

I

"**Y**OU, Hicks," Dart continued, "will be held also on your own testimony, as a possible accessory. The rest of you be ready to be called at any time as witnesses. For the present, however——"

At this moment a newcomer pressed into the room, a large, bluff, red-faced man carrying a physician's bag, and puffing with the exertion of having climbed the stairs.

"Hello, Dart. Got you working, hey?"

"Hello, Dr. Winkler. How long've you been here?"

"Long enough to examine your case."

"Really? I heard some noises downstairs, but I didn't realize it was you. Shake hands with Dr. Archer here. He was called in, pronounced the case, and notified us. And he's a better detective than I am—missed his calling, I think."

"Howdy, doctor," said the florid medical examiner pleasantly. "This case puzzles me somewhat."

"I should think it would," said Dr. Archer. "We have the advantage over you."

"Can't figure out," went on Dr. Winkler, "just what evidence of violence there was to make you call in the police. Couldn't find any myself—looked pretty carefully, too."

"You mean you didn't see a scalp wound over the right ear?"

"Scalp wound? I should say I couldn't. There isn't any."

"No?" Dr. Archer turned to Dart. "Did you see that, Dart, or was it an optical illusion?"

"I saw it," admitted Dart.

"And unless I'm having hallucinations," the local physician went on, "it contained a fresh blood clot which I removed with a gauze dressing that now rests in my bag." He stooped deliberately, procured and displayed the soiled dressing, while the medical examiner looked first at him, then at Dart, as if he was not sure whether to doubt their sanity or his own. Dr. Archer dropped the dressing back into his bag. "Then I probed it for a fracture," he concluded.

"Well," said Winkler, "I don't see how I could've missed anything like that. I went over her from head to foot, and if she wasn't a cardiorenal I never saw one——"

"You went—where?"

"I went over her from head to foot—every inch——"

"*Her?*" burst from Dart.

"Yes—her. She's been dead for hours——"

"Wait a minute. Doctor Winkler," said Dr. Archer, "we aren't discussing the same subject. I'm talking about the victim of this crime, a man known as Frimbo."

"A man! Well, if that corpse downstairs is a man, somebody played an awful dirty trick on him."

"Stand fast, everybody!" ordered Dart. "Tynes, take charge here till I get back. Come on, you medicos. Let's get this thing straight."

Out of the room and down the stairs they hurried,

Archer, Dart, and Winkler. The door of Crouch's front room was open, but the couch on which the dead man had been placed was in a position that could not be seen from the hall. So far did Dr. Archer out-distance the others that by the time they got inside the room, he was already standing in the middle of the floor, staring dumbfoundedly at an unquestionably unoccupied couch.

"The elusive corpse," he murmured, as the other two came up. "First a man, then a woman, then—a memory."

"He was on that couch!" Dart said. "Where's Day? The cop covering the front? Day! Come here!"

Officer Day, large, cheese-colored, and bovine, loomed in the doorway. "Yas, suh."

"Day, where's the body that was on this couch?"

"Body? On that couch?" Day's face was blank as an egg.

"Are you on duty down here—or are you in a trance?"

" 'Deed, I ain' seen no body on that couch, chief. The only body down here is back yonder in the room where the telephone is. On a table under a sheet."

"He's right there," said Winkler.

"Day, don't repeat this question, please: When did you first come into this room?"

"When the medical examiner come. I took him in and showed him back yonder, but I didn' stay to look—I come right back here to my post."

"When you first came here tonight, didn't you see the corpse on this couch?"

"No 'ndeed. I was the last one in. You and the doc

went in there and left the rest of us here in the hall. I couldn't see 'round the door. And when you come out, yo' orders to me was 'cover the front.' And I been coverin' it." Officer Day was a little resentful of Detective Dart's implied censure. "When the medical examiner got here I took him in. And they sho' wasn't no corpse on no couch then. Only corpse in here was back yonder, under the sheet. Natchelly I figured that was it."

"You would. Doc——"

But Dr. Archer was already returning from a quick trip to the rear room. "It's a woman all right," he said. "Frimbo is apparently A.W.O.L. Inconsiderate of him, isn't it?"

"Listen, Day," Dart said, refraining with difficulty from explosive language. "Has anyone come through this door since you came down here?"

"No 'ndeed. Nobody but him." He pointed to Dr. Winkler. "The undertaker started in, but when I told him what had happened he asked where y'all was, and I told him upstairs yonder, so he went straight up. Then, when he come down again, he went on out. Asked me to turn out the lights and slam this door when we was through, that's all."

"All right, Day. That's all. You keep on covering the front. Don't let it get away from you. Doc, you and the M. E. wait here and keep your eyes open. I'll tear this shack loose if necessary—nobody's going to get away with a stunt like that."

"Wait a second," said Dr. Archer. "How long has it been since we were down here?"

"Damn!" exploded Dart, looking at his watch. "Over an hour."

"Well," the local physician said, "whoever removed that stiff has had plenty of time to get it off the premises long before now. Just a hasty harum-scarum search won't dig up a thing, do you think?"

"I can't help it," Dart replied impatiently. "I've got to look, haven't I?" And out of the door he sped and bounded up the stairs.

2

The tall, pale, bespectacled Dr. Archer summarized the situation for the medical examiner's benefit while they waited. He described how they had found the strange instrument of death and later the club, devised of a human femur, which must have delivered the blow. He gave the evidence in support of his estimate of the period during which death had occurred, the medical examiner readily approving its probability.

"Testimony indicated," the local physician went on, "and Dart checked each witness against the others, that the two women and one of the six men present were very unlikely as suspects. Any one of the other five men, four of them visitors and one the assistant or servant, could have committed the crime. One of them, an obvious drug addict, even admitted having a hand in it—rather convincingly, too; although the person who voluntarily comes forward with an admission is usually ignored——"

"Some day," the medical examiner grinned, "that

sort of suspect is going to be ignored once too often—
he'll turn out guilty in spite of his admission."

"Well, there's more to this chap's admission than just
an admission. He had a good motive—believed that
Frimbo was slowly killing his brother by some mystic
spell, which only Frimbo's own death could break. And
he indicated, too, that he had a paid accomplice. That,
plus his obvious belief in the superstition, was what
really lent a little credibility to his admission. But there
was another motive brought out by Dart: One of the
other men was a policy-runner. He said Frimbo had a
winning system that was being used to break his boss's
rival, and that the rival might have found it out and
eliminated Frimbo in self-defense. Even so, of course,
the actual murderer would have to be one of those five
men present. Because one of them had to take that club
from the front room back to the middle room where
we found it—it couldn't move by itself, even if it was a
thigh-bone once. Of course, the same thing applies to
the handkerchief. There was the servant too, who managed to disappear completely just before the murder
was discovered. He'd hardly kill the goose that laid his
golden eggs, though."

"But he did disappear?"

"To the naked eye."

"What about the undertaker who came in and went
out?"

"He didn't enter the front room at any time. You
see, both the handkerchief and the club were unquestionably in the front room before Frimbo was killed
with them. The undertaker, or anybody else, would have

had to be in that room at some time—and so be seen by the others—to have got possession of those two objects.— And the undertaker had every apparent reason to want Frimbo to stay alive. Frimbo paid him outrageously high rent—and always on time."

"So who did it?"

"Well, I'll give you a list—if I don't forget somebody —in the order of their probable guilt. First is Jenkins, against whom both the clues point. It's his handkerchief, as two others testify. What makes it look worse for him is that he denies it's his. It may be just apprehension or perversity that makes him deny it—he's a hard-boiled, grouchy sort of person; but it looks on the face of it, more like he's covering up. But worse still, his right thumb print was identified on the club—which, again, he'd denied touching."

"Dart's holding him then?"

"Has to. And that's evidence that even a smart lawyer —which Jenkins probably can't afford—couldn't easily explain away. Then next, I should say, is Doty Hicks, the drug-addict, about whom I just told you. Possibly the accomplice he admits paying is Jenkins. Then—let's see—then would come Spencer—the number-king mentioned by the runner, Spider Webb. Not Spencer himself, of course, but some one of those present, paid by Spencer. That again suggests Jenkins, who might be in Spencer's employ. Or the railroad porter, Jones—Easley Jones. He might be Spencer's agent, though he tells a simple, straightforward story which can easily be checked; and there isn't a scrap of evidence against him. In fact he went in to see Frimbo first and Frimbo talked to him, as well as to three others following him. Obviously even an African mystic couldn't tell fortunes through a throat plugged up as tightly as Frimbo's was."

"Not unless he used sign language," commented the medical examiner.

"Which he couldn't in the dark," answered Dr. Archer. "Well next—the servant, against whom the only charge is his disappearance. He could figure as somebody's agent too, I suppose. But it wasn't his thumb print on the club, nor his handkerchief. Then there was Brown, a likable sort of Harlem roustabout, who, however, did not leave the front room till after the attack on Frimbo. And finally the two women, who didn't even know the man had been killed till we told them, some time after examining him."

"Well, you know how the books tell it. It's always the least likely person."

"In that case, evidence or no evidence, the guilty party is Mrs. Aramintha Snead, devout church-member and long-suffering housewife."

"Oh, no. You've very adroitly neglected to mention the really most unlikely person. I'm thinking of the physician on the case. Dr. Archer is the name, I believe?"

"Quite possible," Dr. Archer returned gravely. "Motive—professional jealousy."

"If that theory applied here," the medical examiner laughed, "I'd have to clear out myself. I'm obviously the murderer: I was ten miles away when it happened."

"Of course. You put Jenkins' thumb pri
club by telephoto, and the handkerchief——

"I blew the handkerchief out of Jenkins' pocket and down Frimbo's throat by means of a special electric fan!"

*"Some day I'm going to write a murder mystery," mused Dr. Archer, "that will baffle and astound the world. The murderer will turn out to be the most likely suspect."

Fore Shadow

Irony on the author who was a Physicist

"You'd never write another," said the medical examiner.

more ironic because the author died after this book

3

For half an hour, Perry Dart and three of the more experienced bluecoats searched the house. They prowled from roof to cellar in vain. At one moment, Dart thought he had discovered an adequate hiding-place beneath the laboratory bench, which stretched across the posterior wall of the rear on the second floor; for the doors to the cabinets under the bench were locked. But he soon saw that this was an impossible lead: the two doors were not adjacent; an easily opened compartment was between them filled with mechanical bric-a-brac; and the size of this and all the other unlocked compartments indicated that the locked ones were far too small to accommodate a full sized cadaver.

Again a possibility appeared in the old dumbwaiter shaft, which extended from the basement to the first floor. But inspection of this, both from above and below, disclosed that it did not contain even the dumbwaiter which must originally have occupied it. A few

Maybe the culprit came into the room through the broken dumbwaiter so no one could see him and get Frimbo from behind

old ropes and a set of pulleys dangled from its roof, at the level of the first floor ceiling; between these, flashlights revealed nothing but musty space.

Eventually, the detective returned alone to the two physicians. He was still grim and angry, but thoroughly composed again. "Somebody," he said, "is going to get in trouble."

The medical examiner grinned.

"What do you make of it?"

"Only one thing to make of it—you can't prove a murder without a corpse. It's an old trick, but it's the last thing I'd expect up here." ✳

"Somebody's smart," commented Dr. Archer.

"Exactly. And the somebody isn't working alone. Everybody who could possibly have done the job is upstairs in that room now; not a single suspect has been down here since we left the body. Every one of them has been under some policeman's eye."

"The undertaker was down here."

"In the hall, but not in this room. Day might not be as bright as his name would indicate, but surely he could see whether Crouch came in here. Day says positively that he didn't; he went straight up, and came down and went straight out. He couldn't get back in here any other way without being seen, either. The back yard and back door are covered. The roof is covered. Every possible entrance and exit have been covered from almost the moment we left this room with Frimbo on that couch."

"Then," Dr. Archer said, "the fact of the matter must be that the gentleman is still in our midst. Maybe you're dealing with secret passages and mysterious compartments."

"Wouldn't be surprised," said the medical examiner amusedly. "He was a man of mystery, wasn't he? He ought to have a few hidden chambers and such."

"We can take care of them," Dart said. "I'll have a departmental expert here early tomorrow morning—even if it is Sunday. This morning, as a matter of fact. We'll go over the house with a pair of micrometer calipers. There never was a secret chamber that didn't take up space. And one thing is sure: Jenkins knows who did this. Whoever paid him, paid for the removal of the corpse also. It's the final stroke—protects everybody, you see. No corpse, no killing. Damn!"

"Somehow," Dr. Archer reflected, "I've a very uncomfortable feeling that something is wrong."

"Not really?"

"I mean something in the way we've been reasoning. It's so easy to ignore the obvious. What obvious circumstance can we have been ignoring?" He deliberated without benefit of the others' aid. Rather suddenly he drew a breath. "No," he contradicted his own inspiration, "that's a little too obvious. And yet——"

"What the dickens are you mumbling about?" Dart asked, with pardonable impatience.

"Let's divide all the suspects," said Dr. Archer, "whom we have considered here tonight into two groups. The first will be a group about whom we can definitely say they couldn't have made off with this body. The second will be a group about whom we can't say that."

"Go ahead."

"All right. Everybody that's been here will fall into the first group—except one."

"Who?"

"The servant."

"Mmm."

"Nobody knows that servant's whereabouts since he bowed Jenkins into Frimbo's room. And if it's a matter of knowing the layout, he ought to be more qualified than anybody else to bring off this last bit of sleight-of-hand."

"How'll we prove it?"

"Find him. He has all the additional information you need. He's your key."

"If he didn't leave before we got here."

"In that case he couldn't have got back to recover the remains—not if all avenues were covered. So that he may still be—with his gruesome companion. Keep your avenues guarded until you can go over the place with—calipers, did you say? And even if he isn't here, he's got to be found. I suspect his remarks on this whole matter would save us considerable energy, even if he didn't remove the body."

"All right, doc, I accept your suggestion. But Jenkins is a bird in the hand, and I think we can persuade him to talk. Hicks, too, may have something more to say under the right circumstances. And I've a mind to hold the other two also until the body is found. A few pertinent suggestions might improve their knowledge of the case. But it may be better to let 'em go, and have 'em trailed. Find out more that way. Yep—I'm going to have everybody I let out of here tonight trailed. I won't even tell 'em about this. That's the idea——"

"Well," the medical examiner sighed, gathering himself for departure, "I can't examine what isn't here. When you guys get a body let me know. But don't find it till I've had a few hours' sleep. And no more false alarms, please."

"O.K., Dr. Winkler. It won't be a false alarm next time."

"Good-night, doctor."

Before the outside door slammed behind the departing medical examiner, Dart had reached the telephone in the rear room. He got headquarters, made a brief preliminary report of the case, and instituted a sharp lookout, through police radio broadcast and all the other devices under headquarters' control, for a Negro of the servant's description, and any clues leading to possible recovery of the dead body.

Then he and the doctor returned to the death chamber above.

CHAPTER FIFTEEN

I

"**G**REAT day in the mornin'!" exclaimed Mrs. Aramintha Snead. "What under the sun is it now?"

"Sit tight, everybody," advised Tynes. "They'll be right back."

" 'Twouldn' be so bad," commented Easley Jones good-humoredly, "if we was sittin'—tight or loose. But my dawgs is 'bout to let me down."

As for the customary volubility of Bubber, that had for the moment fled. The actuality of his friend's arrest had shocked him even more than it had Jinx, for Jinx had half-anticipated it, while Bubber hadn't given the possibility a thought. He stood near his long, lanky, uncomely friend, looking rather helplessly into his face. Jinx was scowling glumly into the distance. Finally Bubber spoke:

"Did you hear what the man said?"

"Hmph!" grunted Jinx.

"Is you got any idea what it means?"

"Hmph!" Jinx grunted again.

"Hmph hell-ie!" returned Bubber, sufficiently absorbed in his ally's predicament to be oblivious of the heretofore hampering presence of ladies. "Here you is headed straight for the fryin'-pan, and all you can do is grunt. What in the world is you tol' the man to make him think you done it?"

"Tol' him little as I could," muttered Jinx.

"Well, brother, you better get to talkin'. This here's serious."

"You tellin' me?"

"Somebody got to tell you. You don' seem to have sense enough to see it for yo'self. Look here—did you have a hand in this thing sho' 'nough?"

"Hmph!" said Jinx.

"Well, you could 'a. Man might 'a said sump'm 'bout yo' ancestors, and you might 'a forgot yo'self and busted him one. It's possible."

"I tol' 'em what the man said—word for word—near as I could. This is what I get for that."

"Guess you jes' born for evil, boy. Good luck come yo' way, take one look at you, and turn 'round and run. You sho' you ain't done it?"

"Hmph," issued a fourth time from the tall boy's nose.

"Listen, Jinx. 'Hmph' don' mean nothin' in no language. You better learn to say 'no' and say it loud and frequent. You didn't fall asleep while the man was talkin' to you? Did y'?"

"How'm I go'n' sleep with all that light in my eyes?"

"Shuh, man, I've seen you sleep with the sun in yo' eyes."

"Hadn' been for you," Jinx grumbled, "I wouldn' be in this mess."

"Hadn' been for me? Listen to the fool! What'd I have to do with it?"

"You tol' the man that was my han'kerchief, didn' y'?"

" 'Cose I did. It was yo' han'kerchief. But I sho' didn' tell 'im that was yo' finger print on that club yonder."

" 'Tain' no finger print o' mine. I ain' touched no club."

"Now wait a minute, big boy. Don' give the man no argument 'bout no finger print. You in trouble enough now. This ain't the first time yo' fingers got away from you."

"And 'tain't the first time yo' tongue's got away from you. You talk too doggone much."

"Maybe. But everything I've said tonight is a whisper side o' what that finger print says. That thing shouts out loud."

2

Mrs. Aramintha Snead came up to them. "Young man," she addressed Jinx, "your time has come. I'm gonna pray for you."

At this, everyone exchanged uncomfortable, apprehensive glances, and Bubber, gathering the full significance of the church lady's intention, looked at Jinx as if the latter's time had indeed come.

"Stand one side, son," ordered the lady, elbowing Bubber well out of the way.

"Yas'm," said Bubber helplessly, his face a picture of distress.

"Young man, does you know the Ten Commandments?"

Jinx could only look at her.

"Does you know the *six'* commandment? Don't know even a single one of the commandments, does y'? Well, you's a hopeless sinner. You know that, don't y'? Hopeless—doomed—on yo' way," her voice trembled and rose, "to burn in hell, where the fire is not quenched and the worm dieth not."

"Lady, he ain't no worm," protested Bubber.

"Hush yo' mouf!" she rebuked; then resumed her more holy tone. "If you'd 'a' obeyed the commandments, you wouldn't 'a' been a sinner and you wouldn't 'a' sinned. But how could you obey 'em when you didn' even know 'em?"

The silence accompanying her pause proved that this was an unanswerable point.

"If you'd obeyed the six' commandment," her voice was low and impressive, "you wouldn't 'a' killed this conjure-man here tonight. 'Cause the six' commandment say, *'Thou shalt not kill!'* And now you done broke it. Done broke it—done kilt one o' yo' fellow men. Don' matter whether he was good or bad—you done kilt him —laid 'im out cold in the flesh. The Good Book say 'A eye for a eye and a toof for a toof.' And inasmuch as you did it unto him, it shall likewise be done unto you. And you got to go befo' that great tribunal on high and 'splain why—'splain why you done it. They's only one thing, you can do now—repent. Repent, sinner, befo' it is too late!"

"Can I do it for 'im, lady?" Bubber offered helpfully.

"Let us pray," said Mrs. Snead serenely. "Let us pray."

She stood erect, she folded her arms, she closed her prominent eyes. That helped. But the benefit to Jinx of what followed was extremely doubtful.

"Lawd, here he is. His earthly form returns to the dust frum whence it came, and befo' his undyin' soul goes to eternal judgment, we want to pray for 'im. We know he's got to go. We know that soon his mortal shell will be molderin' in the ground. It ain't for that we prayin'—it ain't for that——"

"The hell it ain't," devoutly mumbled Bubber.

"Hit's for his soul we prayin'—his soul so deep-dyed, so steeped, so black in sin. Wash him, Lawd. Wash him and he shall be whiter than snow. Take from him every stain of transgression, and bleach him out like a clean garment in the sunlight of righteousness."

For an unconscionable length of time she went on lamenting the hopeless sinner's iniquitous past, that had culminated in so shameful a present, and picturing the special torments reserved in hell for the impenitent dead.

"We know he's a hopeless sinner. But, oh, make him to see his sins—make him know it was wrong to steal, wrong to gamble, wrong to drink, wrong to swear, wrong to lie, and wrong to kill—and make him fall on his knees and confess unto salvation befo' it is too late. Make him realize that though he can't save his body, they's still time to save his soul. So that when that las' day comes, and he reaches Jordan's chilly shore, and Death puts forth his cold icy hand and lays it on his shoulder and whispers, 'Come,' he can rise up with a smile and say, 'I'm ready—done made my peace callin', and election sho', done cast off this old no'count flesh and took on the spirit.'"

Then she opened her eyes and looked at the young man for whose soul she had so long pleaded. "There now," she said, "Don't you feel better?"

"No, ma'am," said Jinx.

"Lawd have mercy!" breathed the lady, and shaking her head sadly from side to side, she abandoned him to the fate of the unrepentant, returning to her place with the air of one who at least has done his duty.

3

When the second search was over and the detective and the physician returned to the room where the others waited, they found a restless and bewildered company.

"What was it, doc?" Bubber promptly wanted to know, "a boy or a girl?"

"Neither," said the physician.

"Mph!" grunted Bubber. "Was Frimbo like that too? It's gettin' so you don' know who to trust, ain't it?"

"Brown," said Detective Dart, "you heard what I told Jenkins before I went out?"

"Sho' did."

"He's a good friend of yours, isn't he?"

"Who—Jenkins? Friend o' mine? No 'ndeed."

"What do you mean?"

"I mean I barely know the nigger. Up till night befo' las' we was perfect strangers."

"You were pretty chummy with him tonight. You and he came here together."

"Purely accidental, mistuh. Jes' happen' to meet him on the street; he was on his way here; I come along too, thinkin' the man might gimme some high lowdown. Chummy? Shuh! Didn' you and the doc burst in on us in the front room there where we was almost 'bout to fight? Friend o' mine! 'Deed you wrong there, brother. I don' have nothin' to do with gangsters, gunmen, killers, or no folks like that. I lives above reproach. Ask anybody."

Jinx's jaw sagged, his scowl faded into a stare of amazement. It was perhaps the first time in his life when he had failed to greet the unexpected obdurately. Not even the announcement of his arrest for murder had jolted him as did this. He had never been excessively articulate, but his silence now was the silence of one struck dumb.

"All right, Brown," Dart said. "I'm glad to hear that."

"Yes, *suh*," vowed Bubber, but he did not look at Jinx.

"Now listen, you people," went on Dart. "I'm letting you go, with the exception of Jenkins and Hicks, but you're not to leave town until further word from me. Jones, that means you too. I'm sorry to have you lose any time from your job, but you may have to. Can you manage it?"

"Yas, indeed," smiled Easley Jones. "I'm layin' over till Monday anyhow, y'see, and another day or two won' matter. I can fix it up with the boss-man—no trouble 'tall."

"Good. Then you and the others are free to go."

The word "go" was scarcely out of his mouth before the whole place went suddenly black.

"Hey—what the hell!"

Even the hall lights were gone. In the sudden dark, Mrs. Snead screamed aloud, "Sweet Jesus have mercy!" There was a quick soft rustle and bustle. Dart remembered that Jinx was nearest to the hall-door. "Look out for Jenkins!" he yelled. "Block that door—he's pullin' a fast one!"

He reached into his pocket for the flashlight he had dropped there, and at the same time Dr. Archer remembered his. The two fine beams of white light shot forth together, toward the spot where Jinx had been standing; he was not there. The lights swept toward the door, to reveal Officer Green, who had automatically obstructed the exit, earnestly embracing Jinx's long form, and experiencing no small difficulty in holding the young man back. At the same time Jinx looked back over his shoulder and saw the two spots of light. To him they must have appeared to be the malevolent eyes of some gigantic monster; for with a supreme effort he wriggled out of Green's uncertain hold, and might have fled down the stairs and out into the night, had he not tripped and fallen in the hall. Green, following him blindly, tripped over him, landed upon him, and so remained until Dart's pursuing flashlight revealed the tableau.

"Smart boy," muttered the detective grimly, for it did not seem to him that Jinx's behavior might have been occasioned by momentary panic. "Who's workin' with you? Who switched off those lights? Where's the switch?"

Under Green's weight, it was all Jinx could do to answer, "Dam' 'f I know!"

"Oh, no? Got bracelets, Green? Use 'em. Where the——"

A deep strong voice in the middle of the death room struck silence to all the rising babel.

"Wait!"

Profound, abrupt quiet.

"You will find a switch in this room beside the rear door."

Somebody drew a single sharp startled breath. Dr. Archer, who had not moved from where he had been standing, swung his light around toward the sound. It fell on the head and shoulders of a stranger, seated in Frimbo's chair.

Through the subsequent silence came Martha Crouch's voice, uttering one lone, incredulous word:

"Frimbo!"

From the hall Dart called: "Find that switch!" One of the patrolmen stationed inside the room obeyed. The horizontal beam, and the bright sharp extension light came on together as suddenly as they had gone out. Dart came rushing back into the room. He halted, staring like everyone else with utterly unbelieving eyes at the figure that sat in the chair from which the dead body had been removed: a black man wearing a black robe and a black silk head-band; a man with fine, almost delicate features, gleaming, deep-set black eyes, and an expression of supreme intelligence and tranquillity.

Quickly, ere Dart could speak, Martha Crouch stepped forward in wide-eyed wonder.

"Frimbo—you're—alive . . . ?"

"Yes, I am alive," said the deep clear voice of the man in the chair. Something just less than a smile touched the handsome dark face.

"But they said—they said you were dead——"

"They were correct," affirmed Frimbo, without emotion.

CHAPTER SIXTEEN

I

EVERYONE in the room perceptibly shrank. So terrible a thing, so calmly said, at once impelled them to flight and held them captive.

"My Gawd!" breathed Aramintha Snead. "The man done come back!" And she with the others drew away staring and terrified. For a moment it seemed they would have fled, had the air not been turned to jelly, holding them fast. "He done done a Lazarus!" Bubber Brown whispered.

But Perry Dart's amazement gave way to exasperation. He stepped forward. "Say, what is all this, anyway? Who the devil are you?"

There was something extraordinarily disconcerting in the unwavering deep-set black eyes of the man in the chair. Even the redoubtable Dart must have felt the penetrating, yet impenetrable calmness and vitality of that undisturbed gaze as it switched to meet his own.

"I am Frimbo. You heard this lady?"

"Oh, yea? Then who was killed?"

"I was."

"You were, were you? I suppose you've risen from the dead?"

"It is not the first time I have outwitted death, my friend."

He can't be Frimbo unless maybe the
Servant posed as Frimbo!?

THE CONJURE-MAN DIES   171

"Do you mean to sit there and tell me that you are the man I saw lying dead on that couch downstairs?"

"I am the man. And if you will be patient, I will try to explain the matter to your satisfaction."

"But how did you—what did you do? Where did you go? What's the idea dousing the lights? What do you think we are, anyway?"

"I think you are a man of intelligence, who will appreciate that coöperation achieves more than antagonism. I trust I am correct?"

"Go ahead—talk," said Dart gruffly.

"Thank you. I hope you will understand. The facts are these: At the time I was attacked—I am uncertain myself of the precise moment, for time is of little importance to me personally—I was in a state of what you would probably call suspended animation. More exactly, I was wholly immune to activities of the immediate present, for I had projected my mind into the future—that gentleman's future—Mr. Jenkins'. During that period I was assaulted—murderously. Physically, I *was* murdered. Mentally I could not be, because mentally I was elsewhere. Do you see?"

"I never heard of such thing," said Dart, but he spoke uncertainly, for nothing could have been more impressive than this cool, deliberate deep voice, stating a mystic paradox in terms of level reason.

"Your profession, Mr. Dart," returned Frimbo, "should embrace an understanding of such matters. They do occur, I assure you, but at the moment I must not take the time to convince you personally. I can, if necessary. Now, since my apparently lifeless body, which you and Dr. Archer abandoned downstairs, was not seriously damaged in any vital particular, the return of consciousness, which is to say, the return of present mental activity, was naturally accompanied by a return of physical activity also. In short, I came to. I realized what must have happened. Naturally, I decided to assist your further efforts.

"But I have certain aversions, Mr. Dart. One is to be impeded physically, particularly by such worthy but annoying persons as gigantic minions of the law. I therefore desired to return to this room, where you were, without being obstructed by your deputies. It was not difficult to reach my laboratory without being detected, but the hallway there could not be so easily negotiated. And so I adopted the simple, if theatrical, device of completing my journey under cover of darkness. It was much simpler and pleasanter for me, you see."

For the first time tonight Dart was uncertain of procedure. Nothing in his training, thorough as it had been, covered this situation where, with a murder on the verge of solution and the definitely incriminated assailant in handcuffs, the victim walked in, sat down, and pronounced himself thoroughly alive. It swept the very foundation out from under the structure which his careful reasoning had erected and rendered it all utterly and absurdly useless. So, for the present at least, it seemed.

But Frimbo continued with a statement altogether startling in its implications:

"The fact remains, of course, that a murder was committed. I live, but someone killed me. Someone is guilty." The voice took on a new hardness. "Someone must pay the penalty."

Something in that suggestion brought method back into Dart's mind. "Where were you when we were searching the house just now?" said he.

"Obviously, we simply were not in the same place at the same time. That is nothing extraordinary."

"How do I know it was you who was killed?"

"You saw me, did you not? My identity is easy to establish. Mrs. Crouch knows me, as she has indicated, by sight. The other visitors may not have been able to see me well, but they will perhaps recognize my voice."

"Sho' is the same voice," vowed Jinx, unaware that he was testifying against himself.

"Are you sure of that?" Dart asked.

"Sho' is," repeated Jinx, and the others murmured assent.

"Well," Dart turned to the doctor, "at least it wasn't the servant doing the talking."

But Dr. Archer now spoke. "I beg your pardon, Dart, but may I point out that it is of no consequence whether this gentleman is Frimbo or not. The only question of importance is whether he is the man whom we saw downstairs."

Thereupon Frimbo said, "Dr. Archer, who pronounced me dead, will naturally be most reluctant to identify me with the corpse, since the implication would be that he had been mistaken in his original pronouncement. Thereupon I must insist that he examine me now."

The physician was slightly surprised. "I should think you would prefer someone less prejudiced," he said.

"On the contrary. If you identify me with the man you yourself pronounced dead, there can be no further question. You are the only person who would be reluctant to do so. You will allow only the most reliable evidence to overcome that reluctance."

Dr. Archer stared for a moment from behind his spectacles into the serene dark face of this astonishing fellow, sensing for the first time perhaps how his own irrepressible curiosity was to lead him shortly into an investigation of the most extraordinary personality he had ever confronted.

Then he went over to the seated figure. "Will you please remove your head-band? The wound would hardly be healed so soon."

"You will find the wound unhealed," said Frimbo, complying. The silken headdress removed, there appeared a small white dressing affixed by adhesive, over the right temple. "Look beneath the dressing," suggested the African.

Dr. Archer appreciated the ever so faintly malicious little irony, for he answered gravely:

"I shall look even further than that."

He detached the dressing, removed it, and examined a short scalp wound thus disclosed, a wound apparently identical with the one he had probed over an hour ago.

"I delayed a moment to dress it, of course," said Frimbo.

The physician inspected carefully every peculiarity of feature that might answer the question. To the lay eye, certainly there was nothing in this strikingly vivid countenance to recall that other death-distorted visage. But violent death—or even near death—often performs strange transfigurations. Dr. Archer eventually stood erect.

"As nearly as I can determine," he said, "this is the same man. I should request him to submit to a further test, however, before I commit myself finally—a test which will require some little time."

"Whatever the doctor wishes," agreed Frimbo.

"I have in my bag a small amount of blood on a dressing with which I swabbed the wound before probing it. There are one or two tests which can be used as convincing evidence, provided I may have a sample of your blood now for comparison."

"An excellent idea, doctor. Here"—Frimbo drew back the wide sleeve of his black satin robe, baring a well-formed forearm—"help yourself."

The physician promptly secured a tourniquet just above the elbow, moistened a sponge with alcohol, swabbed a small area, where large superficial veins stood out prominently, carefully removed a needle from its sterile tube container, deftly inserted it into a vein, caught a few drops of blood in the tube, loosed the tourniquet, withdrew the needle, and pressed firmly a moment with his swab on the point of puncture.

"Thank you," he said, the operation over.

"How long will this take you, doc?" Dart asked.

"At least an hour. Perhaps two. I'll have to go back to my office to do it."

"You will do the usual agglutination tests, of course?" Frimbo inquired.

"Yes," said Dr. Archer, unable to veil his astonishment that this apparent charlatan should even know there were such tests. "You are familiar with them?"

"Perfectly. I am somewhat of a biologist, you see. Psychology is really a branch of biology."

"You subscribe to the Spencerian classification?" Dr. Archer said.

It was Frimbo's turn to express surprise, which appeared in the slight lift of his lids.

"In that particular, yes."

"I should like to discuss the subject with you."

"I should be very glad indeed. I have met no one competent to do so for years. Today is Sunday. Why not later today?"

"At what hour?"

"Seven this evening?"

"Splendid."

"I shall look forward to seeing you."

2

At this point, a surreptitious remark from Bubber, who had been unwontedly silent, drew attention back to the matter in hand.

"He sho' can talk—for a dead man, can't he?"

"Listen, Frimbo," said Dart. "You say you were killed. All right. Who killed you?"

"I don't know, I'm sure."

"Why don't you?"

"I have tried to explain, Mr. Dart, that I was in a mental state equivalent to being absent. My entire mind was elsewhere—contemplating that gentleman's future. I can no more answer your question than if I had been sound asleep."

"Oh, I see. Would it be asking too much of this strange power of yours if I suggested that you use it to determine the identity of your assailant?"

"I'm glad you suggested it, even ironically. I was reluctant to interfere with your methods. You already have what you believe to be damning evidence against Jenkins. You may be right. But you still have to make sure of the items of motive and possible complicity. Is that not true?"

"Yes."

"Since I am the victim and thus the most personally interested party, I suggest that you allow me to solve this matter for you."

"How?"

"By the use of what you sarcastically call my strange power. If you will have all the suspects here on Monday night at eleven, I will provide you with the complete story of what took place here tonight and why."

"What are you going to do—reconstruct the crime?"

"In a sense, yes."

"Why can't you do that now? All the suspects are

here. Here's Jenkins. His finger print on the club that
inflicted that wound can't mean but one thing—he
handled that club. Why don't you just read his mind
and find out what made him do it?"

"It's not so simple as that, my friend. Such a thing
requires preparation. Tonight there is not time. And I
am tired. But see, I am not suggesting that you neglect
doing any single thing that you would have done anyway. Proceed as if I had not returned—I insist that my
being alive does not alter the fundamental criminal aspect of this case—proceed, hold whom you will, determine such facts as you can by every means at your
disposal, establish your case—then accept my suggestion,
if you care to, simply as a corroboration of what you
have concluded. Consider what I shall show you on
Monday night as just a check on what you already
know."

Dart was impressed by the turn of the suggestion.
"I suppose," he mused, "I could change the charge to
felonious assault——"

Frimbo said, "You are working on a common fallacy,
my friend. You are making the common assumption
that any creature who is alive cannot have been dead.
This is pure assumption. If a body which has presented
all the aspects of death, resumes the functions of life,
we explain the whole thing away merely by saying, 'He
was not dead.' We thus repudiate all our own criteria
of death, you see. I cannot think in this self-contradic-
tory fashion. Physically, I was dead by all the standards
accepted throughout the years as evidence of death. I

was so pronounced by this physician, who has already shown himself to be unusually competent. Had I been anyone else on earth, I should still be dead. But because I have developed special abilities and can separate my mental from my physical activities, the circumstances were such that I could resume the aspects of life. Why must you, on that account, assume that the death was any less actual than the life? Why must you change the charge from murder, which it unquestionably was, to assault, which is only part of the story? Must I pay a premium for special abilities? Must I continually re-expose myself to a criminal who has already carried out his purpose? He has killed—let him die also. If he is able, as I was, to resume life afterwards, I am sure I shall have no objection."

Dart shook his head. "No living person could convince a judge or a jury, that he'd been really murdered. Even if I believed your argument, which I don't, I couldn't arrest this man for murder. A conviction of murder requires the production of a corpse—or tangible evidence of a corpse. I can't present you as a corpse. I'd be the joke of the force."

"Perhaps you are right," Frimbo conceded. "I had not considered the—force."

"Still," Dr. Archer injected, "Mr. Frimbo's suggestion can do no harm. All he says is proceed as if he had not returned. That's what you'd have done anyway. Then, if you like, he will produce additional evidence—Monday night. Personally, I'd like to see it."

"So would I," Dart admitted. "Don't misunderstand

me. My only point is that if this is the same man, it's no longer murder."

"There's still plenty to be answered, though," the doctor reminded him. "Jenkins' stout denial in the face of the strongest evidence, the probability of complicity, the motive——"

"And," popped unexpectedly from Bubber, "where that flunky disappeared to, all of a sudden."

Frimbo apparently rarely smiled, but now his awesome dark face relaxed a little. "That need not worry you. My assistant has been with me a long time. He is like a brother. He lives here. He could not possibly be guilty of this crime."

"Then," inquired Bubber, "how come he hauled hips so fast?"

"He is free to leave at eleven every night. It is our understanding and our custom. At that hour tonight, he no doubt took his departure as usual."

"Departure for where—if he lives here?" asked Dart.

"Even servants are entitled to their hour or two of relaxation. He takes his at that time. You need have no doubts about him. Even if I found him guilty, I should not press charges. And I assure you he will be present Monday night."

Later, Detective Dart conveyed to Dr. Archer the considerations which had influenced his decision. First, it had been his experience that in Harlem the most effective method of crime detection was to give your man enough rope with which to hang himself. If Jenkins' denial was true, in whole or part, careful observation of the behavior of the other suspects would reveal something incriminating. Believing himself free and unwatched, the actual criminal—or accomplice—would soon betray himself. The forty-eight hour interval would reveal much about all the suspects. Secondly, if any suspect demurred on the matter of returning or actually failed to return on Monday night, that fact, together with whatever was discovered meanwhile by trailers, would carry its own weight. In short, it was Dart's persuasion that in Harlem one learned most by seeking least—to force an issue was to seal it in silence forever.

And therefore, he now complied with the suggestion that the company be reassembled here on Monday night.

"Very well. I agree. Jenkins and Hicks will be returned under guard. Do any of you other ladies and gentlemen feel that you will be unable to be present?"

No one demurred.

"It is understood, then, that you will be present here at eleven P.M. on Monday. That is all. You are free to go."

The visitors departed, each in his own manner: Jinx, shackled to Officer Green, glowered unforgivingly at Bubber, who for once did not indulge in an opportunity to mock. Doty Hicks glared helplessly at the superbly calm figure of the man whose death he had admittedly sought and failed to effect. Martha Crouch seemed about to stop and speak to Frimbo, but simply smiled and said, "Good-night." Easley Jones and Aramintha Snead made their way out almost stumblingly, so unable were they to remove their fascinated stares from the man who had died and now lived.

3

The detective and the doctor took leave of each other in the street below.

"I will start this test tonight and finish it in the morning," promised the latter. "You'll get the result as soon as I am reasonably certain of it."

"Could he really be the same guy, doc? Is that suspended animation stuff on the level?"

"Cases have been reported. This is the first in my experience."

"You sound skeptical."

"I am more than skeptical in this case, my suspicious friend. I am positively repudiative. Somehow, I stubbornly cling to the belief that the man I examined was dead, completely and permanently."

"What? Well, why didn't——"

"And I too am of the common persuasion which Mr. Frimbo so logically exposed, that one who comes to life was never dead. Logic to the contrary notwithstanding, I still believe the dead stay dead. And, while the corpse may be hard to produce, I still believe you have a murder on your hands."

"But you practically admitted he was the same man. Why?"

"I found no evidence to the contrary—nothing decisive. He looked enough like the dead man, and he had an identically similar wound."

"Explainable how?"

"Self-inflicted, perhaps."

"Not unless he had seen the original."

"If he removed the corpse, he did see the original."

"Then why didn't you spring that removable bridge on him? I saw you look at his teeth."

"Because his teeth were perfect."

"What! Why, that would have shown he wasn't the same man right there!"

"Wait a minute now. When the bridge was first found, we considered the possibilities: It might be the corpse's, it might be his assailant's——"

"And decided it must be his—the corpse's."

"But we didn't check that up by going back to the corpse at once. We said we'd do so when the medical examiner arrived. But when the medical examiner arrived the corpse was gone."

"But you just said Frimbo's teeth were perfect. So the bridge can't possibly be his."

"That doesn't prove it belonged to the corpse. It might or might not—we never did establish the point."

"That's right—we didn't," Dart admitted.

"Which allows for a third possibility which we haven't even considered—that the bridge may belong to neither the victim nor the assailant. It could conceivably belong to anybody."

"You've got me there. Anybody who'd ever been in that room could have dropped it."

"Yes—out of a pocket with a hole in it—after having found the thing on the street."

"All Frimbo would have to do would be know nothing about it."

"Exactly. The identification of the ownership of that bridge is to find the person it was made for. And it must fit that person. So you see I had only a conviction—no tangible support whatever. It would have been worse than useless to show our cards then and there. But now, if these two blood specimens reposing in my bag present certain differences which I anticipate, I shall advise you to proceed with the total demolition of yonder dwelling—a vandalism which you have already contemplated, I believe?"

"Gosh, doc, it would be so much easier in French. Say it in French."

"And if you shouldn't find the elusive corpse there— a possibility with which I have already annoyed you tonight—you may proceed to demolish the house next to the right, then the next to the left, and so on until all Harlem lies in ruins. An excellent suggestion, I must say. You, after all, would only be doing your duty, while ever so many people would be infinitely better off if all Harlem did lie in ruins."

"And if we do find a corpse, Frimbo becomes a suspect himself!"

"With things to explain."

Dart whistled. "What a mess that would be!"

"Testicles," mused the other.

"All right, doc. It's irregular, of course, but I believe

it's the best way. And I'd rather work with you than—some others. I'm dependin' on you."

"You have the house covered?"

"Sewed up back and front. And we'll keep it sewed up from now till we're satisfied."

"Satisfied—hm—have you reflected on the futility of satisfaction, Dart?"

"Never at one o'clock in the morning, doc. So long. Thanks a lot. See you in Macy's window."

"Shouldn't be at all surprised," murmured Dr. John Archer.

CHAPTER SEVENTEEN

I

WITH an unquestionable sense of humor, the sun grinned down upon the proud pageantry of Seventh Avenue's Sunday noontime, beaming just a little more brightly and warmly than was strictly necessary for a day in February. Accordingly, the brisk air was tempered a little, and the flocks that flowed out from the innumerable churches could amble along at a more leisurely pace than winter usually permitted. This gave his celestial majesty time to observe with greater relish the colorful variety of this weekly promenade: the women with complexions from cream to black coffee and with costumes, individually and collectively, running the range of the rainbow; the men with derbies, canes, high collars, spats, and a dignity peculiar to doormen, chauffeurs, and headwaiters.

Bubber Brown had his place in the sun, too, and he swaggered proudly along with the others, for although Bubber was molded on the general plan of a sphere, his imitation camel's hair overcoat was designed to produce an illusion of slenderness and height, with broad shoulders, a narrowly belted waist and skirts long enough to conceal the extraordinary bowing of his legs. Although he boasted no derby, no cane, and no spats, still with his

186

collar turned swankily up, the brim of his felt hat snapped nattily down, and his hands thrust nonchalantly into his coat pockets, even the rotund Bubber achieved fair semblance of a swagger.

This he maintained as he moved in the stream of church people by humming low yet lustily the anything but Christian song of the moment:

"I'll be glad when you're dead, you rascal you. . . ."

On he strolled past churches, drugstores, ice-cream parlors, cigar stores, restaurants, and speakeasies. Acquaintances standing in entrances or passing him by offered the genial insults which were characteristic Harlem greetings:

"What you say, blacker'n me?"

"How you doin', short-order?"

"Ole Eight-Ball! Where you rollin', boy?"

In each instance, Bubber returned some equivalent reply, grinned, waved, and passed on. He breathed deeply of the keen sweet air, appraised casually the trim, dark-eyed girls, admired the swift humming motors that flashed down the Avenue.

But at frequent intervals a frown ruffled his customarily bland countenance, and now and then he foreswore his humming and bowed his head in meditation, shaking it vainly from side to side.

When he reached the corner of 135th Street, he stopped. The stream flowed on past him. He looked westward toward the precinct station-house. Heaving a tremendous sigh, he turned and headed in that direction.

But when he reached the station-house, instead of

stopping, he strode on past it as rapidly as if no destination had been further from his mind. At Eighth Avenue
he turned south and walked three blocks, then east toward Seventh again. A moment later he halted, aware
of a commotion just across the street.

This was a quiet side street, but people were stopping
to look. Others, appearing from nowhere, began to run
toward the point of agitation, and soon dozens were converging upon the scene like refuse toward a drain. Bubber approached the rim of the clutter of onlookers and
craned his neck with normal curiosity.

The scene was the front stoop of an apartment house.
Two men and a girl were engaged in loud and earnest
disagreement.

"He did!" the girl accused hotly. "He come up to me
on that corner——"

"If you was jes' man enough to admit it," menaced
her champion.

"Aw, boogy, go diddle," the accused said contemp-
tuously. "I never even seen your——"

Clearly, whatever his epithet might have signified at
other times, at this moment it meant action; for hardly
had Bubber time to comment, "Uh-oh—that's trouble——" before the girl's protector had smacked the
offender quite off the stoop and into the crowd.

The latter, somewhat like a ball on an elastic, came
instantaneously and miraculously back at the other. As
he flew forward, the girl was heard to yell, "Look out,
Jim! He's got a knife!" Jim somehow flung off the
attack for the moment and reached for his hip. Ap-

parently every onlooker saw that sinister gesture at the same instant, for the crowd, with one accord, dispersed as quickly and positively as a moment ago it had converged upon this spot—as though indeed, some sudden obstruction had caused the drain to belch back. Two quick loud pistol reports punctuated that divergent scattering. Inquisitive dark heads thrust out of surrounding windows vanished. The victim lay huddled with wide staring eyes at the foot of the stoop, and the man with the gun and his girl sped back into the foyer, appropriated the empty elevator, banged the gate shut, and vanished upward.

[handwritten margin note: 2nd death as predicted in Bubbers "moon signs"]

2

Bubber did not slacken his rapid pace till he was back at the corner of Eighth Avenue and 135th Street, a few feet from the precinct station. Then he removed his hat and with his bright-colored handkerchief mopped his beaded brow and swore.

"Damn! What a place! What is this—a epidemic?" The thought recalled his superstition. He opened his mouth and gazed awestruck into space. "Jordan River! That's number two! One las' night and another one today. Wonder whose turn it'll be nex'?" *[handwritten: ✗]*

Inadvertently, pondering the horror of the mysterious, he allowed his feet to wander whither they listed. They conveyed him slowly back toward the station-house, the abrupt presence of which struck so suddenly upon his consciousness as almost to startle him into further flight.

But his feet were in no mood for further flight; they clung there to the pavement while Bubber's original purpose returned and made itself felt.

For a moment he stood hesitant before the imposing new structure, peering uncertainly in. There was no visible activity. He moved closer to the entrance, gazed into the spacious, not uninviting foyer, looked up and down the street and into the foyer again.

"They's an excuse," he mumbled, "for gettin' dragged into jail, but jes' walkin' in of yo' own free will—ain' no sense in that. . . ."

Nevertheless, with an air of final resolution, he mounted the steps, tried and opened the door. "Hope it works jes' as easy from the other side," he said, and entered.

He approached the desk sergeant.

"Y'all got a boy in here name Jinx Jenkins?"

"When was he brought in?"

"Las' night."

"Charge?"

"Suh?"

"What charge?"

"Couldn' been no charge, broke as he was."

"What was he brought in for—drunk, fightin', or what?"

"Oh. He didn' do nothin'. He jes' got in the wrong house."

"Whose house?"

"Frimbo's. You know—the conjure-man."

"Oh—that case. Sure he's here. Why?"

"Can I see him?"

"What for?"

"Well, y'see, he figgers sump'm I said put him in a bad light. I jes' wanted to let him know how come I said it, that's all."

"Oh, that's all, huh? Well that ain't enough."

But the lieutenant on duty happened to be crossing the foyer at the time and heard part of the conversation. He knew the circumstances of the case, and had planned to be present at the questioning for which, in part, Jinx was being held. With the quick grasp of every opportunity for information that marks the team-work of a well-trained investigative organization, he nodded significantly to the sergeant and promptly departed to arrange a complete recording of all that should transpire between Jinx and his visitor.

"You a friend o' his?" the sergeant asked.

"No—we ain' no special friends," said Bubber. "But I don't aim we should be no special enemies neither."

"I see. Well, in that case, I guess I could let you see him a few minutes. But no monkey-business, y'understand?"

"Monkey-business in a jail-house, mistuh? Do I look dumb, sho' 'nough?"

"O.K."

3

In due time and through proper channels, it came to pass that Bubber confronted his tall lean friend, who stood gloomily behind a fine steel grille.

"Hello, Judas," was Jinx's dark greeting.

"Boy," Bubber said, "it's everybody's privilege to be dumb, but they ain' no sense in abusin' it the way you do."

"Is that what you come here to say?"

"I done nearly had what I come here to say scared out o' me. I done seen number two."

"Number two?"

"Yea, man."

"Number two—that's what the little boy said to his mammy. You big and black enough to——"

"Death on the moon, boy. First one las' night, second one today—not ten minutes ago—'round on 132nd Street. Two boogies got in a li'l argument over a gal, and first thing you know—bong—bong! There was one of 'em stretched out dead on the ground and me lookin' at him."

"No."

"Yea, man. This Harlem is jes' too bad. But I tol' you I'm go'n' stare three corpses in the face. They's one mo' yet."

"Hmph. And you call me dumb."

"What you mean?"

"That wasn' no corpse you stared in the face las' night. Las' I remember, he was sittin' up in that chair talkin' pretty lively, like a natchel man."

"Yea, but he ain' no natchel man—he's a conjure-man. He was sho' 'nough dead, jes' like he said. He 'jes knows sump'm, that's all."

THE CONJURE-MAN DIES 193

"He knows sump'm, I don't doubt that. Tol' me plenty. But any time a man knows enough to come to life after he's dead, he knows too much."

"Reckon that's how come he got kilt, 'cause he knows too much. Sho' was the same man though, wasn't he?"

"Far as I could see. But 'course that don' mean much —all coons look alike to me."

There was a moment's silence, whereupon Jinx added, with meaning, "And no matter how well you know 'em, you can't trust 'em."

"Listen, boy, you all wrong. 'Course I know you can't help it, 'cause what few brains you had is done dried up and been sneezed out long ago. But even you ought to be able to see my point."

" 'Cose I see yo' point. Yo' point was, you was savin' yo' own black hide. If you admit you a friend o' mine, maybe you inhale some jail-air too. Jes' like all boogies —jes' let the man say 'Boo!' and yo' shirt tail roll up yo' back like a window shade."

"All right—all right. But see if this can penetrate yo' hard, kinky head. What good am I——"

"None whatsoever."

"Wait a minute, will you please? What good am I to you if I'm right here in jail alongside o' you?"

"What good is you to me anywhere?"

"Well, if I'm out, at least I got a chance to find out who done it, ain't I?"

Jinx relented a little, reluctantly comprehending.

"Yea, you got a chance," he muttered. "But you go'n'

need mo'n a chance to find out who done that. Right under my nose, too, with me sittin' there—and if I seen anybody, you did."

"Well cheer up, long boy. You ain' got nothin' to worry 'bout. The man's alive and you heard what the detective said—all they can hold you for is assault."

"No," reflected Jinx sardonically. "I ain' got nothin' to worry 'bout. They tell me the most I can get for assault is twenty years."

"Twenty—whiches?"

"Years. Them things growin' out the side o' yo' head. And all twenty of 'em jes' that color. It sho' is a dark outlook."

"Mph!"

"Who's gruntin' now?"

"Both of us. But shuh, man, they can't do that to you."

"I know they can't. You know they can't. But do they know they can't?"

"Don't worry, boy. Leave everything to me. I'll find out who done this if it takes me the whole twenty years."

"Hmph! Well, it's time you done sump'm right. When you could 'a kep' yo' mouth shut, you was talkin'. 'Sho' that's Jinx's handkerchief.' And when you could 'a talked, you kep' yo' mouth shut. 'Friend o' mine? No 'ndeed!'—All right. Whatever you go'n' do, get to doin' it, 'cause these accommodations don't suit me. Twenty years! Twenty years from now Harlem'll be full o' Chinamen."

"Don't blame me for all of it. I never would 'a' been in the conjure-man's place if you hadn't said 'come on let's go.' "

"What you go'n' do?"

"I'm go'n' do some detectin', that's what. What's use o' bein' a private detective if I can't help out a friend? I'm workin' on a theory already, boy."

"First work you done since you quit haulin' ashes for the city."

"That was good trainin' for a detective. I used to figure out jes' what happened the night befo' by what I found in the ash can nex' mornin'. If I see a torn nightgown and a empty whiskey bottle——"

"I've heard all 'bout that. What's yo' theory?"

"The flunky, boy. He done it, sho's you born. I'm go'n' find him and trick him into a confession."

"What makes you think he done it?"

" 'Cause he run away, first thing."

"But didn't you hear the man say he was s'posed to leave by eleven o'clock?"

"That would make it all the easier for him, wouldn't it? If he s'posed to be gone th'ain't nothin' suspicious 'bout him bein' gone, don't you see?"

"M-m."

"He figured on that."

"How'n hell'd he get my handkerchief?"

"He took it out yo' pocket. 'Member when Doty Hicks fell down in a faint and we all scrambled 'round and helped him up?"

"Yea——"

"That's when he took it."

"He could 'a'. But what would he want to kill his boss for?"

"Boy, ain't you ever had a boss? They's times when you feel like killin' the best boss in the world, if you could get away with it."

"Well, whoever you hang it on, it's all right with me."

"If worse comes to worse," Bubber's voice sank to a whisper, "I can swear I seen him take yo' handkerchief out yo' pocket."

"No," Jinx demurred, "ain' no need o' you goin' to hell jes' 'cause I go to jail."

"I'm go'n' get you out o' this."

"When you startin'?"

"Tonight."

"Don' hurry. Nex' week'll be plenty o' time."

"Tonight. By tomorrer I'll have the dope on that flunky. You watch."

"I'm watchin'," said Jinx. "And all I got to say is, Sherlock, do yo' stuff."

CHAPTER EIGHTEEN

BY ELEVEN-THIRTY the same Sunday morning,
Dr. Archer had completed his morning calls—
both of them. He returned to his office, where he found
three gentlemen awaiting him. Two were patients, the
third was Detective Perry Dart.

"Urgent?" he asked Dart.

"Nope. Take the others."

The others were soon disposed of; the first pleaded a
bad cold and got his liquor prescription, the second
pleaded hard times and borrowed three dollars.

"Come in here," the physician then summoned Dart,
and led the way through his treatment room with its
adjustable table, porcelain stands, glass-doored steel cabinets shining with bright—and mostly virgin—instruments, into a smaller side room which had done duty as
a butler's pantry in the days before Harlem changed
color.

"Something like Frimbo's," commented the detective,
looking admiringly around.

"In part, yes. That is, Frimbo has some clinical stuff,
but that's only a fraction of his, while it's all of mine.
He has chemistry apparatus that a physician's lab would
never need except for research, and few practicing physicians have time for that kind of research. More than

that, he has some electrical stuff there that only a physicist or mechanic would have, and I'm sure I saw something like a television receptor on one end of the bench
—remember that affair like a big lens set in a square
box? Those specimens sort of stole the show and we
didn't take time to examine around carefully. But all
I've got is what's necessary for routine clinical tests—
some glassware, a few standard reagents, a centrifuge, a
microscope, and that's about all."

"I guess all labs look alike to me."

"Well, there's enough here to investigate certain prop-
erties of our friend's blood, any day. If the two specimens present no differences that we can determine, we're
stumped—so far as murder goes. But if they do——"

"Is this something new, doc?"

"New? No, why?"

"Well, of course I knew they could tell whether it
was human blood. I know of plenty of cases where blood
was found on a weapon, and the suspect claimed it was
chicken's blood or sheep's blood, but the doctors came
along and showed it was human. I should think that
would be hard enough."

"Not so hard. A chap—Gay, I believe—sensitized
some lab animals—guinea pigs or rabbits or whatever
happened to be around—to various serums. You see, if
you do it right, you can inject a little serum into an
animal and he'll develop what they call antibodies for
that serum. Antibody's a substance which the blood
manufactures to combat certain things that get into it
but haven't any business there. But the point is that each

antibody is specific—hostile to just one certain thing. From the viewpoint of the health of the human family, that's too bad. Be swell if you could just inject a little of anything and get a general immunity to everything. But from the viewpoint of criminology it's useful, because if you're smart enough, you can tell whether your suspect is lying or not about the blood on his weapon. You just dissolve your blood off the weapon, and test it against the sensitized blood from each of your known animals. When you get a reaction you know, your unknown is the same as the one which reacted to it. See?"

Dart shook his head.

"I'll take you guys' word for that stuff. But if it's that hard to tell human blood from other kinds, I should think it would be still harder to tell one human's blood from another human's blood." Dart looked around. "And I don't see the first guinea pig."

"So it would seem. But there are many ways in which one man's blood differs from another's. Take the Wasserman reaction. Mine may be negative and yours positive——"

"Hold on, doc, don't get personal."

"Or we may both be positive, but different in degree."

"That's better."

"And there are plenty of other germs, which, like the germ of syphilis, bring about definite changes in the blood. In many cases these changes can be determined, so that you can say that this blood came from a fellow who had so-and-so, while that blood came from a fellow who didn't have so-and-so."

"Go ahead. How about Frimbo's?"

"Or take blood transfusions. You know everybody can't give his blood to everybody—in many cases it would be fatal—was fatal before blood types were known about. Now it's known a man might be eager to give his blood to save his sweetheart, and yet that might be the quickest way of killing her."

Dart's black eyes were alive with interest.

"That's right. I remember——"

"That's because one blood may contain something that doesn't harmonize with something in another blood."

"Like what, doc?"

"It's mainly a matter of serum and red corpuscles. Some serum will destroy some corpuscles——"

"Oh, I see," said Dart.

"So to make sure this doesn't happen, every transfusion now has to be preceded by a certain blood examination known as typing. Couple of bright gentlemen named Janski and Moss looked into the matter not so many years ago and found that all human blood falls into four general types. Since then a flock of sub-types have been established, but the four basic ones still suffice for ordinary procedures. Everybody falls into one of the four groups—and stays there."

Dart was eagerly curious.

"And Frimbo's blood isn't in the same group with the other?"

"I don't know. Haven't tested it out yet—just got ready and had to go deliver twins. That allowed you to get here just in time for the performance. But for intra-human differences, you'd hardly find any two people with every degree of every blood reaction precisely identical."   ✗   *Unless twins?*

"Do your stuff, doc. I'm getting nervous."

"All right. Now look. See this?" He held up a test tube in the bottom of which was a small amount of pinkish fluid. "This is the unknown serum, extracted from the dressing with which I sponged the wound in the dead man's scalp. It's diluted, of course, and discolored because of haemolysis of the red cells——"

"Don't mind me, doc. Go right ahead."

"——but that doesn't matter much. And this tube is Frimbo's serum, and this is a suspension of Frimbo's red cells, which I made last night. By the way, Dart, would you give up some of your blood to find this thing out?"

"How much, doc?"

"He hesitates in the pursuit of his duty," murmured the doctor. "Well, never mind—I may not need it. I may not even need my own."

"You mean you were figuring on bleeding yourself, too?"

"I happen to know I'm under Type II. You remember I mentioned that all tests are checks against a known specimen."

"And you've got to have a known specimen?"

"Unless we're very lucky. We may be able to prove these two specimens different without actually having to type them. Well, now look. We'll take this capillary pipette and remove a drop of this unknown serum and place it thus on a microscopic slide. Then we'll take a nichrome loop so, and remove a loopful of Professor Frimbo's best red cells, and stir them gently into the drop of serum, thus, spreading same smoothly into a small circular area in this manner. Watch carefully. The hand is quicker than the eye. Now then, a cover glass, and under the microscope it goes. We adjust the low power with a few deft turns and gaze into the mysteries of the beyond. Dart, we seldom reflect upon what goes on at the other end of the barrel of a microscope: challenge, conquest, combat, victory, defeat, life, death, reproduction—every possible relationship of living beings —the very birth of the world there in a droplet of moisture." With both eyes open he was manipulating the fine adjustment. "Do you know what a fellow said to me once? I came up behind him and asked him what he was staring down his mike so steadily for—what did he hope to find? He said one word without looking up. He said, 'God.'" He focused the instrument satisfactorily, peered a moment, then stood aside, "You and I are more practical, aren't we? All we hope to find is a murderer. Come on—try your luck."

"Me?"

"Of course. Look, look, and keep looking. If you see anything happen, don't keep it a secret."

Dart, squinting one eye shut, gazed with the other down the barrel. "A lot of little reddish dots," he announced.

"What are they doing?"

"Nothing." Dart grinned. "Must be Negro blood."

"Jest not, my friend. It is Sunday. All blood reposes. But keep looking."

"Well, maybe they are moving a little. Hey—sure! They *are* moving—so slow you can hardly see it, though."

"In what direction?"

"Every direction. Boy, this is good. They can't make up their minds."

"That sounds as though——"

"Hey—Judas Priest—what's this? Look, doc!"

"You look and tell me about it. I might let my imagination run away with me."

"These things are going into a huddle. No—into a flock of huddles. No kidding—they're slowly collecting in little bunches."

"Are you sure?"

"Am I sure? What does it mean, doc? Here, take a look."

Dr. Archer complied. "Hm—I think I can safely say your observations are correct—though 'agglutination' is a far more elegant term than 'huddle.'"

"But what's the answer?"

"The answer is that nobody's red cells could conceivably behave like that in their own serum. Not even a magician's."

"You mean that's the destruction you were talking about?"

"Yes, sir. The first step in it. That's as far as we need

to go in vitro. In vivo, the process goes on to dissolution, disintegration, haemolysis—oh, there's lots of nice words you can call it. But whatever you call it, this serum gives those corpuscles—hell."

Dart's eyes glowed.

"Then Frimbo and the corpse were two different people?"

"And still are. And you and I are two lucky people, because we don't have to play school any longer—not with these, anyway."

"The son of a bedbug! I'm going to put him *under* the jail—trying to kid somebody like that. Where's my hat?"

"What's your hurry, mister? He isn't going anywhere."

"How do I know he isn't?"

"Can he get out without being seen by your men?"

"That's right. But why wait?"

"If you grab him now—if you even let him suspect what we know, he'll close up like a vault. My humble opinion is that he's got a lot of information you need —if he gets lockjaw, you'll never convict him."

"Then what's your idea?"

"Indulge me, my friend. I'm smart. I want to keep that appointment with him this evening——"

"He may be back in Bunghola, or wherever he hails from, by then."

"Not the slightest chance. Frimbo is staging a party tomorrow night for just one reason—he's going to fasten the blame for that murder, as he still calls it, and rightly, on somebody—somebody else. Your best bet is to have all the counter-evidence ready to confront him with at the same time. Don't worry, he'll be there."

"Well this certainly is enough to make him a suspect."

"You've got suspects enough already. What you want now is a murderer. It's true that Frimbo was not the corpse. This proves that. It is also true that he must have managed to make away with the corpse; then, to cover that, masqueraded as the corpse—even inflicted a wound on his head resembling that of the corpse." Dr. Archer could talk very plainly and directly on occasion. "But there are lots of things between that conclusion and proof of his being the murderer. All that we know is that Frimbo lied. We do not know why he lied. And he isn't the only liar in this case—Jenkins lied, probably Hicks lied, for all I know Webb lied——"

"Say that reminds me! That Webb was on the right track. He was telling the truth, at least in part. I meant to tell you, but I got so interested in this other thing. There was a knock-down and drag-out shooting this morning on 132nd Street. Apparently an argument over a girl, but who do you suppose the victim was? One of Brandon's best-known runners. Yes, sir. Well, it took the boys exactly forty-five minutes to nab the guy that did it. And who do you s'pose he was? Spencer's first lieutenant, boy named Eagle Watson. Of course he'll get out of it—good lawyers and all—girl'll swear the victim attacked her and turned on him when he came to her rescue—plenty o' bona fide witnesses—self-defense—easy.

But we know what's behind it—and Webb told the truth about it. There actually is a Spencer-Brandon policy feud on; Spencer's getting the worst of it, and he's declared war on the whole Brandon outfit. The reason why he's getting the worst of it can only be because he's losing a lot of money and losing it fast, and the reason he declares war on the rival outfit is because he figures they are responsible. If he figures that, he may have got wind of this Frimbo's having a hand in it and tried to pull a fast one last night. Only that doesn't hitch up with this blood business at all, does it?"

"There was once a man—nice fellow, too, even though he was a policeman—who delivered some remarks on premature conclusions. His idea was to fit conclusions to facts, as I recall, not facts to conclusions. And he admitted—nay, insisted—that, by such a system, it would only be necessary to accumulate enough facts and they'd sort of draw their own conclusions. You will observe that this fellow was a lineal descendant of Francis Bacon—despite their difference of complexion—in that he inherited the tendency to reason inductively rather than deductively. But such is the frailty of human-kind that even this fortunate chap occasionally fell into the error of letting his imagination, instead of his observation, draw the conclusions; whereupon he would suddenly look about in bewilderment and say that something didn't hitch up with something."

"O.K., doc. The point of all that being it's still too soon to speculate?"

"The point being that where more facts can be gathered, it is always too soon to speculate."

"Well—I guess he'll keep. But if you let him get away from me——"

"My dear fellow, permit me to remind you that in that case the situation would be no different from what it was before I suggested the blood comparison."

"Beg your pardon, doc. But what about the corpse? We've got to have a corpse—you know that. If it's still somewhere in that house, Frimbo's going to have plenty of time to destroy it."

"Have you—if I'm not too personal—ever tried to destroy a corpse, Dart?"

"Almost impossible to destroy it completely by ordinary methods. But there are acids. As much stuff as he's got there——"

"You searched the house pretty well."

"Yes, but we've got experts that do nothing else, doc. They could find places that I wouldn't dream of looking for. They measure and calculate and reconstruct to scale, and when they get through, there isn't a place left big enough to hide a bedbug in."

"They take time, though, and their presence would arouse Frimbo's suspicions and hostility. Believe me, Dart—Frimbo himself is the only answer to this riddle. Jump him too soon and you'll destroy the only chance. I'm sure of that. I'm as curious about this thing as you are. I'm funny that way. And I'd like to see you and the local boys get the credit for this whole thing—not a lot of Philistines from downtown. You said you were depending on me. All right. Do that. And let me depend on you."

"Gee, doc, I didn't realize you were as interested as all that. It sure would mean a lot to me personally to get credit for this. We don't grab off a funny one like this often. If that's really how you feel about it——"

"Fine. Now all you've got to do is make no report of this last finding and hold off Frimbo till I'm through with him. Before tomorrow night I hope to have a pretty good idea of what makes him go 'round. After all, a gentleman who turns out to be one of the suspects in his own murder case deserves a little personal consideration."

"A suspect in his own murder—say, that's right! That's a brand-new one on me! But he's smart all right. Wonder why he didn't object to the blood test? He must have known it might prove incriminating."

"Of course he knew it. But what could he do? To refuse would have put him in a bad light too. All he could gracefully do was acquiesce and take a chance on the two bloods being so much alike that the small amount of the unknown would be exhausted before we could distinguish it from his own. That failing, he would simply have to depend on his wits. Did you hear him ask me whether I would use the ordinary agglutination tests? He's ready with an alibi for this lie right now, I'll bet you. That's another reason for not rushing in yet. We've got to get something he can't anticipate."

Dart looked at the physician with genuine admiration.

"Doc, you're all right, no lie. You ought to've been a detective."

"I am a detective," the other returned. "All my training and all my activities are those of a detective. The criminal I chase is as prime a rascal as you'll ever find—assailant, thief, murderer—disease. In each case I get, it's my job to track disease down, identify it, and arrest it. What else is diagnosis and treatment?"

"I never thought of it that way."

"In this Frimbo case, I'm your consultant—by your personal invitation. I'm going to make as extensive an examination as I can before I draw my conclusions. Your allowing me to do so is proper professional courtesy—a rare thing for which I thank you deeply." He bowed solemnly to the grinning Dart. "And meanwhile you will be finding out every move of every visitor to that place last night?"

"Right. They're all being tailed this minute. And I've already checked everybody's story, even the undertaker's. They're all O.K. Brown came around to the precinct this morning to see Jenkins—they eavesdropped on him but didn't get anything except that Jenkins is still denying guilt. And his friend is willing to perjure himself to save him."

"I still find it hard to believe that Jenkins, even for the dirty lucre you so cogently brought forward, actually did this. Jenkins is a hard one all right, but it's all external. He's probably got the heart of a baby, and has to masquerade as a tough customer to protect himself."

"As you like. But that very masquerade could lead

him into something from which he couldn't turn back."

"But not murder."

"Well, explain how he masqueraded his finger print onto that club and you'll do him a great favor."

"He may be lying about not touching the club the same as he is about the handkerchief."

"He's lying all right if he says he didn't touch that club. There's no other way the print could have got there."

"Isn't there?" the physician said, but the detective missed the skepticism in the tone and went on with his enumeration.

"Doty Hick's brother really is sick with T.B. and refuses to go to a hospital. I told you this morning about the killing that harmonizes with Webb's story. And Easley Jones has been employed by the Pullman Company for ten years—the man spoke very highly of him. I went by the Forty Club last night after leaving you. Three different members told me Crouch the undertaker had been there as he said."

"What about the women?"

"Well, you yourself vouched for Mrs. Crouch. And I'm almost willing to vouch for that other one. If she's got anything to do with this, I have."

"I was wondering about that. Have you?"

"Sure, doc," Dart's bright smile flashed. "I'm the detective on the case, didn't you know?"

"Do you know who committed the crime?"

"Not for certain."

"I see. Then you couldn't have done it yourself. Because if you had, you'd know who did it and it would be a simple matter for you to track yourself down and arrest yourself. Of course you might have done it in your sleep."

"So might you."

"I have a perfect alibi, my friend. Doctors never sleep. If it isn't poker it's childbirth—a pair of aces or a pair of pickaninnies."

"Seriously, doc, there's one objection to your trying to get something on Frimbo tonight."

"What?"

"Why do you suppose that guy was so quick to invite you back alone? Because you're his chief worry. You may be the cause of putting him on the frying-pan. He's evil. He must know your purpose. And if you get too warm, he'll try to rub you out."

"He'll find me quite indelible, I'm sure," Dr. Archer said.

CHAPTER NINETEEN

I

JOHN ARCHER opened a desk drawer and picked up a revolver which lay there. He gazed thoughtfully upon it a moment, then gently replaced it. He shut the drawer, turned and made his way out of the house. His front door closed behind him, and he stood contemplating the high narrow edifice across the dark street. It was two minutes to seven; the air was sharp and ill-disposed and snapped at him in passing. Absently he hunched his ulster higher about his shoulders, thrust his hands, free of the customary bag, deep into his pockets and studied Frimbo's shadowy dwelling. Rearing a little above its fellows, it was like a tall man peering over the heads of a crowd. "Wonder if I'm expected?" the physician mused. As if in answer, two second-story windows suddenly lighted up, like eyes abruptly opened.

"I am expected." Slowly he crossed the dim street, halted again at the foot of the stoop to resume his meditative stare, then resolutely mounted to the door and, finding it unlocked, entered.

His host was awaiting him at the head of the stairs. Frimbo's tall figure was clad tonight in a dressing-gown of figured maroon silk; this, with a soft shirt open at the throat, and the absence of any native headdress, gave him a matter-of-fact appearance quite different from that of the night before. Tonight he might have been any well-favored Harlemite taking his ease on a Sunday evening in leisure which he could afford and intended to enjoy.

But the deep-set eyes still held their peculiar glow, and the low resonant voice was the same.

"Let us go up to the library," he said. "It will be more comfortable."

He reached into the front room as they passed and snapped a wall switch, leaving the room dark. "I turned those on for your benefit, doctor. We must not be disturbed by other visitors. I have been looking forward to seeing you."

He led the way to that rear third-floor chamber which the physician had visited the night before.

"Choose your own chair—you will find most of them comfortable." The man's attitude was entirely disarming, but Dr. Archer took a chair that was disposed diagonally in a corner with bookshelves to either side.

Frimbo smiled.

"I have some fair sherry and some execrable Scotch," he offered.

"Thank you. You evidently prefer the sherry—I'll follow your example."

Shortly the wine had been procured from the adjacent kitchen; glasses were filled—from the same container, the physician noted; cigarettes were lighted; Frimbo seated himself on the divan before the fireplace, in which artificial logs glowed realistically.

"You were speaking," he said, as if almost a whole day had not intervened, "of Herbert Spencer's classification of the sciences."

"Yes," the physician said. "Psychology considered as the physiology of the nervous system."

Easily and quickly they began to talk with that quick intellectual recognition which characterizes similarly reflective minds. Dr. Archer's apprehensions faded away and shortly he and his host were eagerly embarked on discussions that at once made them old friends: the hopelessness of applying physico-chemical methods to psychological problems; the nature of matter and mind and the possible relations between them; the current researches of physics, in which matter apparently vanished into energy, and Frimbo's own hypothesis that probably mind did likewise. Time sped. At the end of an hour Frimbo was saying:

"But as long as this mental energy remains mental, it cannot be demonstrated. It is like potential energy—to be appreciated it must be transformed into heat, light, motion—some form that can be grasped and measured. Still, by assuming its existence, just as we do that of potential energy, we harmonize psychology with mechanistic science."

"You astonish me," said the doctor. "I thought you were a mystic, not a mechanist."

"This," returned Frimbo, "*is* mysticism—an undemonstrable belief. Pure faith in anything is mysticism. Our very faith in reason is a kind of mysticism."

"You certainly have the gift of harmonizing apparently opposite concepts. You should be a king—there'd be no conflicting parties under your régime."

"I am a king."

For a moment the physician looked at the serene dark countenance much as if he were seeing his first case of some unusual but clear-cut disease. Frimbo, however, tranquilly took a sip of sherry, gently replaced the fragile glass on a low table at his elbow, and allowed the phantom of a smile to soften his countenance.

"You forget," he said, lighting a fresh cigarette, "that I am an African native." There was a pride in the statement that was almost an affront. "I am of Buwongo, an independent territory to the northeast of Liberia, with a population of approximately a million people. My younger brother rules there in my stead." A reminiscent air descended momentarily upon him. "Often I long to go back, but it would be dull. I am too fond of adventure."

"Dull!" Archer exclaimed. "Why—most people would consider that an extraordinarily exciting life."

"Most people who know nothing of it. Excitement lies in the challenge of strange surroundings. To encounter life in the African brush would exhilarate you, certainly. But for the same reasons, life in a metropolis exhilarates me. The bush would be a challenge to all your resources. The city is a similar challenge to mine."

"But you can't be so unaccustomed to this now. You have finished an American college, you have mastered

the ways of our thinking enough to have original con-
tributions of your own to make—surely all that is behind you once and for all."

"No," said Frimbo softly. "There are things one
never forgets."

"You make me very curious."

The kindled black eyes regarded him intently a long
moment. Then Frimbo said, "Perhaps I should satisfy that
curiosity somewhat . . . if you care to listen. . . ."

And the dark philosopher who called himself king,
with a faraway look in his eyes and a rise and fall in
his deep low voice, painted a picture twenty years past
and five thousand miles away.

2

"In some countries night settles gently like a bird
fluttering down into foliage; in Buwongo it drops pre-
cipitately like a bird that has been shot. It is as if the
descending sun backed unaware upon the rim of a distant mountain, tripped on the peak, and tumbled head-
long out of sight into the valley beyond. The bright day
has been mysterious enough—the blank, blue sky, the
level rice fields, the arrogant palms, the steaming jungle.
But it is obvious, bold mystery—it must reveal itself before it can strike. Night clothes it in invisibility, renders
it subtle, indeterminate, ominous. Brings it close.

"All day we have traveled southward—my father, a
hundred fighting men, and I. I am only twelve, but that
is enough. I must now begin to take part in the feasts

of our tributary villages. We are on the way to Kimalu, a town of a thousand people. I am very tired—but I am the eldest son of a chief. I stride proudly beside my tireless father. Some day I shall be like him, tall, straight, strong; I shall wear the scarlet loin cloth and the white headdress of superior rank. I must not falter. We have not stopped for food or drink—for shall we not feast lavishly tonight? We have ignored the beckoning paths that lead off our main trail—paths to other villages, to cool green tributaries of the Niger, to who knows what animal's hideout. And in the flattening rays of the sinking sun we at last see the rice fields outside our destination and presently the far off thatched roofs of Kimalu's dwellings. We are on a slight rise of ground. Yet before we can reach Kimalu, night overtakes us and devours us.

"But already there is the glow of village fires, a hundred spots of wavering yellow light; and shortly we enter Kimalu, my father leading, with me by his side, the men in double file behind us. All fatigue drops away as the shouts of greeting and welcome deluge our company like a refreshing shower.

"The ceremonies are scheduled to begin three hours hence, at the height of the moon. Meanwhile preparations go on. Our company is welcomed respectfully by the elderly headman, who receives with effusive thanks our two bullocks, each suspended by its feet on a horizontal pole and carried on the shoulders of eight of our carriers. These will augment the feast that follows the ceremony and help provide for our party on the morrow. We are conducted to the central square before the dwelling of the headman, a large house, thatch-roofed, walled with palm and bamboo, and surrounded by a high rampart of tall interlaced *timwe* trunks, the sharpened top of each one treated with a poison that is death to touch. Even the most venomous snake could not crawl over that rampart and live. The square is large enough to accommodate all the people of the village, for here they must assemble at regular intervals to hear the issuing of edicts relative to their governing laws and their local and national taxes. Here too, the headman sits in judgment every other day and pronounces upon both moral and civil offenders sentences ranging from temporary banishment to castration—the latter a more dreaded penalty than beheading.

"Around the enormous square, as we enter it, we see many fires, over which stews are simmering in kettles, and barbecues of boar, bullock, or antelope are roasting on poles. Savory odors quicken our nostrils, cause our mouths to water. But we may not yet satisfy our appetites. First we must wash and rest. And so we go down to the edge of the river beside which the village lies; there is a broad clearing and a shallow bit of beach upon which more fires burn for illumination and protection. Here we wash. Then we return to the rim of the square and stretch out to doze and rest till the feast begins.

"It is the Malindo—the feast of procreation—and of all the rites of all our forty-eight tribes, none is more completely symbolic. An extremely wide circle—one hundred and fifty feet in diameter—of firewood has been laid in the center of the square. Outside this at

[margin handwritten note: The ooze on the chair, perhaps the same poison?]

intervals are piles of more firewood, short dry branches of fragrant trees.

"At the height of the moon, the headman gives the signal for the ceremony to begin. The band of drummers, stationed to one side of the rampart gate, is ready. The drums are hollow logs; one end is open; over the other is stretched a tympanum of boarskin; they lie horizontally side by side; vary in length from two to twenty feet, but are so placed that the closed ends are in alignment facing the circle of firewood; they vary in diameter also, but even the smallest is a foot high. Each drummer sits astride his instrument above its closed end, upon which he plays with his bare hands and fingers.

"At the chief's signal, the player of the largest drum stretches his arms high over his head and brings the heels of both hands down hard on the face of his instrument. There is a deep, resounding boom, a sound such as no other instrument has ever produced; as low and resonant as the deepest organ note, as startlingly sudden as an explosion. A prowling cat five miles away will halt and cringe at that sound. The stillness that follows trembles in the memory of it; as that tremor dwindles the drummer strikes again—the cadence is established. Again, again. Slowly, steadily the great drum booms, a measure so large, so stately, so majestic, that all that follows is subordinated to it and partakes of its dignity.

"The people of the village have already gathered around the margin of the square; some sit on the ground, some stand, all are raptly intent. My father is seated on a platform directly in front of the rampart gate; I am

on his left, the headman on his right, our hundred men
seated on the ground further along. There is no movement anywhere save the flicker of low fires, and no
sound save the steady tremendous boom of the great
drum.

"But now something is happening, for a new note
creeps subtly into the slow period of the drumbeat—another smaller drum, then another, then another, sound-
ing a submeasure of lesser beats, quicker pulsations that
originate in the parent sound and lift away from it like
dwindling echoes. From the far side of the clearing a
procession of shadowy figures emerges, and in their
midst appear six men bearing on their shoulders a large
square chest. The figures move slowly, in time with the
fundamental measure, till they are on this side of the
circle of firewood; then the six bearers turn toward the
circle, and the others, in front of them and behind them,
turn toward us. The bearers, still in time, move forward
toward the circle, step over the wood with their burden,
and deposit it in the center of the ring, while the others,
also keeping to the measure, approach our position,
about face, and seat themselves on the ground to either
side of our platform.

"Still another motif now enters the rhythmic cadence
—all the remaining drums, at first softly, almost im-
perceptibly, then more definitely, take up this new,
lighter, quicker variation, which weaves itself into the
major pattern like brocaded figures into damask—the
whole a rich fabric of strength, delicacy, and incredible
complexity of design. And now a file of torches appears

far across the clearing, comes closer—they seem number-less, but are forty-eight, I know—one for each of our tribes. And we see that they are borne aloft, each in the hand of a slim naked girl whose dancing movements are in accord with the new lighter measure of the drums. The file passes before us, each member gracefully main-taining the rhythmic motif, till, equally spaced, they face the circle, each the stem of a bright flower in a swaying garland of flame.

"For a few minutes they dance thus, keeping their relative positions around the circle, but advancing peri-odically a few feet toward the center then withdrawing; and they do this so perfectly in unison that, while their feet and bodily gestures obey the lighter, quicker rhythm, their advances and retreats are tuned to the original, fundamental pulse, and the flares in their hands become jewels of flame, set in a magic ring which con-tracts . . . dilates . . . contracts . . . dilates . . . like a living heart, pumping blood. Then, with a sudden swell and dwindling of the lesser drums, there is a ter-minal, maximal contracture—the girls have advanced quite to the circle of firewood, dropped their torches upon it each at her respective point; have then, without seeming to lose a rhythmic movement, executed a final retreat—faded back from the circle like so many shad-ows, and fallen on the ground perfectly straight, each in a radial line, each as motionless as if she were bound to a spoke of some gigantic wheel.

"The great circle of wood soon kindles into an un-broken ring of fire, symbol of eternal passion; and as the flames mount, the drumming grows louder and more turbulent, as if the fire were bringing it to a boil. A warrior, whose oiled skin gleams in the light, leaps through the flames into the inside of the circle, reaches the large square chest in the center, unfastens and turns back the lid, and vanishes through the far rim of the fire.

"Every eye is focused on the chest beyond the flames. There is a slight shift of the rhythm—so slight as entirely to escape an unaccustomed ear. But the dancing girls catch it, and instantly are on their feet again in another figure of their ceremonial gesture—a languorous, lithe, sinuous twist with which they again advance toward the fiery circle. They incorporate into this figure of their dance movements whereby they take branches from the extra piles and toss them into the fire. The blaze mounts steadily. No one is noticing the girls now, however; no one is aware of the pervasive incense from the fragrant burning wood. For something is rising from the chest—the head of a gigantic black python, that rears four—five—six feet above the rim and swings about bewildered by the encircling fire.

"Now the warrior reappears, holding aloft in his two hands an infant of the tribe. Swiftly, with the infant so held as to be out of reach of the licking flames, again he bounds through the fire into the circle. At the same time the most beautiful maiden of the tribe, her bare body oiled like the warrior's, appears within the ring from the opposite side. The python, still bewildered, swings back and forth. The warrior and the maiden dance three times in opposite directions around the serpent. And now, though none has seen it happen, the girl has the infant in her arms; the python, sensing danger in the entrapping flames and the tumult of the drums, withdraws into his chest. The warrior closes and fastens the lid and vanishes through the far wall of fire. The drums have gone mad. The girl, holding the baby aloft in both hands, faces us, dashes forward with a cry that transcends the crescendo of drumming, a shriek like that of a woman in the last spasm of labor, leaps high through the blaze, runs toward our platform, and gently lays the unharmed infant at our feet. . . ."

3

There was a long silence. Frimbo sat looking into the flickering mock-embers on his artificial hearth, seeing those faraway genuine ones of woods that burned with a fragrance like incense. John Archer was silent and still, absorbed in the other man's fine dark face. Perhaps he was wondering, "Could this man have committed a murder? Whom would he want to kill? Why? What is he—charlatan or prophet? What is his part in this puzzle—what indeed is not possible to this mind that in a moment steps out of cold abstract reason into the warm symbolic beauty of a barbaric rite?"

But what the physician actually said was, "Rather a dangerous ceremony, isn't it?"

Frimbo gathered himself back into the present, smiled, and answered, "Are conception and birth without danger?"

After a moment the doctor said, "My own youth was so utterly different."

"Yet perhaps as interesting to me as mine would have been to you."

"The age of twelve," laughed the other, "recalls nothing more exciting than a strawberry festival in the vestry of my father's church."

"Your father was a minister?"

"Yes. He died shortly after I finished college. I wanted to study medicine. One of my profs had a wealthy friend. He saw me through. I've been practicing nearly ten years—and haven't finished paying him back yet. That's my biography. Hardly dramatic, is it?"

"You have omitted the drama, my friend. Your father's struggle to educate you, his clinging on to life just to see you complete a college training—which had been denied him; your desperate helplessness, facing the probability of not being able to go on into medicine; the impending alternative of teaching school in some Negro academy; the thrill of discovering help; the rigid economy, to keep the final amount of your debt as low as possible—the summers of menial work as a bell boy or waiter or porter somewhere, constantly taking orders from your inferiors, both white and black; the license to practice—and nothing to start on; more menial work —months of it—to accumulate enough for a down payment on your equipment; the first case that paid you and the next dozen that didn't; the prolonged struggle against your initial material handicaps—the resentment you feel at this moment against your inability to do what you are mentally equipped to do. If drama is struggle, my friend, your life is a perfect play."

Dr. Archer stared.

"I swear! You actually are something of a seer, aren't you?"

"Not at all. You told me all that in the few words you spoke. I filled in the gaps, that is all. I have done more with less. It is my livelihood."

"But—how? The accuracy of detail——"

"Even if it were as curious as you suggest, it should occasion no great wonder. It would be a simple matter of transforming energy, nothing more. So-called mental telepathy, even, is no mystery, so considered. Surely the human organism cannot create anything more than itself; but it has created the radio-broadcasting set and receiving set. Must there not be within the organism, then, some counterpart of these? I assure you, doctor, that this complex mechanism which we call the living body contains its broadcasting set and its receiving set, and signals sent out in the form of invisible, inaudible, radiant energy may be picked up and converted into sight and sound by a human receiving set properly tuned in."

He paused while the doctor sat speechless. Then he continued:

"But this is much simpler than that. Is it at all mystifying that you should walk into a sick room, make

certain examinations, and say, 'This patient has so-and-
so. He got it in such-and-such a way approximately so
long ago; he has these-and-these changes in such-and-
such organs; he will die in such-and-such a fashion in
approximately so long'? No. I have merely practiced
observation to the degree of great proficiency; that, together with complete faith in a certain philosophy en-
ables me to do what seems mystifying. I can study a
person's face and tell his past, present, and future."

The physician smiled. "Even his name?"

"That is never necessary," smiled Frimbo in the same
spirit. "He always manages to tell me that without
knowing it. There are tricks in all trades, of course. But
fundamentally I deceive no one."

"I can understand your ability to tell the present—
even the past, in a general way. But the future——"

"The future is as inevitably the outcome of the present as the present is of the past. That is the philosophy
I mentioned."

"Determinism?"

"If you like. But a determinism so complete as to
include everything—physical and mental. An applied
determinism."

"I don't see how there can be any such thing as an
applied determinism."

"Because——?"

"Because to apply it is to deny it. Assuming the ability
to 'apply' anything is free will, pure and simple."

"You are correct," agreed Frimbo, "as far as you go."

"Why," the doctor continued warmly, "anyone who

achieved a true freedom of will—a will that had no reference to its past—was not molded in every decision by its own history—a power that could step out of things and act as a cause without being itself an effect—good heavens!—such a creature would be a god!"

"Not quite a god, perhaps," said the other softly.

"What do you mean?"

"I mean that such a creature would be a god only to those bound by a deterministic order like ours. But you forget that ours is not—cannot be—the only order in the universe. There must be others—orders more complex perhaps than our simple cause-and-effect. Imagine, for instance, an order in which a cause followed its effect instead of preceding it—someone has already brought forward evidence of such a possibility. A creature of such an order could act upon our order in ways that would be utterly inconceivable to us. So far as our system is concerned, he would have complete freedom of will, for he would be subject only to his order, not to ours."

"That's too much metaphysics for me," confessed the physician. "Come on back to this little earth."

"Even on this little earth," said Frimbo, "minds occasionally arise that belong to another order. We call them prophets."

"And have you ever known a prophet?"

"I know," said the other in an almost inaudible voice, "that it is possible to escape this order and assume another."

"How do you know?"

"Because I can do it."

Had he shouted instead of whispering, John Archer could not have exhibited greater amazement.

"You can—what?"

"Do not ask me how. That is my secret. But we have talked together enough now for you to know I do not say anything lightly. And I tell you in all seriousness that here, in a world of rigidly determined causes and effects, Frimbo is free—as free as a being of another order."

The doctor simply could not speak.

"It is thus I am able to be of service to those who come to me. I act upon their lives. I do not have to upset their order. I simply change the velocity of what is going on. I am a catalyst. I accelerate or retard a reaction without entering into it. This changes the cross currents, so that the coincidences are different from what they would otherwise be. A husband reaches home twenty minutes too soon. A traveler misses his train—and escapes death in a wreck. Simple, is it not?"

"You've certainly retarded my reactions," said Dr. Archer. "You've paralyzed me."

4

It was ten o'clock when finally the physician rose to go. They had talked on diverse and curious topics, but no topic had been so diverse and curious as the extraordinary mind of Frimbo himself. He seemed to grasp the essentials of every discussion and whatever arose brought forth from him some peculiar and startling view that the physician had never hitherto considered. Dr. Archer had come to observe and found himself the object of the observation. To be sure, Frimbo had told how, as an adventurous lad, he had been sent to a mission school in Liberia; how at twenty he had assumed the leadership of his nation, his father having been fatally injured in a hunting expedition; but after a year, had turned it over to his brother, who was ten months younger than he, and had departed for America to acquire knowledge of western civilization—America because of his American mission school beginning. He had studied under private tutors for three years in preparation for college; had been irregularly allowed to take entrance examinations and had passed brilliantly; but had acquired a bitter prejudice against the dominant race that had seemed to be opposing his purpose. Many episodes had fostered this bitterness, making it the more acute in one accustomed to absolute authority and domination. But all this, even as it was being told, had somehow increased the physician's sense of failure in this first meeting. It was too much under Frimbo's direction. And so he suggested another call on the morrow, to which Frimbo agreed promptly.

"I have a little experiment in which you would be interested," he said.

"I had really intended to discuss the mystery of this assault," the doctor declared. "Perhaps we can do that tomorrow?"

Frimbo smiled.

"Mystery? That is no mystery. It is a problem in logic, and perfectly calculable. I have one or two short-cuts which I shall apply tomorrow night, of course, merely to save time. But genuine mystery is incalculable. It is all around us—we look upon it every day and do not wonder at it at all. We are fools, my friend. We grow excited over a ripple, but exhibit no curiosity over the depth of the stream. The profoundest mysteries are those things which we blandly accept without question. See. You are almost white. I am almost black. Find out why, and you will have solved a mystery."

"You don't think the causes of a mere death a worthy problem?"

"The causes of *a* death? No. The causes of death, yes. The causes of life and death and variation, yes. But what on earth does it really matter who killed Frimbo—except to Frimbo?"

They stood a moment in silence. Presently Frimbo added in an almost bitter murmur:

"The rest of the world would do better to concern itself with why Frimbo was black."

Dr. Archer shook hands and departed. He went out into the night in somewhat the state of mind of one waking from odd dreams in a dark room. A little later he was mounting his own stoop. Before opening his door he stopped for a moment, looking back at the house across the street. With a hand on the knob, he shook his head and, contrary to his custom, indulged in a popular phrase:

"What a man!" he said softly.

CHAPTER TWENTY

I

EVENING had fallen and still Bubber Brown, Inc., had not been able to decide on a proper course of action. He had wandered about Harlem's streets unaware of its Sunday-best liveliness and color. Sly, come-hither eyes that fell upon him had kindled no sheikish response, trim silken calves had not even momentarily captured his dull, drifting stare, bright laughter of strolling dark crowds had not warmed his weary heart. Even his swagger had forsaken him. He had rolled along, a frankly bow-legged man, and the mind behind his blank features had rolled likewise, a rudderless bark on a troubled sea of indecision.

A mystery movie in which the villainous murderer turned out to be a sweet young girl of eighteen had not at all quickened Bubber's imagination. Leaving the theater, he had stopped in Nappy Shank's Café for supper; but the pigtails and hoppin'-john, which he meditatively consumed there from a platter on a white porcelain counter, likewise yielded no inspiration.

Eventually, in the early evening, his wandering brought him to Henry Patmore's Pool Room, and after standing about for a few minutes watching the ivory balls click, he made his way to the rear room where blackjack was the attraction.

231

An impish fate so contrived matters that the first player he saw was Spider Webb, whose detention he had brought about the night before. Spider at first glared at him, then grinned a trifle too pleasantly.

"Detective Brown, as I live!" he greeted. "Do you guys know the detective? Who you squealin' on to-night, detective?"

Bubber had forgotten until now Spider's threat last night. The abrupt reminder further upset his already unsteady poise. It was clear now that Spider really meant to square the account. To conceal his discomfiture, Bubber calmly seated himself at the table and bought two dollars' worth of chips.

"Deal me in," said he casually, ignoring Spider Webb.

"Sure—deal him in. He's a good guy."

Had the situation been normal it is likely that Bubber would promptly have lost his two dollars, got up, and departed. But inasmuch as his mind was now on anything but the cards, his customarily disastrous judgment was quite eliminated, and the laws of chance had an opportunity to operate to his advantage. In the course of an hour he had acquired twenty dollars' worth of his fellow players' chips and had become too fascinated at the miraculous, steady growth of his pile to leave the game. And of course, no one, not even an ordinarily poor gambler like Bubber, could run away from luck, not only because of what he might miss thereby but also because the losers expected a sporting chance to win back their money and could become remarkably disagreeable if it should be denied them.

But Bubber continued to win, the only disturbing part of this being that most of his gain was Spider Webb's loss. He did not know that Spider was gambling with money collected from policy-players, money that must be turned in early tomorrow morning; but he knew that Spider was taking risks that one rarely took with one's own hard-earned cash. And he soon saw whither this was directed. For whenever Bubber won a deal by holding a blackjack, Spider grimly undertook to break him by "stopping the bank"—that is by wagering at every opportunity an amount equal to whatever Bubber possessed, hoping thus to pluck him clean on the turn of a single hand.

With luck running in Bubber's direction, however, this plunging soon proved disastrous to Spider. By the time Bubber's twenty dollars had swelled to forty, Spider, certain that the moment was at hand when the tide must turn, "stopped" the forty dollars with all he had. Chance chose that moment to give Bubber another blackjack. Spider's curses were gems.

The heavy loser had now no recourse save to leave the game, and he did so with ill grace. A few minutes later, one Red Williams, a hanger-on at Pat's who was everybody's friend or enemy as profitable opportunity might direct, came into the card room from the pool parlor and called Bubber aside.

"Is you won money from Spider Webb?" he inquired in a low tone that clearly indicated the importance of what hung on the answer.

"Sho'," admitted Bubber. "Does it pain you too?"

"Listen. I heard Spider talkin' to Tiger Shade jes' now. Seem like Spider had it in for you anyhow. I don't know what you done to him befo', but whatever 'twas he could 'a' scrambled you with pleasure. But when you ups and wins his money too, that jes' 'bout set 'im on fire. Fu'thermo', that wasn't his money he los'—that was players' money. If he don' turn in nothin' in the mornin', his boss Spencer knows he's been stealin' and that's his hips. If any o' his players git lucky and hit and don't git paid, that's his hips too. Either way it's his hips. So from what I heard him whisperin' to his boy, Tiger, he's plannin' to substitute yo' hips fo' his'n."

"Talk sense, man. What you mean?"

"Mean Tiger is done agreed to lay for you and remove both yo' winnin's and yo' school-gal complexion. Tonight."

"You sho'?"

"I heard 'em. You better slip on out befo' they git wise you onto 'em."

"O. K. Thanks."

"Thanks? Is that all it's worth to you—much as you done won?"

"Wait a minute." Bubber made extravagant excuses to the house and cashed his chips. He returned to the waiting informer and handed him a dollar. "Here—git yo'self a pint o' gut-bucket. See y' later."

Sourly, Red Williams gazed upon the bill in his hand. "Hmph!" grumbled he. "Is this all that nigger thinks his life is worth?" Then he grinned. "But it won't be worth this much when Tiger Shade git hold of 'im. No, *suh!*"

2

Bubber sought to elude those who conspired against him by making a hasty exit through the barroom instead of through the poolroom, where apparently the plot had been hatched. This would have been wholly successful had not Tiger Shade already taken his stand on the sidewalk outside, between the poolroom and barroom entrances.

"Hello, there, Bubber, ol' boy," he greeted as Bubber came out and started to walk rapidly away.

It was perhaps the most unwelcome greeting Bubber had ever heard. He returned it hurriedly and would have kept going, but the Tiger called pleasantly, "Hey, wait a minute—I'm goin' your way. What's y' hurry?"

"Got a heavy date and I'm way late," came over Bubber's shoulder.

But in what seemed like three strides, the Tiger had overtaken and was beside him. For Tiger Shade was by a fair margin the tallest, widest, and thickest man in Harlem. He was bigger than the gigantic Officer Small, one of Bubber's companions of last night—and one for whose presence Bubber would have been most grateful now. And the Tiger was as bad as he was big. His was no simulated malice like Jinx's, no feigned ill-humor arising as a sort of defense mechanism; no, the Tiger simply enjoyed a congenital absence of sympathy. This had been too extreme even for those occupations where it might have been considered an advantage. He might have been a great boxer, but he simply could not remember to take the rules seriously. When he got interested in putting an opponent out, he saw no sound objection to doing so by hitting him below the belt or by snapping his head back with one hand and smiting him on the Adam's apple with the other. And when the opponent thus disposed of lay writhing or gasping as the case might be, Tiger always thought the hisses of the crowd were meant for the fallen weakling.

Hence he didn't rise high in the pugilistic firmament; but nobody crossed his path in that lowly part of Harlem where he moved. His reputation was known, and his history of destruction was the more terrible because it was so impersonal. He proceeded in combat as methodically as a machine; was quite as effective when acting for someone else as when acting for himself, and in neither case did he ever exhibit any profound emotion. True, he had a light sense of humor. For example, he had once held an adversary's head in the crook of his elbow and with his free hand torn one of the unfortunate fellow's ears off. He was given to such little drolleries; they amused him much as it amuses a small boy to pull off the wings of a fly; but it was quite as impersonally innocent.

It is hardly accurate to say that Tiger walked along beside Bubber. He walked along above Bubber, looming ominously like a prodigious shadow, and fully as tenacious. He did so without effort, smoothly, taking approximately one step to Bubber's three; he glided. Bubber bounced along hurriedly, explaining how he had allowed the time to get away from him and must rush but did not want to inconvenience his unexpected companion by so swift a pace. Tiger assured him that the pace was anything but exhausting.

It was about the hour at which his moonsign had appeared to him on the night before. "Wonder do you see yo'self when you dead?" he asked himself. "Maybe the third one is me!"

"Huh?" inquired Tiger.

"Nothin'. Jes' thinkin' out loud."

It was a mistake that he did not make again. But what he thought further, as the two progressed southward along Harlem's Fifth Avenue, was evident from what he presently did.

"I ain't got but one chance to shake this boogy loose. That's 'cause he don't know that I know what he's aimin' to do. He didn't see Red come in the card-room and tell me the bad news. So the thing to do is surprise him; got to stay here on the Avenue till I get a chance to duck around a corner and run like hell up a side street. By the time he realize' what I've done, not expectin' me to know nothin', I'll have a start on him. When he look he won't see nothin' but the soles o' my feet. I'll be runnin' so fas' he'll think I'm layin' down.—But what's the use runnin' if I ain' got no place to run to? Lemme see. Hot damn—I got it! The doctor—right in the next street. I was goin' to see him anyhow, see if he could tell me how to help Jinx. Now I *got* to see him. Feet, get ready. And fo' Gawd's sake keep out o' each other's way!"

They crossed 130th Street. As they mounted the far curb and would have passed the building line, suddenly Bubber pointed in astonishment. "Good-night! Look a yonder! Done been a accident!" And as Tiger Shade innocently peered ahead, the trickster did a right turn, snatched off his hat, and flew.

He had estimated Tiger's reaction correctly. Tiger even walked on past the building line before he realized that he was alone, and Bubber was at the physician's stoop before Tiger's pursuit got under way.

The front door was at that moment opening to let out a patient who had come to see the doctor and found him out. The patient was in a bad humor. He needed treatment for certain scratches, abrasions, and bruises which his physiognomy had sustained before he had been able to subdue a violent wife. The wife had taken it upon herself to follow a certain private detective to a certain private residence the night before, and had come thus to discover her husband in an unexplainably trouserless state. The misunderstanding which had arisen then had waxed into an energetic physical encounter this morning; and though the lady had been duly subdued, she had, so to speak, made her mark first. Further the patient's present ill humor had been increased by the difficulty of getting a physician on a Sunday evening. Dr. Archer had been his fifth unsuccessful attempt, and he emerged from the hallway, where a housekeeper had told him the doctor was out for the evening, in a state of repressed, scowling rage which was the more rancorous because it was facially painful to scowl. Indeed he was at the moment praying to high heaven that the blippety-blipped so-and-so that got him in the jam in the first place be delivered into his hands just for sixty seconds.

It was therefore not coincidence but the efficacy of honest prayer which brought Bubber bounding up the stoop just as the large, disappointed gentleman turned to descend. There was just enough light before the door closed for each to recognize the other. And it might have inspired a new philosophy of the organism had some competent observer been there to see how so utterly different emotions in so utterly dissimilar men produced so completely identical reactions: malicious glee on the gentleman's part, consternation on Bubber's, but abrupt and total immobility in both cases. Before action could relieve that mutual paralysis, Tiger Shade was at hand.

At such moments, imbecility becomes genius. Bubber, accordingly, became a superman. "Come on, boy!" he shouted to the leaping Tiger. "Here he is—this the guy I was chasin'! He grabbed my money at the corner and run! Come on, let's get 'im!" Whereupon he lunged upward and tackled the dumbfounded husband about the knees. Tiger, whose real interest lay in recovering the money, of which he was to receive part, hesitated now but a moment; swept up the stairs and lay hold of the accused, whom Bubber promptly released below. When Doctor Archer's housekeeper opened the door again to see what the sudden rumpus was about, her astonished eyes beheld two heavyweights engaged in a wrestling match. It ended as she watched.

"Hand it over," she heard the victor, sitting astride the other, advise.

"I ain't been near no corner!" panted the uncomfortable underling. "I'm after that tubby runt, too! Where'd he go? Lemme up! Which a way'd he go?"

"Get off my stoop, you hoodlums," cried the outraged housekeeper, "else I'll call the police. Go on now! Get off o' my stoop!"

Her admonitions were unnecessary. Bubber's absence was sufficient evidence of his stratagem. Tiger desisted, whipping about just in time to see the elusive Bubber enter the house directly opposite across the street and carefully close the door behind him.

"There he goes!" exclaimed he. "Come on—let's get him!"

3

Across the street they sped, scuffled up the brownstone stoop and burst through the door. Tiger, who was first, glanced up the stairs, which the fugitive could not possibly yet have traversed.

"He's down here some place—on this floor. Let's look. Come on."

His new ally hesitated.

"Say—you know what this is?"

"What?"

"This place is a undertaker's parlor!"

"I don't care if it's a undertaker's bathroom, I'm goin' in here and look for that boogy. He can't pull no fast one on me like that."

They found Undertaker Crouch's rooms invitingly accessible and apparently quite empty. They went into the parlor and stopped. There was a faint funeral fragrance in the air, and a strange, unnatural quiet over all that immediately subdued their movements to cautious tiptoeing and their voices to low muttering.

"I ain' crazy 'bout lookin' for nobody in here," announced the husband.

"Aw, what you scared o'?" the Tiger reassured him. "Dead folks ain' no trouble."

"They ain' no trouble to me—I don't get that close to 'em."

"Well—you don't see none do you?"

"I ain' looked. First one I see, I bids you both good-evenin'."

"I thought you wanted some o' this guy?"

"Some of him? In a place like this, I couldn't use two of him. My mind wouldn't be on what I was doin'."

"Well, I'm go'n' get 'im tonight. He's got eighty bucks o' my buddy's dough. If he gives me the slip tonight, them bucks is long gone."

"And if I hear any funny noises, I'm long gone."

"Come on. Let's look back yonder."

"Go ahead—I'll wait for you."

"He's tricky—it'll take both of us to find 'im."

"O.K. I'm behind you. But I ain't lettin' nothin' get 'tween me and the door."

"Did you leave it open?"

"I sho' did."

But the words were no sooner out of his mouth than the door was heard to swing gently shut.

"The wind," explained Tiger Shade.

"Oh, yea?"

"What else could it be?"

"The Spirit of St. Louis for all I know."

"Come on."

"What you waitin' for?"

"Come on."

"O.K. Start out. If you turn round and don't see me you'll know I jes' lost my enthusiasm."

None too eagerly, Tiger started out, followed by his reluctant ally. Several tubbed palms stood supercilious and motionless along the walls, and these the two searchers eyed distrustfully as they passed. They reached the wide doorway of the rear room without noting any evidence of their quarry. The rear room was dark save for what shadowy illumination reached it from the dim light of the parlor. Close together, the husband peering around the more venturesome Tiger, their wide eyes trying vainly to discern the contents of the room, they halted on the threshold.

It occurred to both of them to feel for a switch-button on the wall beside the door, and still eyeing the shadows they simultaneously felt. Contact with an open live wire could have given either no greater shock than he got at this unexpected contact with a hand. For one palsied moment their fingers stuck together as if to an electrified object which, once grasped, could not be released. Then the husband snatched his hand away, wheeled and took the first stride in flight. Only the first. The Tiger, having wheeled also, was so close behind him as to be able to grab him from behind, and his comrade, not knowing what held him, gave a hoarse moan, slipped on the polished hardwood floor, and sprawled.

"Hey you dumbbell," muttered Tiger, recovered and master of himself again, but still noticeably dyspnœic. "That was only me. Come on—snap out of this monkey-business."

"I felt a human hand!" the other whispered getting up sheepishly.

"Well, don't I look human?"

"Was it you? Huh—well—yea, you look human all right. But if you grab hold o' me the next time I start to run, you won't look human no mo'. You'll look like you been ridin' a wild steer."

"Come on. That guy is hidin' in there."

"Somehow I done los' interest in that guy."

At this moment a curious sound rose to their ears.

"What's *that*?"

It was startlingly close—a distinct chorus of voices singing. Even the words of the song were easily distinguishable:

> "*Am I born to die?*
> *Oh, am I born to die?*
> *Lord, am I born to die—*
> *To lay this body down?*"

"What kind o' house is this?"

Tiger's wealth of reassurance was rapidly being exhausted. "Can't you think o' none o' the answers? That's somebody's radio."

> "*One of these mornings bright and fair,*
> *Lay this body down—*
> *Going to take my wings and try the air,*
> *Lay this body down—*
> *Lord am I born to die?*"

"No radio never sounded like that. Them's sho' 'nough voices and they's in this house."

> "*Oh, am I born to die*
> *To lay this body down?*"

"Not me!"

"Listen," said Tiger. "That's only a radio. Let's give this place one mo' look. He got to be in there. If he can go in there, so can we."

"All right. But no holdin' in the clinches."

Again, in the closest possible formation and in utter silence, they advanced to the rear room door.

"Whyn't you feel for the light ag'in?"

"Wait. I'll strike a match." The Tiger did so with none too steady fingers. By its fluttering, feeble, yellow flare two pairs of dilated eyes surveyed what could be seen of the room—a large desk on the right in the far corner, two windows in the back wall, a chair or two, and—

"Lawd have mercy—look a yonder!"

But the Tiger had needed no such admonition—he was looking with one hundred percent of his eyesight. Along the left wall stretched a long table, upon which, covered with a sheet, lay an unmistakably human form.

The match went out.

The pair stood momentarily cataleptic, their eyes fixed on the body which, once seen, remained now vaguely but positively visible even in the shadows. Before their shock passed a mysterious thing, an awful thing, began to happen, holding them fast in a horrified moment of fascination: slowly the white form moved in the shadow, seemed to change shape, to lift and widen like vapor. At the moment when their very eyeballs seemed about to burst, singing voices came again with that disturbing query:

"Am I born to die?"

Their spastic paralysis broke into convulsions of activity.

"Not here!" gasped the husband. And this time Tiger Shade did not overtake him till they both hit the sidewalk at the base of the front stoop and headed in opposite directions for more light.

Bubber, sitting fully erect now on the side of the

table, cast the sheet aside and stood up with a sigh of relief. "Frimbo ain't got a thing on me," said he. "If that ain't risin' from the dead, what is it?"

But the chorus of the singing was disturbing him as much as it had his pursuers. While allowing the latter time to retreat to a safe distance he decided to investigate the former. "Might as well find out all I can 'bout this morgue. Which a way——?"

He listened. He moved toward the door which led from the room directly into the back of the first-floor balcony. At the head of the stairs leading down to the basement he saw light below, and realized that the sound was coming from that direction. The singing had stopped. Just over his head, in the flight above, soft footsteps were distinctly audible. He waited, listening. Presently the front door clicked shut.

"Wonder if that was that flunky goin' out?"

It was too late to attempt to follow, however, and so he pursued his present investigation. The singing had stopped. Bubber went on down the stairs as noiselessly as he could. In the hall below, which corresponded to its fellows above, he paused and listened again. The light he had seen came from a door which was only partly open; the prowler could not see around it without going too close. But he heard significant sounds:

"Is they anybody heah," a deep evangelic voice was saying, "what don't expect to shake my hand up in glory?"

"No!" shouted a number of voices.

"The spirit of the Lord has been in this place to-night!"

"Yes!" avowed the chorus.

"Did you feel it?"

"Yes!"

"Did it stir yo' soul?"

"Yes, Jesus!"

"Move you to do good deeds?"

"Yes, indeed. Amen, brother!"

"Aw right then. Now let's take up the collection."

Silence, abrupt and unanimous.

Bubber grinned in the hall outside. "Church meetin' —and 'bout to break up."

He was right. Some of the members of the little group that evidently used Crouch's meeting-room Sundays were already shamelessly heading for the hall door, en route to the freer manifestations of divine presence out of doors. Bubber retreated to the rear of the hall so as to attract no attention, and found himself at the head of the cellar stairs. It occurred to him that his tour of inspection might as well include the cellar, especially since that would allow the occupants of the meeting-room time to take up their collection and depart. Then he could return and investigate the basement floor.

4

He had procured at a drugstore during his wanderings today, an inexpensive pocket flashlight in imitation of the physician and detective who had found such devices so useful last night. This he now produced and by its light started down the cellar stairs. He had to proceed cautiously for this staircase was not so firmly constructed as those above; but he was soon in the furnace-room below the sidewalk level, and his small pencil of light traced the objects which his predecessors had observed the night before: the furnace, the coal bin, the nondescript junk about the floor, the pile of trunks, boxes, and barrels up front. He saw the central droplight but could not turn it on, since its switch was at the head of the stairs he had already passed.

And so he moved inquisitively forward toward the pile of objects up front. A few minutes of nosing about revealed nothing exciting, and he became conscious that the sounds of shuffling feet overhead had stopped.

He was about to abandon the cellar, whose chilly dampness was beginning to penetrate, when, without sound or warning, the center droplight went on. Feeble as it was, its effect was startling in the extreme, and Bubber felt for the moment trapped and helpless. He recovered his wits enough to crouch down among the shadows of the objects around him, and slowly came to realize that no one else was in the place. He awaited a footfall on the staircase. None came. At the moment when curiosity would have overcome better judgment, he heard a sound which came from beyond the stairs, toward the distant back wall. Cautiously looking around the corner of a packing case, he saw a figure emerge from the dimness. The figure approached the foot of the stairs, and Bubber saw that it was Frimbo, bareheaded, clad in a black dressing-gown. Frimbo carefully and silently went up the stairs; there was the sound of a bolt sliding; then Frimbo came down again.

Fortunately Bubber's protection was now nothing so unstable as an outspread wardrobe trunk, for he was quite unmindful of anything but the strange man's movements. And curious enough they were. Frimbo grew dim again in the shadow, then reëmerged with a paper bundle in his arms. He laid this down several feet from, and in front of the furnace, which was against the left wall and facing toward the center. The bundle thus rested almost directly beneath the droplight, and Bubber could see that its paper wrapping had a greasy appearance, as if its contents had been dripping with oil. Frimbo went to the furnace door and flung it wide. The red of the bright coals touched his awesome face to a glow, contrasting oddly with the yellow light behind him. He seized a long-handled shovel standing beside the furnace and returning, lifted the bundle upon it, reapproached the open door and thrust the thing in. The ignition of the package was instantaneous, the flames from it belching out of the aperture before Frimbo closed it. Now he replaced the shovel, went up the stairs again, unbolted the door at the top, came down, and disappeared in the darkness at the rear. There was a soft sound like the one that had heralded Frimbo's appearance, and a moment later the center light went out.

Among all the bewildering questions which must have presented themselves to Bubber now, the greatest was surely, "What's he burnin'?" For a long time, perhaps half an hour, the spy remained where he was, afraid to move. Eventually, the compelling impulse to look into the furnace and trust to providence for escape, if necessary, moved him out of his refuge and toward the fire.

Every foot or two he stopped to make sure there was no sound. It was clear that Frimbo had some means of traveling about the house other than the stairs, and it was probable that he would not return to the cellar without switching on the light from whatever distant connection he had contrived. But Bubber had to re-assure himself somewhat as to the mysterious avenue of approach before satisfying his major curiosity. He invaded the territory through which Frimbo had departed, and could discover no ordinary exit. There was no cellar door leading up to the back yard; the walls were solid cement. All that he could find was the base of the dumb-waiter shaft, and his little beam of light, directed up the channel, was sufficient to disclose, some feet above, the dangling gears and broken ropes which attested the uselessness of the device.

In a state of mind which the shifting shadows about him did nothing to relieve, he quickly returned to the furnace and flung open the door. Whatever Frimbo had used to accelerate combustion had already reduced his bundle to a fragile-looking char; its more susceptible parts had already stopped blazing, and the remainder lay crumbling like the embers of a frame house that has burned down. Pocketing his light and working by the illumination from the coals, Bubber took the shovel and, with as little noise as possible, gently retrieved a part of what had been consigned to the flames. He laid it, shovel and all, on the floor, shut the furnace, and examined it with his flash. So intent was he now that it would have been easy to approach and catch him unawares. But the contents of the shovel, from which the glow had already faded, presented nothing susceptible to Bubber's knowledge; his puzzled stare disclosed to him only that he must get the find out of this place and subject it to more expert inspection.

It did not take him long to find a wooden box into which he could deposit what he had retrieved. Having done so, he replaced the shovel beside the furnace, and with the box under one arm, quietly mounted the stairs. The basement floor was dark. He did not stop to investigate that now, however, but, succeeding in making his exit by way of the basement front door, without a moment's delay he ran across the street to Dr. Archer's house and, no less excitedly than twenty-four hours before, rang the front-door bell.

Again the doctor himself answered the summons.

"Hello, Brown! What's up?"

"I done 'scovered sump'm!"

"In that box? What?"

"You'll have to answer that, doc. Damn 'f I know."

"Come in."

5

In the warmth and brightness of the physician's consulting-room, Bubber related what he had seen and done.

Meanwhile the doctor was examining the contents of the box on his desk, poking about in it with a long paper knife. He stopped poking suddenly, then, very gently resumed. Much of what he touched crumbled dryly apart. At last he looked up.

"I should say you have discovered something."

"What is it, doc?"

"How long did you say this burned?"

" 'Bout half an hour. Took me that long to make up my mind to get it out."

"Are you sure it didn't burn longer?"

"With me snoopin' 'round 'spectin' to be bumped off any second? No, *suh!* If it was half an hour that was half an hour too long."

"Did it blaze when he first put it in the furnace?"

" 'Deed it did. Looked like it was 'bout to explode."

"Let me see now. How could he have treated human flesh so as to make it so quickly destructible by fire?" The doctor mused, apparently forgetting Bubber's presence. "Alcohol would dehydrate it, if he could infiltrate the tissues pretty well. He could do that by injecting through the jugulars and carotids. But the alcohol would evaporate—that would explain the rapid oxidation. Greasy? Oh, I have it! He's simply reinjected with an inflammable oil—kerosene, probably. Of course. Hm—what a man!"

"Doc, would you mind tellin' me what you talkin' 'bout?"

"Have you any idea what this stuff is?"

"No, suh."

The 'ail Frimbo's body

"It's what's left of a human head, neck and shoulder, a trifle over-cooked."

"Great day in the mornin'!"

"Quite so. The extent of destruction has been sped up by treating the dead tissues with substances which quickly reduced the water content and heightened the imflammability. Maybe alcohol and kerosene—maybe chemicals even more efficient—it doesn't matter."

He stopped his poking and gently lifted from the box an irregular, stiff, fragile cinder. He placed it very carefully on a piece of white paper on his desk.

"This is exhibit A. Notice anything? No, don't handle it—it's too crumbly and we can't afford to lose it. What do you——"

"Ain't them teeth?" Bubber pointed to three little lumps in the char.

"Yes. And apparently the only ones that haven't fallen loose. I believe we may be able to use them. Further, this cinder represents parts of two bones, the maxillary, in which the upper teeth are set, and the sphenoid which joins it at about this point."

"You don't mean to tell me?" gaped Bubber.

"I do. I do indeed. And I mean to tell you this also: that the presence of the sphenoid, or most of it, in a relatively free state like this is proof that its owner has left this world. On this bone, in life, rests a considerable part of the brain."

"S'posin' a guy's brainless, like Jinx?"

"Even Jinx couldn't make it without his sphenoid. So you see that in that fragile bit of the fruit of the crematory, we have an extraordinary bit of evidence. We have proof of a death. You see that?"

"Oh, sho' I see that."

"And we may have a means of identifying the corpse. You see that?"

"Well, that ain't quite so clear."

"Never mind. It will be. And finally we have your testimony to the effect that Frimbo was destroying this material."

"Huh. Don't look so good for Mr. Frimbo, do it?"

"Thanks to your discovery, it doesn't."

"Will that help Jinx out?"

"Possibly. Even probably. But the case against Frimbo is not quite complete, you see, even with this."

" 'Tain't? What mo' you need?"

"It might be important to know who was killed, don't you think?"

"Tha's right. Who?"

"I'm sure I don't know. Maybe nobody. These may be the remains of an old stiff he was dissecting—who knows? That we must find out. And there is one more thing to learn—Frimbo's motive. Not only whom did he kill—if anybody—but why?"

"Why you reckon?"

"That may be a hard point to convey to you, Mr. Brown, so late in the evening. But this much I will tell you. You see, while you have been ruminating in the depths of Frimbo's cellar, I have been ruminating in the depths of my mind."

"I hope 'tain't as full of trash as that cellar was."

"It has its share of rubbish, I'm not ashamed to say. But what it holds just now is the growing conviction that Frimbo is a paranoiac."

"A—which?"

"A paranoiac."

"The dirty son of a gun. Ought to be ashamed o' hisself, huh?"

"And so, my worthy collaborator, if you don't mind leaving this precious clue in my hands, I'll spend a little time and energy now freshening my mind on homicidal tendencies in paranoia—a most frequent symptom, if I recall correctly."

"Jes' what I was thinkin'," agreed Bubber. "Well, I'll come 'round again tomorrow, doc. I was on my way here tonight, but I got sorta side-tracked. I thought you might be able to tell me how to help Jinx out."

"If this is any indication," smiled the doctor, pointing to the evidence, "the best thing you can do for Jinx is to get side-tracked again."

Bubber thought over the day's episodes, grinned and shook his head.

"Uh—uh," he demurred resolutely. "He ain't wuth it, doc."

CHAPTER TWENTY-ONE

I

"IN THIS respect," Dr. Archer confessed to Detective Dart, who sat facing him across his desk the next morning, "Frimbo would call me a mystic. I have implicit faith in something I really can't prove."

"Is it a secret?"

"Yes, but I'll share it with you. I believe that the body, of which these humble remnants are ample evidence, is the same as the one I pronounced dead on Saturday night."

"Shouldn't think there'd be any doubt about that."

"There isn't. That's the mysticism of it. There isn't any doubt about it in my mind. But I haven't proved it. I have only yielded to a strong suspicion: somebody is killed, the body disappears. Frimbo steps up claiming to be the body. He is lying as our little blood test proved, and later he is seen destroying vital parts of a body. This might be another body, but I am too confirmed a mystic to believe so. I am satisfied to assume it is the same."

"You know damn well it's the same," said the practical Dart.

"We won't argue the point," smiled Dr. Archer. "Assuming it is the same—there will be reasons why Frimbo destroys a murdered man."

"Protecting himself."

"An omnipresent possibility. The victim was sped into the beyond either by Frimbo himself or by someone in league with Frimbo, whom Frimbo is trying to protect. Yes. But do you recall that we drew the same conclusions about Jinx Jenkins?"

"Well—bad as this looks for the conjure-man, it doesn't remove the evidence against Jenkins. That handkerchief could be explained, but that club—and the way he tried to scram when the lights went out——"

"Very well. Nor does it eliminate the actuality of a feud between the two policy kings, Spencer and Brandon, in which that runner was an unfortunate sacrifice yesterday. Personally, I pay no more attention to that than I do to the ravings of Doty Hicks."

"Me, personally," responded Dart, "I pay attention to both of 'em. I suspect 'em all till facts let 'em out. And I still think that the simplest thing may be so. Why make it hard? Hicks or Brandon, the one out of superstition, the other out of greed, either one may have hired Jenkins to do the job. Jenkins somehow didn't get Frimbo but got—say! I know—he got Frimbo's flunky! That's your dead body! The flunky!"

The physician demurred.

"Inspiration has its defects. Remember. The flunky ushered Jenkins to the entrance of the room. Jenkins went in. The victim was already in the chair waiting. Would the flunky have obligingly hurried around through the hall and got in place just so that Mr. Jen-

kins could dispose of him? That would be simple indeed
—too simple."

"Well, maybe I'm prejudiced. But——"

"You are. Because that isn't all you ignore. Why
would Frimbo claim to be the victim if what you suggest
were true? Why would he destroy the body of his servant? One would rather expect him to want to find and
punish the murderer."

"All right, doc. You can out-talk me. You give us the
answer."

"I'm only part way through the problem. But I had
an interesting interview with the gentleman last night.
And I'm reasonably sure he's a full-fledged paranoiac."

"Too bad. If he was a Mason, now, or an Odd Fellow——"

"A paranoiac is a very special kind of a nut."

"Well, now, that's more like it. What's so special
about this kind of a nut?"

"First, he has an extremely bright mind. Even flashes
of brilliance."

"This bird is bright, all right."

"You don't know the half of it. You should hear him
tie you up in mental knots the way he did me. Next
thing, he has some trouble—some unfortunate experience, some maladjustment, or something—that starts
him to believing the world is against him. He develops
a delusion of persecution. Frimbo concealed his pretty
well, but it cropped out once or twice. He came to
America to study and had some trouble getting into

college. He took it personally, and attributed it to his color."

"Where's the delusion in that?"

"The delusion in that is that plenty of students the same color, but with more satisfactory formal preparation, have no such difficulty. Also that plenty the same color with unsatisfactory preparation don't draw the same conclusion. And also that plenty *without* his generous inheritance of pigment and with unsatisfactory preparation have the same difficulty and don't draw the same conclusion."

"Call it a delusion if you want to——"

"Thanks. Now your paranoiac couldn't live if something didn't offset that plaguing conviction. So he develops another delusion to balance it. He says, 'Well, since I'm so persecuted, I must be a great guy.' He gets a delusion of grandeur."

"I know flocks of paranoiacs."

"Me too. But you don't know any with the kind of delusion of grandeur that Frimbo has. It's the most curious thing—and yet perfectly in case. You see, his first reaction to the persecution idea was flight into study. He got steeped in deterministic philosophy."

"What the hell is that?"

"The doctrine that everything, physical and mental, is inevitably a result of some previous cause. Well, Frimbo evidently accepted the logic of that philosophy, and that molded his particular delusion of grandeur. He said, 'Yes, everything is determined—nature, the

will of man, his decisions, his choices—all are the prod-
ucts of their antecedents. This is the order of our existence. *But I—Frimbo—I am a creature of another order.*
I can step out of the order of this existence and become,
with respect to it, a free agent, independent of it, yet
able to act upon it, reading past and present and modi-
fying the future. Persecution cannot touch me—I am
above it.' Do you see, Dart? Does it mean anything to
you?"

"Not a damn thing. But it doesn't have to. Go on
from there."

"Well, there you are—still paranoia. But when it gets
as bad as in Frimbo's case, they get dangerous. They get
homicidal. Either the first delusion moves them to eliminate their supposed persecutors, or the second generates
such a contempt for their inferiors that they will remove them for any reason they choose."

"Gee! Nice people to ride in the subway with. Are
you sure about this guy?"

"Reasonably. I'm going back for more evidence today."

"So he can remove you?"

"Not likely. I think he's taken a fancy to me. That's
another symptom—they make quick decisions—accept
certain people into their confidence as promptly as they
repudiate others. I seem to be such a confidant. Something I said or did Saturday night appealed to him.
That's why he accepted me so quickly—invited me back
—took me in—exchanged confidences with me. No

normal mind under similar circumstances would have done so."

"Well—be careful. I don't mind nuts when they're nuts. But when they're as fancy as that they may be poison."

"Don't worry. I know antidotes."

After a pause, Dart said:

"But who the hell did he kill?"

"You mean who's dead? We only surmise that Frimbo——"

"I mean who was the bird on the couch?"

"Have you that removable bridge in your pocket?"

"Sure. Here it is. What of it?"

"I don't dare hope anything. But let's see." He took the small device. Its two teeth were set in a dental compound tinted to resemble gums and its tiny gold clamps reached out from either end to grasp the teeth nearest the gap it bridged.

"Look." The doctor pointed to the three teeth in the bony char which still lay on the piece of white paper. "Upper left bicuspid, a two-space gap, and two molars. That means first bicuspid and second and third molars. Now this bridge. Second bicuspid and first molar. See?"

"Don't you ever talk English?"

"The gap, Dart, old swoop, corresponds to the bridge."

"Yea—but you yourself said that doesn't prove anything. It's got to fit. Fit perfect."

"Oh, thou of little faith. Well, here goes. Pray we don't break up the evidence trying to get a perfect fit." With deft and gentle fingers, the physician brought the bridge clamps in contact with the abutments of the cinder and ever so cautiously edged them in place, a millimeter at a time. He heaved a sigh.

"There you are, skeptic. The gums are gone of course. But the distance between the teeth has been maintained, thanks to the high fusion point of calcium salts. Am I plain?"

"You are—but appearances are deceiving."

"Here's one you can depend on. Find out who belongs to this bridge and you'll know who, to put it quite literally, got it in the neck on Saturday night."

Dart reached for the bridge.

"Gently, kind friend," warned the doctor. "That's your case—maybe. And leave it in place."

"There's probably," observed the detective, "three thousand and three of these things made every day in this hamlet. All you want me to find out is whose this was."

"That's all. It'll be easy. See your dentist——"

"I know—twice a year. What time'll you be back here?"

"Four o'clock. And bring that club with you."

"Right. I'll see you—if Frimbo lets you out whole."

2

With the clue resting like a jewel upon soft cotton in a small wooden box, Detective Dart sought out one Dr. Chisholm Dell, known to his friends, including Perry Dart, as Chizzy. Chizzy was a young man of swarthy complexion, stocky build, and unfailing good humor, whose Seventh Avenue office had become a meeting-place for most of the time-killing youth of Harlem—ex-students, confidence boys, insurance agents, promoters, and other self-confessed "hustlers." The occasional presence of a pretty dancing girl from Connie's or the Cotton Club, presumably as a patient awaiting her turn, kept the boys lingering hopefully about Chizzy's reception room.

Detective Dart was not deceived, however, and rose promptly when Chizzy, in white tunic, came out of his operating-room.

"Can you give the law a hot minute?"

"I couldn't give anybody anything right now," grinned Chizzy. "But I'll lend you one. Come on in."

Dart obeyed. He produced his exhibit.

"Take a look."

"What the devil's that?" Chizzy exclaimed after glancing at it.

Dart explained, adding, "As I get it, this bridge is a pretty accurate means of identification. Is that right?"

"I've been practicing ten years," said Chizzy, "and I haven't seen two exactly alike yet."

"Good. Now is there any way to tell who this belonged to?"

"Sure. Whose bone is it?"

"Don't be funny. Would I ask for help if I knew that?"

Chizzy considered. "Well—it can be narrowed down, certainly. I can tell you one thing."

"No?"

"Sure. That bridge is less than two months old."

"Yea?"

"See this part here that looks like gums?"

"Is that what it's supposed to look like?"

"Yea. That's a new dental compound called deckalite. Deckalite has been on the market only two months. I haven't made a case yet."

"Know anybody in Harlem that might have?"

"When you limit it to Harlem, that makes it easy. Do you know it was made in Harlem?"

"No. But it was made for a Harlemite. The likelihood is that he went to a local dentist."

"I doubt it. I haven't seen a patient for so long I believe all the Harlemites must be going to Brooklyn for their teeth. But if he did go to a Harlem dentist, it's easy."

"Hurry up."

"Well, you see there are only two dental mechanics up here that can handle deckalite. As it's a recent product it requires a special technique. Not one of the regular dentists knows it, I'm sure. Whoever your unknown friend went to would just take the impression and send it to one of those two men to be made up. All you've got to do is to go to each of the two mechanics, find out what dentist he's made deckalite uppers for, go back to the referring dentist and trace down your particular bridge."

"Beautiful," said Dart. "Two names and addresses, please."

Chizzy complied. "You'll find 'em in now, sitting down with their chins in their hands, wishing for something to do."

"Thanks, Chizzy. If you weren't so damned funny-lookin', I'd kiss you."

"Is that all that prevents you?" Chizzy called—but Dart was already banging the outside door behind him.

3

"Come into my laboratory, doctor," Frimbo invited Dr. Archer. "I'm glad you could return, because, if you remember, I promised to demonstrate to you a little experiment. Let's see, this time you have your bag, haven't you? Good. Have you a gauze dressing?"

Dr. Archer produced the requested article and handed it over. Frimbo removed it from the small, sealed tissue paper envelope which kept it dry and sterile, and dropped it into a sealed glass beaker. Then he rolled up the left sleeve of his robe, the one he had worn the night before.

"Please, doctor, remove a few cubic centimeters of blood. Put a little in that test tube there, which contains a crystal of sodium citrate to prevent clotting, and the rest in the empty tube beside it. You will be interested in this, I'm sure."

The physician applied a tourniquet, procured a syringe, touched a distended vein of Frimbo's forearm with alcohol, and obeyed the latter's directions. Frimbo, the tourniquet removed, pressed the swabbing sponge on the point of puncture a moment, then discarded it and dropped his sleeve.

"Now, doctor, there are my red cells, are they not?" He indicated the first tube. "And in a moment we shall have a little of my serum in this other tube, as soon as the blood clots and squeezes the serum out." They awaited this process in silence.

"Good. Now I take your sterile dressing and pour onto it some of my serum. In a general way, now, this dressing might have wiped a bloody wound on some part of my body—except that it has upon it only serum instead of whole blood. A mere short cut to my little demonstration. I return the dressing to the beaker and add a few cubic centimeters of distilled water from this bottle. Then I remove the dressing, thus, leaving, you see, a dilute sample of my serum in the beaker."

"Yes," Dr. Archer said thoughtfully.

"Now on this slide, with this loop, I place a drop of my diluted serum"—he stressed "my" whenever he used it—"and mix with it a loopful of my red cells, so. Now. Will you observe with the microscope there, what takes place?"

The doctor put the slide on the stage of the microscope, adjusted the low power, and looked long and intently. Eventually he looked up. He was obviously astonished.

"Apparently your serum agglutinates its own cells. But that's impossible. One part of your blood couldn't destroy another—and you remain alive."

"Perhaps I am dead," murmured Frimbo. "But there

is a much simpler explanation: Your dressings are
dently treated with some material which is hostile
red cells. In such a procedure as this, where the serum
has to be soaked out of the dressing, this hostile material
is soaked out also. It is this material that is responsible
for the phenomenon which we usually attribute to
hostile serum. Let us prove this."

Thereupon he repeated the experiment, discarding
the dressing, and using a dilution of his serum made directly in another test tube. This time the microscope
disclosed no clumping of red cells.

"You see?" the African said.

The doctor looked at him. "Why did you show me
this?" he asked.

"Because I did not wish you to interpret falsely any
observations you might have made in your investigation
of night before last."

"Thank you," Dr. Archer said. "And may I say that
you are the most remarkable person I have ever met in
my life."

"Being remarkable also in my lack of modesty,"
smiled the other, "I quite agree with you. Tell me. How
do you like my little laboratory?"

"It certainly reveals as unusual combination of inter-
ests. Biology, chemistry, electricity——"

"The electricity is, with me, but a convenience. The
biochemistry is vital to my existence."

"Isn't that a television receiver over there?"

"Yes. I made it."

"Small, isn't it?"

267

evi-
to

v originality."

١ my curiosity; you have taken
confidence, and if I presume
. But you seem so absorbed in more
pursuits—have you no lighter moments?
...u think you would have to relax—at least occasionally—to offset your habitual concentration."

"I assure you I have—lighter moments," smiled the other.

"You are a bachelor?"

"Yes."

"And bachelors—you may look upon this as a confession if you like—are notoriously prone to seek relaxation in feminine company."

"I assure you," Frimbo returned easily, "that I am not abnormal in that respect. I admit I have denied myself little. I have even been, on occasion, indiscreet in my affairs of the heart—perhaps still am. But," he promptly grew serious, "this," he waved his hand at the surrounding apparatus, "this is my real pleasure. The other is necessary to comfort, like blowing one's nose. This I choose—I seek—because I like it. Or," he added after a pause, "because a part of it lifts me out of the common order of things."

"What do you mean?" The voice of Dr. Archer was not too eager.

"I mean that here in this room I perform the rite, which has been a secret of my family for many generations, whereby I am able to escape the set pattern of cause and effect. I wish I might share that secret with you, because you are the only person I have ever met who has the intelligence to comprehend it and the balance not to abuse it. And also because"—his voice dropped—"I am aware of the possibility that I may never use it again."

The doctor drew breath sharply. But he said quietly:

"It is always the greatest tragedy that a profound discovery should remain unshared."

"Yes. Yet it must be so. It is the oath of my dynasty. I can only name it for you." He paused. Then, "We call it the rite of the gonad."

"The rite of the gonad." With the greatest difficulty the physician withheld his glance from the direction of the shelf whereon he had observed a specimen jar containing sex glands.

"Yes," Frimbo said, a distant look creeping into his deep-set eyes. "The germplasm, of which the gonad is the only existing sample, is the unbroken heritage of the past. It is protoplasm which has been continuously maintained throughout thousands of generations. It's the only vital matter which goes back in a continuous line to the remotest origins of the organism. It is therefore the only matter which brings into the present every influence which the past has imprinted upon life. It is the epitome of the past. He who can learn its use can be master of his past. And he who can master his past—that man is free."

For a time there was complete silence. Presently Dr. Archer said, "You have been very kind. I must go now. I shall see you tonight."

"Yes. Tonight." A trace of irony entered the low voice. "Tonight we shall solve a mystery. An important mystery."

"Your death," said the doctor.

"My death—or my life. I am not sure."

"You—are not sure?"

"The life of this flesh, my friend."

"I do not follow you."

"Do not be surprised. Released of this flesh, I should be freer than ever."

"You mean—you think you may be—released?"

"I do not know. It is not important now. But Saturday night, an odd thing happened to me. I was talking to the man, Jenkins. I had projected my mind into his life. I could foresee his immediate future—up till to-night. Then everything went blank. There was nothing. I was as if struck blind. I could see no further. You see what that means?"

"A sort of premonition?"

"So it would be called. To me it is more than that. It meant the end. Whether of Jenkins' body or mine, I can not say at the moment. I was with him, of him, so to speak. But you see—the abrupt termination which cut off my vision could be either his—or—mine."

The doctor could say nothing. He turned, went out, and slowly descended the stairs.

CHAPTER TWENTY-TWO

I

AGAIN Bubber Brown called on his friend Jinx Jenkins and again was permitted to see him. Jinx had never been of cheerful mien; but today he had sunk below the nadir of despondency as his glum countenance attested. But Bubber wore a halo of hope and his face was a garland of grins.

"Boy, I told you I'd get you out o' this!"

"Where," asked the sardonic prisoner, "is the key to the jail?"

"Far as you concerned, it's on Doc Archer's desk."

"That's a long way from this here lock."

"I been goin' after mo' evidence, boy. And I got it. I give it to the doc and, what I mean, yo' release is jes' a matter of time."

"So is twenty years."

"You' good as out, stringbean."

"Not so long as I'm in. Look." He laid hold of the grille between them and shook it. "That's real, man; that's sump'm I can believe, even the holes. But what you're sayin' don't widen nothin' but yo' mouth."

"Listen. You know what I found?"

And he related, how, at great personal risk, which he ignored because of his friend's predicament, he had

271

voluntarily entered the stronghold of mystery and death, ignored the undertaker's several corpses—four or five of them lying around like chickens on a counter —descended past the company of voodoo worshipers who would have killed him on sight for spying on their secrets, and so into the pit of horror, where the furnace was merely a blind for the crematory habits of the conjure-man.

"He come straight out o' the wall," he related, "and me there hidin' lookin' at him. Come through the wall like a ghost."

"Ghos'es," Jinx demurred, "is white. Everybody know that."

"And so was I," avowed Bubber.

"Well," Jinx conceded, "you might 'a' turned white at that—when you seen Frimbo come out o' that wall."

Bubber went on with his story. "And," he eventually concluded, "when Doc Archer seen what I'd found, he said that settled it."

"Settled what?"

"That proved somebody's been killed sho' 'nough. See?"

Jinx gazed a long time upon his short, round friend. Finally he said, "Wait a minute. I know I didn't hear this thing straight. You say that what you found proves it was murder?"

"Sho' it do."

"Boy, I don't know how to thank you."

"Oh that's all right. You'd 'a' done the same for me."

"First you get me pulled in on a charge of assault. But

you ain' satisfied with that. Tha's only twenty years. You got to go snoopin' around till you get the charge changed to murder. My pal."

"But—but——"

"But my ash can. You talkin' 'bout dumbness and ignorance. Well, you sho' ought to know—you invented 'em. All right; now what you go'n' do? You got me sittin' right in the electric fryin'-pan. Somebody got to throw the switch. You done arranged that too?"

"Listen, boy. All I'm doin' is tryin' to find enough facts to clear you. You ain't guilty sho' 'nough, is you?"

"I didn't think so. But you got me b'lievin' I must be. If you keep on bein' helpful, I reckon I'll jes' have to break down and confess."

"Well, what would you 'a' done?"

"What would I 'a' done? First place, I wouldn' 'a' been there. Second place, if the man wanted to burn up sump'm in his own furnace, he could 'a' burned it. He could 'a' got in the furnace and burned hisself up for all I'd 'a' cared. But you—you got to run up and stop the thing from burnin'—you rather see me burn."

"Aw man, quit talkin' lamb-yap. If Frimbo's tryin' to get rid o' remains, who's responsible for 'em bein' remains? Frimbo, of course. Frimbo put his flunky up to killin' somebody; then he got the flunky away and tried to get rid o' the remains."

"Yea? Well, I don' see Frimbo in this jail house. I'm here. I'm holdin' the well-known bag. And all you doin' is fillin' it."

"I wish I could fill yo' head with some sense. Maybe

when you get yo' big flat feet out on the street again you'll appreciate what I'm doin' for you."

"Oh, I appreciate it now. But I never expect to get a chance to show you how much. That'll be my only dyin' regret."

Bubber gave up. "All right. But you needn' never fear dyin' in nobody's electric chair."

"No?"

"No. Not if they have to put that electric cap on yo' head to kill you. Yo' head is a perfect non-conductor."

With this crushing remark Bubber terminated his call and gloomily departed.

2

"You're ahead of time," said Dr. Archer.

"This won't wait," returned Perry Dart. "It took me less than an hour to get the dope. Here's your club." He laid a package on the desk. "And here," he put the box containing Bubber's discovery down beside the other package, "is your removable deckalite bridge. And I'll bet a week's wages you can't guess who that bridge belonged to."

"I can't risk wages. Who?"

"A tall, slender, dark gentleman by the name of N. Frimbo."

The physician sat forward in his chair behind the desk. The gray eyes behind his spectacles searched Dart's countenance for some symptom of jest. Finding none, they fell to the box, where they rested intently.

"And his address," the detective added, "is the house across the street."

"Unless I've been seeing things," said Dr. Archer, "Frimbo's teeth are very nearly perfect. Those two teeth are certainly present."

"This patient differed from our friend in only one respect."

"How?"

"The dentist who treated him insists that he was cock-eyed."

"I'm beginning to wonder aren't we all?"

"Frimbo's servant was cock-eyed."

"And otherwise much like his master—tall, dark, slender."

"With the same name?"

The physician regarded the detective a solemn moment. "What's in a name?" he said.

3

Before the detective could answer, Dr. Archer's door bell rang again. The caller proved to be Bubber Brown; and a more disconsolate Bubber Brown had never appeared before these two observers.

"Sit down," said the doctor. "Found anything else?"

"Gee, doc," Bubber said, "my boy Jinx is got me worried. He brought up a point I hadn't thought about before."

"What point?"

"Well, if that clue I brought you last night changes

the charge to murder, Jinx'll have to do life at least. 'Cose life in jail with nothin' to worry 'bout, like meals and room rent, has its advantages. But the accommodations is terrible they tell me, and I don't like the idea that I messed my boy up."

"Is that what he thinks?" asked Dart.

" 'Deed he do, mistuh, and it don't sweeten his temper. He's eviler than he would be if he really had killed the man."

"There is evidence that he did kill the man," Dart reminded him.

"Must be sump'm wrong with that evidence. Jinx wouldn't kill nobody."

"I thought you didn't know him so well?"

Bubber was too much concerned for his friend to attempt further subterfuge. "I know that much about him," he said. "That Negro ain't bad sho' 'nough. He's jes' bad-lookin'."

"You yourself identified his handkerchief. It had been stuffed down the victim's throat, you'll remember."

"Well—I knowed he didn't do it befo'. But, far as I see, that proved he didn't do it."

"How?"

"Listen, mistuh. Jinx might 'a' hit somebody with that club jes' sorter thoughtless like. But stuffin' a handkerchief down his throat—that wouldn't even occur to him. He's too dumb to think up a smart trick like that."

"An opinion," Dr. Archer said, "in which I wholly concur. Nothing in Jenkins' character connects him with this offense, either as author or agent. Someone in that room simply made him the dupe."

"Possibly you can explain, then, how his thumb print got on that club," Dart said.

"Possibly I can. In fact I had just that in mind when I asked you to bring it along."

He reached for the first package which Dart had put on the desk, and unwrapped it carefully.

"Remember, we don't know," he observed meanwhile, "that this club or bone actually delivered the blow. There was no blood on it for the simple reason that it had bounced back from the point of impact before hemorrhage, which was moderate, got under way. But it is permissible to assume that it was used."

He lifted the club by its two ends, using the tips of his fingers, and slowly rotated it about its own axis. His glanced shuttled back and forth over the ivory-colored surface. "This is the incriminating print?" he asked, indicating a dark smudge.

"Yes. That's what Tynie photographed."

"He didn't dust the bone with powder first, did he?"

"No. How'd you know?"

"Because there's no powder on it elsewhere. This surface has a thick viscous film over it as though it had been oiled or waxed. It isn't oil or wax. It's a film which oozes from the pores of the incompletely prepared specimens, due to the presence of undestroyed marrow inside. If Tynie had dusted this bone there'd be particles of powder stuck all over it. Fortunately, he looked first and found preparation unnecessary—his print had been prepared for him. Now let's have a look.

"I've a magnifying glass hereabouts somewhere—here it is." He studied the smudge a moment. Then he put the bone down, looked up at Dart and smiled. "Easiest thing in the world," he said.

"What is?"

"Transferring a finger print."

"Are you kidding me, doc?"

"Not at all. Simple statement of fact. The discovery of a finger print is not necessarily any better evidence of its owner's presence than the discovery of any other object belonging to him. Don't misunderstand me. I know that as a means of identification, its value is established. But as proof that the owner's fingers put it where it was found—that's another matter. That is a belief based on an assumption. And the fact that the assumption is usually correct does not make it any the less an assumption."

"But just what is the assumption?"

"That there is but one way to put finger prints on an object, namely, direct contact between the fingers and the object. That is the unconscious assumption that is always made the moment a finger print is discovered. We say 'A-ha, finger print.' We identify it as John Doe's finger print. Then we say, 'A-ha, John Doe was here.'"

"Of course," said Dart. "What else would anyone think?"

"Apparently nothing else. But I assure you that as a matter of demonstrable fact, John Doe may never have been near the place. He may have been ten miles away when his finger print was put on the object."

"You'll have to produce plenty evidence to convince me of that, doc."

"Look. You were perfectly willing to believe that Jinx Jenkins' handkerchief might have been taken by somebody else and put where we found it, weren't you? So willing that you did not arrest him on that evidence alone. But when his thumb print was found on the club—that settled it: Jinx must have had a hand in it. Now, I believe I can show you that, aside from a lot of minor assumptions there, your major assumption could have been wrong. Jinx Jenkins didn't have to be anywhere near this club. His finger print could have been deliberately put on it to incriminate him, just as his handkerchief could have been used as it was for the same purpose."

"I'm looking, doc. Go ahead."

"All right. Let us suppose that I want to rob that safe in the corner. I'd be an awful ass, because I wouldn't get a dime's worth of anything. But I don't know that. I want to rob it and I want the circumstances to incriminate you. I decide that since people think as they do, it would incriminate you if right after the robbery your finger prints—even a lone thumb print—could be demonstrated on that safe door.

"Here is a box of fine grade talcum powder. It's a professional sample, otherwise it wouldn't be so fine. I'll put a little on the arm of your chair—smooth, polished wooden surface. Now grasp the arms of your chair with your hands, as you might if you didn't think I was putting something over on you. Good. Incidentally, look at your thumb—has a fair film of powder, hasn't it? All right. Change seats with me. . . . Now again grasp the arms of your chair naturally. Take your hands away. Look at the right arm of your chair. See anything?"

"Sure. A perfect thumb print in white powder! But——"

"Too early for buts. Get up now and stand behind the chair. You are now ten miles away. All right. Here is a rubber glove, such as I rarely nowadays have the opportunity to use. I put it on my hand thus. The rubber is of course perfectly smooth, and if I wish I can increase the coefficient of adhesion——"

"Wait a minute, doc."

"My error. I can make it just a very little bit sticky by rubbing into the palm of it thus, a bit of vaseline, cold cream or what have you. This is not strictly necessary, but tends to improve the clearness of the transfer. Now, with proper stealth, I approach the talcum-powder thumb print which you have so obligingly left on the arm of your chair. I lean over the chair thus and carefully, as if it were a curved blotter, I roll the heel of my hand once, only once, over our powder print. And you see, I have the powder tracing on my glove.

"Of course this is not your thumb print. It is the negative of your thumb print, or rather, the mirror-image of it. If now I go to the safe and smear a tiny bit of vaseline on the safe door thus, it is a simple matter to

roll your thumb print off my glove onto the black surface of the door. And there it is. Doesn't even have to
be dusted. Photograph it, bring it up on the high contrast paper, and you, my friend, are under arrest for
robbing my safe. Yet you have never been near my safe
and you were ten miles away when the crime was committed."

Perry Dart silently went over to the safe and gazed
upon the smudge of powder. He came back to the desk,
picked up the doctor's hand glass, returned to the safe
door and studied the transferred print. It was not the
crisp image of the original, but the fine granules of
powder, primarily arranged in a definite pattern by the
tiny grooves of his own skin, had not been sufficiently
disarranged by the transposition to obliterate that pattern.

"If you wish," said Dr. Archer, "I can improve on
that beautifully by using the same technique with
printer's ink. It comes up astonishingly when dusted
with finger-print powder afterwards. But this is sufficient to indicate the possibilities."

"You're going to get yourself in trouble thinking
up things like that," muttered the detective.

"I didn't think it up," was the answer. "Our unknown murderer—if any—thought it up and used it.
Only, since he had a light-colored and fairly gummy
object to work toward, he used a black substance instead of a white. I remember getting some of it on my
hand from that chair Brady brought me; possibly the
same chair Jenkins used—or maybe several chair-arms

had been so treated. Lamp-black would do nicely, plain or in a paste like shoe polish. If you examine that print on the bone as you did the one on the safe, you will note a general similarity. Both look as though they might have been put on by a somewhat dirty finger, that's all. Both, however, were actually put on by a smooth-surfaced applicator, which spread the lines just a little, but not too much."

"You know, I thought it was funny Tynes' saying he didn't even have to prepare the thing."

"Still," the physician said, "this only indicates that Jenkins didn't have to touch the club or deliver the blow. It doesn't indicate that he did not actually do so. But something else does."

"What?"

"The position of the print. Even if the transferability of a finger print couldn't be demonstrated, still this print would not prove that Jenkins delivered a blow with this club. On the contrary, it proves that he could not have delivered an effective blow with his thumb in that spot. Look. To deliver an effective blow he would grasp the club in his hand like this—no danger, I'm using my gloved hand and I've wiped off the remains of your thumb print—like this, near the smaller end, so that the condyles—those big bumps which help form the knee part of the bone—would land on the victim's head. Grasping it so, his fingers would surround the shaft thus, completely, and his thumb, you see, would rest on the outside of his fingers; it couldn't possibly produce a print on the surface of the bone because it wouldn't even touch the surface of the bone. But beyond that, the position of the print is near the big end—the clubbing-end here. Notice that the print is close to this condyle and directed obliquely toward it. If your hand grasped this bone so that your thumb fell in that position, your fingers would have to be around the club end like this, and the shaft of the bone, you see, would then fall along your forearm, so that you could not possibly deliver a blow. Any attempt to do so would only endanger your own fingers."

"Gee, doc, you ought to be a lawyer."

"I am. I'm Jenkins' lawyer right now. And I contend, your honor, that if the handkerchief was insufficient basis for indictment, so is the thumb print. Only more so."

"Hot damn!" came an unexpected cry from the admiring Bubber. "Go to it, doc! You're the best!"

4

Bubber's ensuing expressions of appreciation literally carried him away. He backed and sidled out through the doctor's several doors on a transporting flood of gratitude, much like a large rubber ball twisting this way and that on the surface of a flowing stream.

The physician turned again to the detective and smiled. "What does your honor say about Jenkins?"

"Sort of lost my enthusiasm for Jenkins," grinned Dart.

"Well, then, since we're beginning to eliminate, let's attempt a diagnosis."

"O.K. doc. Take 'em one by one. That'll bring up some things I've found out that I haven't told you. I was too interested in Frimbo's servant when I came in."

"Jinx Jenkins."

"Hardly, after your defense."

"Thanks. Doty Hicks."

"Oh, yes. Well, here's the dope on Hicks. Remember, he said that to break Frimbo's spell on his brother it was necessary to put a counter-spell equally fatal on Frimbo. But he had to have somebody's help. The immediate possibility was, of course, that Jenkins was that somebody. But your argument practically eliminates Jenkins on the one hand; and on the other we've found out by further questioning just who he meant. He was talking about a hoodoo artist named Bolus in 132nd Street, who gave him some kind of goofer dust to sprinkle on Frimbo's floor. That's the gray powder we found under the table."

"You found this Bolus?"

"Had no trouble getting a check-up out of him. I told him he was under suspicion for murder, having deliberately conjured and killed a professional competitor. Well, sir, he nearly died himself trying to convince me that his goofer dust was just ordinary coal ashes. Of course, I knew that already. Got the report last night. So then I promised to come back and take him for fraud."

"Doty Hicks, then, is no longer a suspect?"

"Hardly."

"Ironic business all around, Dart. Hicks, in all good faith, put his goofer dust at the feet of a man who may even then have been dead. And he and Jenkins, the only two you could reasonably have held, are probably the least likely suspects of the lot. Well—the two women."

"They're out. We know from checked testimony that they didn't enter the death room till after the thing was done."

"All right by me. Nice girl, Martha Crouch. Easley Jones, the railroad man?"

"Excellent record on his job. Long, faithful service. Hasn't been out of his rooming-house but twice since Saturday night, both times for food."

"Also decidedly untutored—same sort of man that Aramintha Snead is of woman. By no means the character of mind who would think up this particular scheme to incriminate someone else."

"Who's next?"

"Spider Webb."

"Yes, Webb. Well, Webb told a straight story. And Frimbo tried to dispose of the servant's remains. The only way to connect Webb with the crime now is to assume that he and Frimbo were conspiring. But why they'd be conspiring to kill Frimbo's servant—that's beyond me."

"You're sure Webb told a straight story?"

"About the feud, yes. We've gone into it thoroughly. That killing yesterday morning means all I told you it meant. Further, Brandon, Spencer's rival policy king, has disappeared. He always does when somebody has to take the rap."

"That leaves us Frimbo himself."

"Nobody else but."

"Hm—the house is open for suggestions."

"You know, I'm beginning to see daylight in this thing." An idea was growing on Dart. "By Judas! I do see daylight!"

"Show me, O master."

"Look. Suppose Brandon did find out that Frimbo was the cause of his downfall. It's not hard to believe you know. Dumber people than Frimbo are remarkably clever at this number-playing game. They hit on some system and it works. They get so good that bankers actually turn down their bets. Well, Frimbo could have doped out such a system. Suppose he did, and suppose that through it, Spencer was playing heavily with Brandon and winning. Brandon couldn't wipe out Spencer— that would be open confession. But nothing in the world would stop him from trying to wipe out Frimbo. Nothing except that Frimbo isn't easy to get at alone, except at night in a private interview. To take Frimbo, therefore, Brandon's got to finesse. You see?"

"So far."

"So what does he do? He finds somebody who is close to Frimbo, who has access to him, and who is not likely to be suspected. In short, he finds the servant. The servant, who no doubt is already envious of his master's success—the way black servants are with black masters—is offered a big handful of change to put his boss out—any way he can. All right. He agrees. But he's not going to jam himself by doing it during the day when he is known to be in the place alone with Frimbo! He's going to wait till night when the office is full. And he's going to bring the whole thing off in a way that will incriminate somebody else who happens to be present. Wouldn't you? Wait a minute—I know what you're going to say. The answer is that the servant was on the point of carrying the scheme through. He had snatched Jenkins' handkerchief in the scramble there when Doty Hicks fainted. He had already by some scheme such as you just demonstrated got Jenkins' finger print on the club. But Frimbo's smart. Frimbo reads his mind or gets a hunch or anything you want to call it. Frimbo discovers what's up just in time to turn the tables—frustrates the attack and gives the servant his own medicine, club, handkerchief, and all!"

Dart paused to emphasize this twist of interpretation; then went on:

"But Frimbo hasn't got time to dispose of the body then and there. So he exchanges the servant's yellow turban and sash for his own, props the body up in his own chair, hides in the dark and goes on telling visitors their fates, intending to get them all out without arousing any suspicions. But our crusty friend Jenkins discovers the fact that the man talking to him is a corpse —and that changes his plans. See?"

The physician meditated upon this. "You have lapsed into brilliance, Dart," he commented finally. "Brilliance is likely to be blinding. . . . Wasn't it the servant who ushered each visitor to Frimbo's door?"

"Hell, no. That was Frimbo, himself. He took each one to the door, then, while they were going in, blinded by that light, he'd run around, enter the hall door, hide behind the corpse, and talk to 'em."

"All coons look alike, to be sure. But I've seen no sign of external strabismus in either of Frimbo's eyes."

"What?"

"The servant in general resembled Frimbo. But he was cock-eyed. Frimbo isn't. The people who testified all saw the servant and all agreed that he was cock-eyed. Somehow, Dart, I dislike that term—extremely misleading isn't it? But strabismus, now—there's a word! External strabismus—internal strabismus—see how they roll off your tongue."

"I'm particular what rolls off my tongue."

"Nevertheless, external strabismus is not an easily assumed disguise. I have never heard of anyone who could render himself cock-eyed at will."

"You haven't?" grinned Dart. "Ever try cooked whiskey?"

"The phenomenon you have in mind is an illusion— an optical illusion, if you like. The victim enjoys diplopia—the impression of seeing the world double, an impression which he believes cock-eyed people must have at all times. Thus the illusion is twofold: cock-eyed people really don't see double; and the happy inebriate actually has no external strabismus, he has only a transitory internal strabismus. I insist therefore, that, remarkable as Frimbo is, voluntary external strabismus is an accomplishment which we must not grant him lightly. But all this is not the prime objection to your startling vision. The prime objection is that Frimbo would surely not leave thwarted his own plan. Would he?"

"He didn't. Jenkins———"

"He did. Jenkins would have gone on being mystified by Frimbo's revelations, had it not been for Frimbo's own startled words. The thing that made Jenkins jump up and turn the light on the corpse was Frimbo's sudden exclamation, 'Frimbo, why don't you see?' Frimbo would not have said that if he had been planning to get Jenkins and the others out as quickly and unsuspectingly as possible. Something happened to Frimbo about that moment."

"But Jenkins' word is all we have for that remark."

"Jenkins' word, now that he is pretty well exonerated, should be worth something. But even if by itself it isn't, I have Frimbo's word in support."

"You what?"

"Frimbo himself said to me today that he went blind, so to speak, while talking to Jenkins. He saw so far ahead—then everything went blank."

"Hooey."

"All right. Maybe this is hooey too: You say that Frimbo hid behind the corpse near enough to make his voice seem to come from the corpse."

"Yes."

"Then, when Jenkins suddenly jumped up and without warning swung the light around why didn't he see Frimbo hiding?"

"I don't know—maybe Frimbo ducked under the table or some place."

"Hooey. Hooey. An eloquent word, isn't it?"

"Well, the details may not be exact, but that isn't far from what happened. It's the only thing I can think of that even nearly fits the facts."

"Nearly won't do."

"All right, professor. You guess."

"There's something malicious in the way you say that. However, innocent and unsuspecting as I am, I will guess. And I guess, first off, I'll leave out the number racket. That'll make it easier for me, you see."

"But the number racket can't be ignored——"

"Who's doing this guessing?"

"O.K. doc. Guess away."

"I guess the same thing that you guess, that Frimbo killed his servant. But not because of the number racket, or any attack upon him growing out of the number racket."

"But because he's a nut."

"Please—not so bluntly. It sounds crude—robbed of its nuances and subtleties. You transform a portrait into a cartoon. Say, rather, that under the influence of certain compulsions, associated with a rather intricate psychosis, he was impelled to dispose of his servant for definite reasons."

"All right. Say it anyhow you like. But to me it's still because he was a nut."

" 'Nut' in no wise suggests the complexity of our friend's psychology. You recall my description of his condition; its origin in his type of mind, its actual onset in an experience, its primary and secondary delusions."

"Yes. I recall all that."

"Well, here's an item you don't recall because it hasn't been mentioned; Frimbo like other paranoiacs, has a specific act as a part of his compensatory mechanism. This act becomes a necessary routine which must be performed, and naturally takes its form from some earlier aspect of his life. In his case it derives from his native days in Buwongo, his African principality. He calls it the rite of the gonad. And though he declines to describe it, I can imagine what it amounts to. It is nothing more or less than his extracting, in that laboratory of his, a kind of testicular extract with which he periodically treats himself. By so doing, he believes that he partakes of matter actually carrying the impress of all the ages past, and so becomes master of that past."

"Deep stuff. Anything in it?"

"Well, I don't know anything about endocrines. But I should think such a practice would produce some kind of hyper-sexuality. Sex gland deficiency can be helped by such treatment, so perhaps a normal person would become, in some respects, oversexed."

"But sex has played no part in this picture."

"I was only answering your question. To return to my guess. Frimbo has to have sex glands—not those of lower animals such as biological houses use to make their commercial extracts, but human sex glands, carrying, to his mind, the effects of human experience from time immemorial. With the compulsion strong upon him to secure human tissues for his rite, he could easily become as ruthless as a drug addict deprived of his drug. But he would be far more cunning. He would choose a victim who would not be missed, and he would arrange circumstances to incriminate someone else. And the insanely brilliant feature is that he would arrange to have himself appear to be the victim. I do not believe that the unusual devices used to commit this crime and divert suspicion indicate the workings of an ordinary mind or knowledge such as a servant would have. They indicate a sort of crazy ingenuity which would not be conceived and carried out by a normal person. Frimbo is the only one in the crowd whose mind fits the details of this crime."

"Well, you're disagreeing with me only on motive. I say self-defense. You say insanity. But both of us say Frimbo did it. From that point on I should think our difficulties would be alike: the cock-eyed business, the blind spot or whatever it was, and the—what was the other thing?"

"His sudden invisibility if he hid behind the dead servant."

"Yea—that."

"The cock-eyed business, yes. But the other business, no. I did not say that he hid behind the servant. I think he had some device or instrument—I'm not sure just what, but we'll find it—that placed his voice so that it seemed to come from the servant. And I do not say that he acted under the urgency of a sudden encounter. I say that he planned the whole thing ahead, deliberately. Even foresaw the possibility of discovery and arranged to rise from the dead, just for effect, as he did. That would be wholly in character. He even had an alibi ready for my blood test. He showed me this afternoon how I might easily have made an error in the little experiment I showed you. He did not know, of course, that Bubber Brown's discovery was on hand as a perfect check.

"He demonstrated how something in my gauze dressing might throw the test off—it would have been very disturbing indeed if I had not known what he was up to. What he did was to substitute for my gauze a piece which he had previously treated with the dead man's serum. He foresaw every possibility. Far from thwarting his own plans, even that sudden loss of prophetic vision, that premonition, did not change his main course of action. That exclamation, 'Frimbo, why don't you see?' startled Jenkins into action, to be sure, and resulted in our rushing on the scene. But even then he would have removed the body anyway from under our very noses—he could have done so simply by shutting off the lights.

"And there's another difference in our theories: If, as you say, it was just self-defense, he is not shown to be dangerous. He can be held for disposing of the remains, but not for murder; self-defense is manslaughter and is likely to go unpunished. But if, as I say, it is insanity, then he's liable to do the same thing again to some other unfortunate fellow; he must be put away in a cool dry place where he's no longer a menace. Don't you see?"

"That's so. You know, doc, just out of sportsmanship you might let me win an argument once in a while."

"We're not arguing. We're guessing. And I have a curious feeling that smart as we think we are, we're both guessing wrong."

"You're good, doc. Anyway it goes now, you're right."

"At least I know one thing."

"What?"

"I know I saw a new specimen jar on one of Frimbo's shelves today. It was next to the one that we noted before. And it contained two more sex glands."

"Judas H. Priest!" said Perry Dart softly.

CHAPTER TWENTY-THREE

I

FOR the first time since the incarceration of his friend Jinx, Bubber Brown enjoyed a meal. The probability of Jinx's release later tonight, a happy eventuality which Bubber himself had helped bring about, more than restored Bubber's appetite to normal, and he indulged in gleeful anticipation of what he would say to his grouchy comrade upon the latter's return to freedom. Mumbled mockery pushed its way through prodigious mouthfuls of food.

"Uh—huh," emerged stifled but determined through roast beef and mashed potatoes. "Here you is. Yo' flat feet is now out in the free air they probably need plenty of. Now get to thankin' me." A succulent forkful of kale crowded its way in with the roast and potatoes, and all this was stuffed securely back with a large folded layer of soft white bread. Even through this there somehow escaped sounds.

"Boy, you was due to go. Go where? Where do folks go what murder folks? I mean it was upon you. If it hadn' been for me and the doc, you'd be on your way to Swing Swing now. Your can was scheduled to rest on a 'lectric lounging chair—they even had the date set. I ain' kiddin' you, boy. You was jes' like that coffee they advertise on the radio—your can was dated."

The next few phrases were overwhelmed with hot coffee. Bubber grinned and substituted a dish of juicy apple cobbler for his denuded dinner plate. "From now on," he told it, "you listen and I talk, 'cause your head is a total loss to you—jes' extra weight you carryin' around for no purpose." The apple cobbler began miraculously to vanish. "You see, you don't appreciate my brains. I got brains enough for both of us. I don't even have to use all my brains—I got brains in the back o' my head I ain't never used. Some time when you admit how dumb you is, I'll lend you some for a few days, jes' to show you how it feels to have a thought once in a while."

The dessert became a sweet memory, vestiges of which were dislodged with a handy toothpick.

"Now, let's see. Got to be at the place at 'leven o'clock. Guess I'll drop in and see that picture at the Roosevelt Theatre—*Murder Between Drinks*. Wonder 'f I'm go'n' see that third one tonight? Maybe the one in the picture'll be number three. Now there's brains again. Jes' by goin' to see this picture I may save somebody's life. Doggone!—ain't I smart?"

2

Promptly at eleven, Bubber Brown mounted the stoop and entered the house. He started up the stairs toward Frimbo's floor, looking above. He stopped, his eyes popping. He brushed his hand across his lids, and stared again toward the head of the stairs. What he saw persisted. It might have been Saturday night again; for there motionless above him stood the tall, black-robed figure of Frimbo's servant, bright yellow turban and sash gleaming in the dim light, exactly as he had been before, even—yes, there it was—even to the definite cast in one solemn eye.

Bubber blinked twice, wheeled about, and would have vanished through the front door as magically as this corpse had reappeared. But at that particular moment the door opened and Perry Dart with half a dozen policemen obstructed the avenue of escape. Bubber came to in Jinx Jenkins' arms, pointed, and gasped:

"Look! is I dreamin'—or is I dreamin'?"

"What's the matter, Brown?" Dart asked.

"Didn't you say the flunky was the one got cooked?"

"Yes."

"Well, look up yonder! He's there—I seen him!"

"Yeah?" Dart stepped forward, looked up the stairs. He smiled. "So he is, Brown. We must have made a mistake. Come on, let's go—can't let a little error like that worry us."

"So," muttered Jinx, "you is wrong again. What a brain!"

"You can go if you want to, brother," demurred Bubber. "Me—I've never felt the need of fresh air the way I do now. People in this house don't suit me. They jes' don't pay death no mind."

"Come on, Brown," insisted Dart. "I'll need your help. Don't let me down now."

"All right. I'll follow. But don't count on me for

no help. I'm go'n' stay 'live long as I can. I ain't learnt this Lazarus trick yet."

In the hallway above, Dart gave due orders in stationing his men, so that all natural exits were covered. The servant ushered them then to the reception room, where every one was present but Dr. Archer. The detective noted each person in turn: Mrs. Aramintha Snead, Mrs. Martha Crouch, Easley Jones, Doty Hicks, Spider Webb, and Jinx Jenkins, whom he had brought with him.

The physician arrived a moment later. "I summon Frimbo," said the servant who had escorted him in also. The servant bowed. The doctor looked after his retreating form quizzically, then turned to Detective Dart and smiled. Dart grinned back. Bubber observed the exchange and murmured, "You all could see jokes in tombstones, couldn't you?"

Perry Dart said to the physician, "Now what?"

"Wait," answered Dr. Archer. "It's his show."

They waited. Shortly the gold turban and sash returned. "This way, please," said the servitor, and gestured toward the wide entrance to the consulting-room.

"Everybody?"

"Please."

Again the servant retreated by way of the hall. The others, directed by the detective and led by the physician, entered the black chamber from the front room and stood in an expectant semicircle facing the table in the center. Over the far chair, which still sat behind the table just as it had when the body had been found in it, hung the device which projected a horizontal beam of light toward the entrance. Most of the visitors fell to the one or the other side of this beam, but at the distance of the semicircle, its rays diverged enough to include two figures directly in its path, those of Martha Crouch and Spider Webb. Mrs. Crouch's dark eyes were level and clear, her lips slightly compressed, her expression anticipative but not apprehensive. Spider Webb also betrayed interest without profound concern, his countenance manifesting only a sort of furtive malignancy. The rest were mere densities in the penumbra.

3

As they stood watching, the darkness beyond the table condensed into a black figure, much as mist might condense into a cloud. This figure silently came to occupy the chair beneath the light. Then from it issued the low rich voice of Frimbo.

"A return into the past," it said, "observes events in their reverse order. May I therefore ask Mr. Jenkins, who was the last to occupy that chair on Saturday evening, to be the first to do so tonight?"

Nobody moved.

Bubber's sharp whisper came forth.

"Go on, fool. Get yo'self freed."

With obvious and profound reluctance, Jinx's figure moved forward into the light. Those toward one side could see tiny beads of sweat glistening on his freckled countenance. He sidled into the chair on this side of the table, facing the voice and the shadow. His face was brightly illuminated and starkly troubled.

"Mr. Jenkins," Frimbo's voice went on smoothly, "it is again Saturday night. You have come to consult me. All that reached your consciousness is again before you. You will conceal nothing from the eyes of Frimbo. The light shall lay open your mind to me, book-wise. I shall read you. Be silent, please."

There was scant danger of Jinx's being anything else. Even his usual murderous scowl had been erased, and Frimbo's intent contemplation of his face could be sensed by every onlooker. They too were steadily staring upon him from behind or from the side, according to their position, much as if they expected him at any moment to leap to his feet and confess the crime.

Then a change of color came over Jinx's face. Those who were in position to see observed that the light freckled skin over the eminences of his bony countenance was growing darker. Alarmingly the change progressed, like an attack of some grave cyanotic disease. Jinx was actually turning blue. But it at once became apparent that his color was due to a change in the light which illumined him. Slowly that light changed again.

"Each hue," said Frimbo's voice, "makes its particular disclosure."

Jinx became yellow.

"Got to do mo'n that to make a Chinaman out o' him," came Bubber's whisper.

Diabolically red flushed the subject's lean visage, and finally a ghastly green. Throughout it all Frimbo's intense inspection created an atmosphere of vibrant expectancy. One felt that the lines of vision between his eyes and Jinx's face were almost tangible—could be plucked and made to sing like the strings of an instrument.

Eventually Frimbo said, "No," and the spell was broken. "This is not the man." The light came white again. "That is all, Mr. Jenkins."

There was a general sigh of relief. Jinx returned to the circle, where Bubber greeted him with an inevitable comment:

"The red light turned you red, boy, and that green light turned you green. But that white light couldn't do a thing for you. It was jes' wasted."

Frimbo said, "Now, Mr. Webb, please."

But Perry Dart interrupted. "Just a minute, Frimbo." He stepped forward to the side of the table. "Before we go any further, don't you think it fair to have your servant present?"

Frimbo's voice became grave. "I regret that I have already permitted my servant to leave."

"Why did you do that?"

"It is his custom to leave at eleven, may I remind you?"

"And may I remind you that we are investigating a serious crime; also that you promised to have him present."

"I kept my promise. He was here. You all saw him. I did not promise that he would remain after his hours."

"Very well. You say he is gone?"

"Yes."

"He has left the house?"

"Yes."

"Then perhaps you will tell me just how he got out. Every exit is covered by an officer, with orders to bring to me anyone who tries to leave this house."

There was a pause; but Frimbo said easily, "That I cannot tell you. I can tell you, however, that by interrupting this procedure you are defeating your own investigation, with which I am endeavoring to help you."

Dart achieved a trace of Frimbo's own irony. "Your consideration for my interest touches me, Frimbo. I am overwhelmed with gratitude. But your servant is a necessary witness. I must insist on his being here—with you."

"That is impossible."

"Well, now you are at least telling the truth. Or perhaps you can do for him what you did for yourself?"

"You are obscure."

"Look harder, Frimbo. It's the bad lighting. I mean that perhaps you can make him rise from the dead, as you did."

Bubber could not suppress a mumbled, "Come on, Lazarus. Do yo' stuff."

"You believe then," Frimbo said, "that my servant is dead?"

"I know that your servant is dead. I have in my hand positive evidence of his death."

"Of what nature?"

"Evidence that was retrieved from your furnace downstairs by one of my men——"

"Hot damn!" breathed Bubber. "Tell 'em 'bout me!"

"——when you were trying to destroy it. I have a piece of the bone upon which his brain rested during life. I have a removable bridge which is known to be his, and which fits that bone—or rather the teeth in the bone joined to it. Frimbo, this is a farce. You killed your servant, who also went by the name of Frimbo. You slipped around through this house somehow on Saturday night while I was investigating this case, and moved his body to some hiding-place on these premises. You treated that body to make it burn quickly and to make what bone was left crumble easily. You dismembered it and tried to dispose of it by way of your furnace. You were seen doing this by Bubber Brown, who was in your cellar last night and who recovered a part of the bone before it crumbled. To avert suspicion, you masqueraded as your servant by a trick of your eyes. I see no point in continuing this nonsense. You're the guilty party and you're under arrest. Am I still obscure?"

4

For a long moment no other word was spoken. At last Frimbo said quietly:

"Since I am already under arrest, it would be useless, perhaps, to point out certain errors in your charges. . . . However, if you would care to know the truth——"

"You are at liberty to make any statement you please. But don't try anything funny. We've anticipated some of your tricks."

"Tricks," Frimbo said softly, "is an unkind word. The fact is, however, that I have killed no one. It is true that I have disposed of my servant's remains. If that box contains what you say it does, and if Brown was in the cellar when you say he was, he undoubtedly saw me in the course of performing what was nothing more or less than a tribal duty."

"Tribal duty?"

"The servant was a fellow tribesman of mine whom I took in and protected when his venture into this civilization proved to be less fortunate than mine. He was of my clan and entitled to use the name, Frimbo. His distinguishing name, however—what you would call his Christian name, had he not been a heathen and a savage—was N'Ogo. It is our tradition that the spirit of one of our number who meets death at the hands of an—an outsider, can be purged of that disgrace and freed from its flesh only by fire. The body must be burned before sunset of the third day. Since the circumstances made this impossible, I assumed the risk of removing and properly destroying my tribesman's flesh. For that and for whatever penalty attaches to it, I have no regret. My only regret, Mr. Dart, is that you have interrupted, and perhaps for the time defeated, my effort to complete the duty which this death has imposed upon me."

Dart was impressed. The man's total lack of embarrassment, his dignity, his utter composure, could not fail to produce effect.

"Complete the duty———?"

"It is a part of my duty, as the king of my people, to find the killer and bring him to the just punishment which he has earned. In my own land I should take that part of the matter into my own hands. Here in yours it was my intention to find the killer and turn him over to you. But as for killing N'Ogo myself— you would have to be one of us, my friend, to appreciate how horribly absurd that is. I would sooner kill myself than one of my clan. And he—he could not under the most extraordinary circumstances imaginable bring himself to do a thing against his king. He simply could not have committed an offense against me that would have caused me to decree or execute his death. Against one of his own or lower rank, perhaps, but not against me."

The detective, ordinarily prompt in decision, was for the moment bewildered. But habit was strong. "Look here," he said, "how can you prove that what you say is true—that you didn't kill this man?"

"It is not of the slightest importance to me, Mr. Dart, whether you or the authorities you represent believe me or not. My concern is not for my own protection but for the discharge of my obligation as king. If I can not complete my duty to this member of my clan, I do not deserve to have been his king. The greatest humiliation I could suffer would be death at the hands of a strange people. That is no more than he has suffered."

This was an attitude which Dart had never encountered. The complete and convincing unimportance to Frimbo of what was paramount to the detective left the latter for the moment without resource. He was silent, considering. Finally he asked:

"But why did you have to do so much play-acting? Accepting what you say as true, why did you have to pull all that hokum about rising from the dead?"

"Do you not see that it was necessary to my plans? I had to have time in which to dispose of N'Ogo's body. I had to account for its disappearance. It is easy for me to pass undiscovered from almost any part of this house to any other part. I have a lift, electrically operated and practically undiscoverable, in the old dumbwaiter shaft. It travels from this floor to the cellar. What appears on examination to be the roof of the old shaft, with rusty gears and frazzled rope hanging down, is really not the roof but the bottom of the floor of the lift. N'Ogo's remains reposed on that lift, securely hidden, during the latter part of your search. So did I until the proper moment for my entrance. What better way can you think of to account for the disappearance of a body than to claim to be that body? I even wounded myself as N'Ogo had been wounded, in anticipation of the good doctor's examination. I took every possible precaution— even inviting the doctor alone here to determine the extent of his investigations and divert him from the truth if possible."

"What about those sex glands?"

"They too are a part of the tradition. They alone, of

all his flesh, must be preserved as a necessary item in the performance of one of our tribal rites, one which I went so far as to mention to Dr. Archer today. That I can not speak further of, but I think the doctor's excellent mind will comprehend what it can not fully know."

"But this is unheard of. You haven't told the whole story yet. You say you don't know who killed this servant or tribesman of yours. Do you know when he was killed?"

"Not even that. I know only that one of the people who came here to see me killed him, thinking he was I."

"How could anybody make that mistake?"

"Easily. You see, it has always been our custom, as is true of many peoples, that the chief, in whom resides the most important secrets of the nation, should not be unnecessarily exposed to physical danger. Just as a lesser warrior in medieval days donned the white plume of his commander to deceive the enemy and prevent the possibility of their concentrating upon the leader, killing him early, and demoralizing the troops by eliminating competent direction, so with us for many hundreds of years a similar practice has been in effect. The king is prohibited by tribal law from unnecessarily endangering the tribal secrets residing in his person. My servant knew of certain dangers to which I was exposed here. I had devised a mathematical formula whereby I was able to predict a certain probability in the popular policy game of this community. My part in the dwindling fortunes of one of the so-called bankers was discovered through the disloyalty of a disgruntled underling in the rival camp which my information was aiding. The loser intended to eliminate me. Whether this actual killing was his doing or not I am not sure—that was one possibility. There was another.

"At any rate, N'Ogo and I exchanged rôles. It had been so for several days. I am able through a divertissement learned in youth to diverge my eyes as easily as most people converge theirs, and so, to the casual observer, could easily pass for my own servant.

"My servant had only to sit here in this chair in the darkness. I myself, dressed in his costume, would usher the visitor to the entrance there, turn aside, and come down the hall to my laboratory at the rear. There a device of mine enabled me to convince the visitor, now seated in that chair opposite, that it was really I who sat there. This light over my head is far more than a light. It is also a mechanism whereby I can see the illuminated face of whoever occupies that chair, and whereby also I can transmit my voice to this point. It comprises nothing mechanically original or unusual, except, perhaps, its compactness. By means of it, I was able to carry on my observation of a visitor and talk to him quite as if I were really in this chair, except that I could see only his face. Thus, you see, by the use of two rather simple mechanisms, my lift and my light, I enjoyed remarkable freedom of movement and considerable personal security in case of necessity.

"But on Saturday night, I had no need, any more than on any other night, for entering this room. Visitors were always accustomed to paying their fees to the assistant in the hall as they departed. So negative was my assistant's part in this masquerade that I did not—and do not—know just when he was attacked. But the strange experience—what you will call a premonition—that momentarily startled me during Mr. Jenkins' interview made me exclaim in a way that startled him also, so that he jumped up to investigate. The crime had been done before that moment. It was done between the time when some prior visitor rose to go—disappearing from view in my mechanism—and the time when I collected the same visitor's fee in the hall. Or perhaps between the time when I bowed him into this room and reached my laboratory.

"From that point on you know what happened. I could do only what I did do. Tonight I had every reason to believe, before your interruption, that I should determine the identity of the murderer. Perhaps I may do so yet—I have arranged certain traps. In case of the unexpected, Mr. Dart, be careful what you touch——"

A wholly strange voice suddenly shot out from the deep shadow behind Frimbo.

"So it's really you this time, Frimbo? Why weren't you careful what you touched?"

At the last word a pistol banged twice.

In that frozen instant, before any of the dumbfounded bystanders could move, Frimbo's light was abruptly blotted out and the room went utterly black. At the same moment a shriek of unmistakable pain and terror broke through the dark from the direction of the two shots.

"Brady—that light—quick!" came Dart's sharp voice. The powerful extension light flashed brilliantly on.

There was no need for haste, however. Against the wall at the rear of the black-draped chamber, whence the distressed cry had come, everyone saw a figure slumped limply down, as if it would fall but could not. It moaned and twitched as if in a convulsion, and one arm was extended upward as if held by something on the wall.

Dr. Archer reached the figure before the detective, started to lift it, looked up at the point where the hand was clinging, and changed his intention.

"Wait—be careful!" he warned the detective. The man's hand was grasping the handle of the switch-box which occupied that point on the wall. "That handle's live in that position. Here—push it up by lifting him by his clothing—that's it—a little more—I'll push up his elbow—there!" The hand fell free.

Supporting his limp figure between them, they got the man to his feet. They swung him, more unnerved than hurt, around into the light and drew him forward.

It was the railroad porter, Easley Jones.

5

Dr. Archer first did what he could for Frimbo, who, still sitting in the chair, had fallen face-down on the table; lifted his shoulders so that he resumed an erect posture, and began to loosen his clothing in order to examine his wounds. Frimbo, rapidly weakening, yet

was able to lift one hand in protest. He smiled ever so
faintly and managed a low whisper:

"Thank you, my friend, but it is of no use. This is
what I foresaw."

Martha Crouch had come forward like one walking
in a daze. Now she was beside Frimbo. Her face was a
portrait of bewilderment and dread. Frimbo's head sank
forward on his chest.

"The Buwongo secret," he murmured, "dies. . . ."

The young woman put her arm about his sagging
shoulders. Her horror-struck face turned to Dr. Archer,
mutely questioning. He shook his head a little sadly.

"How about the car downstairs, doc?" Dart was
asking. "Shoot right over to Harlem Hospital if you say
so."

Dr. Archer stood beside Frimbo a moment longer
without answering. Then he sighed and turned away.
"It's too late," he said. "Have him taken up to his
room."

He approached Easley Jones, who stood between two
policemen, looking down at the palm of his left hand,
where the live switch handle had burned him. The doctor picked up the railroad porter's hand, inspected it,
dropped it.

"Just what under the sun," he said, looking the man
up and down, "could you have had against Frimbo?"

Easley Jones said nothing. His head remained sullenly
lowered, the bushy kinks standing out like a black wool
wig, the dark freckles sharply defined against pale brown
skin.

"Have you anything to say?" Dart asked him.

Still he was silent.

"You sneaked around in the dark until you were near that switch Frimbo mentioned Saturday night. Then you shot Frimbo from behind, intending to throw off the switch and get back to your place during the excitement. We were looking for something like that, otherwise this extension would have been useless. We plugged it in downstairs on another circuit."

"But it was Frimbo," Dr. Archer said, "who caught him. Frimbo had wired that switch box so that the handle would go live when it was pulled down. Frimbo anticipated all this—he said so. Deliberately exposed himself to another attack in order to catch the killer. He even knew he was going to die."

"What this guy's grudge was I can't imagine. But he's saved us a lot of trouble by trying again. I suppose he would have tried it before if he hadn't known he was being trailed. How'd you know we were trailing you, Jones?"

No answer.

"Incredible," Dr. Archer was muttering. "Nothing about him to suggest the ingenuity——"

"Frimbo!"

The physician swung around, stepped back to Martha Crouch, who had uttered the name as one might cry out in torture. Never on any face had he seen such intense grief.

"Why, Martha—what in the world? Does this mean all that to you?"

Her eyes, wide and dry, stared impotently about in a suppressed frenzy of despair. Clearly, she would have screamed, but could not.

"You mean"—the physician could not bring himself to accept the obvious—"that you and Frimbo——?"

It was as if that name coupled with her own was more than she could endure. She wheeled away from him, and from the sudden tense immobility of her figure he knew that in a moment all that she was now curbing by long self-discipline would explode in one relieving outburst.

Suddenly she about-faced again. This time her eyes, fixed on a point behind John Archer, had in them the madness of hysteria. The doctor manifested an impulse to restrain her as she passed him. He hesitated a trifle too long. Before anyone knew her intention, she had swept like a Fury upon the man whose arms were in the grasp of the two officers. Low words came from between her clenched teeth as her hands tore at his face.

"You—killed—the only man——"

They managed after a moment to pull her away. What shocked her, however, out of that moment of mania into a sudden stupor of immobility was not the firm grasp of friendly hands but the realization that in her tightly closed fingers was a wig of kinky black hair, and that the sleek, black scalp of the man before her, despite the freckles which so well disguised his complexion, was that of her husband, the undertaker, Samuel Crouch.

CHAPTER TWENTY-FOUR

JINX JENKINS, released, and his ally, Bubber
Brown, walked together down Seventh Avenue.
It was shortly after midnight and the Avenue at this
point was alive. The Lafayette Theatre was letting out
somewhat later than usual, flooding the sidewalk with
noisy crowds. Cabs were jostling one another to reach
the curb. Brightly dressed downtowners were streaming
into Connie's Inn next door. Habitués of the curb stood
about in commenting groups, swapping jibes. The two
friends ambled through the animated turbulence, unaware of the gaiety swirling around them, still awed
by the experience through which they had passed.

"Death on the moon, boy," Bubber said. "What'd I
tell you?"

"You tol' me," Jinx unkindly reminded him, "it was
the flunky done it."

"The flunky done plenty," returned Bubber. "Got hisself killed, didn't he?"

"Yea—he done that, all right."

"His name was N'Ogo," Bubber said, "but he went."

They emerged from the bedlam of that carnival
block.

"Smart guy that Frimbo," observed Bubber. "Y'
know, I wouldn't mind bein' kind o' crazy if it made
me that smart."

"That Crouch wasn't no dumbbell."

"Dart say Crouch must 'a' known all about a railroad porter named Easley Jones, and made out he was him."

"Hmph. Guess now he wishes he was him sho' 'nough."

"Sho' was different from his own self—act different, talk different."

"He wasn't so different. He was still actin' and talkin' cullud, only more so."

Bubber's hand was on the roll of bills in his pocket which he had won at blackjack, but his mind was still in Frimbo's death chamber.

"Them artificial freckles—that man must 'a' been kind o' crazy too—jealous crazy—to sit down and think up a thing like that. Freckles sump'm like yourn, only his comes off."

"Mine liked to come off too when I seen who he was. How you reckon he got my finger print on that thing?"

Bubber described with enthusiasm the physician's demonstration.

"Say, that's right," Jinx recalled. "My chair arm was kind o' messy on one side, but I thought it was jes' furniture polish and sorter blotted it off on a clean place."

"Then we got up and went over to the mantelpiece and was talkin' 'bout all them false-faces and things."

"Yea."

"That's when this guy come up and joined the conversation. But he had dropped his hat in your chair.

While he was standin' there talkin' so much, he got your han'kerchief and that club. Then it come his turn to go in to Frimbo. On the way he leaned over your chair to pick up his hat. That's when he got your thumb print—off the clean place. Didn't take him a second."

"The grave-digger," Jinx muttered. "He sho' meant to dig me in, didn't he?"

"If it hadn't been you, 'twould 'a' been somebody else. He jes' didn't mean to lose his wife and his life both. Couldn't blame him for that. Jes' ordinary common sense."

A gay young man on the edge of the pavement burst into song for the benefit of some acquaintance passing by with a girl:

"*I'll be glad when you're dead, you rascal you—*
I'll be glad when you're dead, you rascal you—
Since you won't stop messin' 'round,
I'm go'n' turn yo' damper down—
Oh, you dog—I'll be glad when you're gone!"

"Boy," murmured Bubber, if he only knew what he was singin'."

And deep in meditation the two wandered on side by side down Seventh Avenue.